REALIZING A NEW CULTURE
Realizing a New America and a New World

REALIZING A NEW CULTURE
Realizing a New America and a New World

Norman D. Livergood & Michelle Mairesse

A Dandelion Books Publication
www.dandelionbooks.net
Tempe, Arizona

A Dandelion Books Publication Dandelion Books, LLC Tempe, Arizona

Library of Congress Cataloging-in-Publication Data

Library of Congress Catalog Card Number 2007934659

ISBN 978-0-9789611-5-2, 0-9789611-5-3

Cover and book design by Delaney-Designs, www.delaney-designs.com

Livergood, Norman D. and Michelle Mairesse

Realizing a New Culture: realizing a new america and a new world

Disclaimer and Reader Agreement

Printed in the United States of America Dandelion Books, LLC
www.dandelionbooks.net

Table of Contents

The Saving Remnant   163

The Triumph of a New World Culture   177

About The Authors   181

Index   189

Introduction

by Norman D. Livergood

Worldwide, thinking people are faced with the terror of the demonic **cabal**[1] controlling America and the world. This cabal is engaged in imperialistic conquest of other nations and the obliteration of the American democratic system. We must bring into realization an entirely *new culture* composed of new physical, psychological, and metaphysical principles and structures.

We have no other recourse than to realize[2] a new culture[3]. The criminal cabal has corrupted and contaminated the old culture to the point that if we locate our primary being in that culture we'll become as insane and corrupt as they.

To realize a new culture, we must understand the essence of the philosophical, economic, political, and social realities facing us. For example, unlike the American colonists, we no longer have a free press to use in our struggle against oppression; right-wing Republicans own most American media outlets.

Disaffirming the Old Culture

The American 2000, 2002, and 2004 elections revealed unmistakably that the criminal cabal no longer feels it needs the fig leaf of democracy to mask its fascistic, police-state visage. It also showed that they believed that there were no political, military, or economic countervailing powers--in the old world--to oppose the criminal cabal and its Bush II puppet regime. The 2006 mid-term election represented the American public rising up in momentary protest against the cabal outrages.

The Bush junta has seized the executive, legislative, and judicial branches of American government--and the Democratic party is complicit in the devastation of constitutional safeguards.

It's now apparent that the American Constitution--which during the John Adams administration proved vulnerable to tyranny--can be completely subverted, allowing criminal groups to seize total power and destroy the ideals of a society to assure the welfare of all the people.

> In a very real sense, the Constitution was a coup d'état by the bankers and other "moneyed interests" who were trying to protect their investments in the collapsing post-Revolution economy.
>
> —Michael Hasty, "Uncommon Sense: 21st Century American Revolution,"
> *Online Journal,* December 4, 2004

That world citizens should now be terrorized by the Bush junta shows that the American revolution did *not* bring about a government of the people and for the people. American totalitarianism under the Bush junta reveals that it's necessary to realize a new American and world culture by throwing off the tyranny of internal oppressors.

The criminal hijacking of the American 2000-2004 elections, and the rapidly expanding list of other Bush regime atrocities, forces thinking people worldwide to begin their struggle to realize a new political-economic-social culture.

Realizing a New Culture

I use the phrase "realizing a new culture," in the sense of making real or concrete; giving reality to; being fully aware or cognizant of *a culture that already exists*. As we'll examine in this book, this new culture is composed of pre-

---

[1] The demonic cabal is delineated in Chapter 1.

[2] *Realize:* make real or concrete; give reality to; be fully aware or cognizant of.

[3] *Culture* in its most comprehensive meaning, includes knowledge, belief, art, morals, law, custom, and other capabilities and habits acquired by humans as members of a society. In essence, culture is the sum of all technology and values that make up human life.

existent essences that Plato and other **Perennialist**[4] teachers reveal. Perennialist savants have inhabited this culture since the beginning of humankind, initiating select aspirants into this domain.

It may seem counterproductive to talk about realizing a new culture, because most of us feel that we must live in this current defective and corrupted culture, whether we like it or not. "Realizing a new culture" seems like philosophical nonsense to people who like to think of themselves as hard-headed realists.

But humankind has existed within several different "cultures" during our time on this earth, and similar to what was said in the Declaration of Independence, when a culture and its causative world-view become destructive of human welfare, it is the right--and the necessity--of humans to disaffirm the old world and bring forth a new culture.

> We hold these truths to be self-evident, that all men are created equal, that they are endowed by their Creator with certain unalienable Rights, that among these are Life, Liberty and the pursuit of Happiness . . . That to secure these rights, Governments are instituted among Men, deriving their just powers from the consent of the governed, --That whenever any Form of Government becomes destructive of these ends, it is the Right of the People to alter or to abolish it, and to institute new Government, laying its foundation on such principles and organizing its powers in such form, as to them shall seem most likely to effect their Safety and Happiness.
>
> — *Declaration of Independence, July 4, 1776*

The current criminal cabal's *deliberately constructed* political-economic culture of militaristic imperialism, fascism, and vulture capitalism must be opposed in every possible way, while we recognize the dangers of contact with that insane world. But the old culture's structures of government and economy have been so thoroughly corrupted by the dominating cabal that we must focus most of our efforts on realizing an entirely new culture.

Reality As Socially Constructed

Let's be definite as to what we mean by "realizing a new culture," clarifying our terms of discourse:

Culture: the material and spiritual state of human existence *created by a specific world view*

World-view: A comprehensive perspective that allows humans to discern *essential* meanings, principles, and values; beliefs about the limits and workings of reality shared by the members of a culture and represented in their myths, lore, ceremonies, social conduct, and general values

When we speak of "realizing a new culture," we're referring to humans producing their *reality*, with the totality of its spiritual, metaphysical, sociocultural, and psychological structures. This is somewhat the same sense in which Peter L. Berger and Thomas Luckman speak of "society as a human product" and "the social construction of reality."

> An institutional world, then, is experienced as an objective reality. It has a history that antedates the individual's birth and is not accessible to his biographical recollection. It was there before he was born, and it will be there after his death. This history itself, as the tradition of the existing institutions, has the character of objectivity.
>
> Knowledge about society is thus a realization in the double sense of the word, in the sense of apprehending the objectivated social reality, and in the sense of ongoingly producing this reality.
>
> —Peter L. Berger and Thomas Luckmann, *The Social Construction of Reality: A Treatise in the Sociology of Knowledge*, 1966

---

[4] See the co-author's (NL) recently published book, *The Perennial Tradition*

Realizing a New Reality

We're realizing a new culture in a metaphysical as well as a material sense: a complete new reality, not just a different *conception* of our present reality or a *new paradigm* with which to conceptualize what we recognize at present to be reality. We're realizing a new reality.

Realizing a new culture--a new reality--involves understanding and actualizing concepts and practices which reflect higher, eternal *essences*--what Plato called "ideas" or "forms." These concepts and practices define human nature, relations between humans, and the goals and meaning of human existence.

To realize a new culture we must develop *new people*: humans who understand and act in entirely new ways. To discern essences will require a new kind of person who has achieved philosophical understanding through experience with higher realities and identification with higher consciousness.

The reason we must do this is that the old culture--the old reality--has led to the *evils* that we see staring at us when we turn on our TV sets, when we read our newspapers, surf the Internet, or converse with our neighbors. The old culture is based on faulty conceptions and practices which have led to the horrors of current American cabal totalitarianism. In realizing a new culture, the *new people* must make sure--among other things--that no tyranny such as the United States under the Bush junta can ever rise again.

Previous Cultures

To understand what it requires to realize a new culture, let's review how humans have realized and inhabited various "worlds" in their history. We can say with clear meaning that people in the middle ages lived in an entirely different culture or world than we do today. In describing the Medieval mind-set, Roger Bacon wrote in his *Opus Maius* (1268):

> There are two modes of knowledge, through argument and experience. Argument brings conclusions and compels us to concede them, but it does not cause certainty nor remove doubts in order that the mind may remain at rest in truth, unless this is provided by experience.

Throughout the Middle Ages, European thought stagnated largely because of its conception of knowledge as derived from argument from authority--whether the authority of the Church or the State. Europe languished in intellectual and cultural retrogression during the Dark Ages, while the light of wisdom was preserved and advanced by those they labeled "the infidel Saracen." The reintroduction of the Classical (Greek) Tradition and the Perennial Tradition through the confluence of European and Muslim thought, beginning around 1000 AD, revitalized earlier conceptions of knowledge as derived from experience.

Medieval people suffered under religious and political tyranny because they allowed themselves to be controlled by a world-view that included such retrograde ideas as the divine right of kings--and popes.

A more recent example of a "culture" was the cargo cult created after the second world war in certain South Sea island communities. During the war they had seen airplanes landing on their islands, bringing a wide variety of people and materials.

After the war ended and the planes no longer appeared, the natives on these islands wanted the same thing to happen again. So they made ersatz runways, put fires along the sides of the runways, made wooden huts for a man to sit in to direct the airplanes' landing, with two wooden pieces on his head to resemble headphones and bars of bamboo sticking out like antennas.

The islanders had done everything that fit into their world-view—trying to copy what they had seen. Now they waited for the airplanes to land. They did everything right, completing all aspects of their new culture; everything looked exactly the way it had when the Allied soldier had been there. This cargo cult constituted a culture that followed all the apparent practices and forms of the earlier Allied culture. But the planes didn't land; the supplies didn't arrive. Their world-view had created a false reality.

In exactly the same manner, the old American culture pretended to do everything according to a pattern of "government of the people, by the people, and for the people." But now that the cabal has begun destroying constitutional liberties, the "planes don't land." The pretense of government for the people has been exposed; the emperor has no clothes. The old culture's concepts and practices--as corrupted by the cabal--have inexorably led to the current reign of terror under the Bush junta.

In the sixteenth through eighteenth centuries, Europeans called North America "the new world." But this so-called "new world" was founded on concocted myths such as "the invisible hand of the market," government as above classes and serving only the national interest, slave-labor as essential to the American economy, history as the record of property rights, state-power, and the necessity of war.

If you think that the idea of "realizing a new culture" is nothing but fantasy, then I invite you to examine one of the truly fantastic, unreal inventions of the old culture: the corporation.

> A corporation is an artificial being, invisible, intangible, and existing only in contemplation of law. Being the mere creature of law, it possesses only those properties which the charter of its creation confers upon it, either expressly or as incidental to its very existence . . . Among the most important are immortality, and, if the expression may be allowed, individuality; properties by which a perpetual succession of many persons are considered as the same and may act as a single individual.
>
> —Supreme Court Chief Justice Marshall, *1819*

The Corruption of the Old Culture

We *realize* a new culture through--among other activities--understanding fully the corruption of the old culture perpetrated by the criminal cabal now controlling America.

> President Bush isn't a conservative. He's a radical - the leader of a coalition that deeply dislikes America as it is. Part of that coalition wants to tear down the legacy of Franklin Roosevelt, eviscerating Social Security and, eventually, Medicare. Another part wants to break down the barriers between church and state.
>
> —Paul Krugman, *New York Times*, 11/5/04

The devastation of the old culture has been so craftily carried out by mind-control experts such as Karl Rove, that it's visible only to those who have retained--or newly developed--their full intellectual and spiritual powers and comprehend the eradication of essential human elements from the old culture. We must recognize and work to rectify all the devastation that the criminal cabal is perpetrating:

- People are being conditioned to abnegate their rational minds
- Old values of honesty, justice, and fair competition are being replaced by the intrigues of deliberate lying, politically-motivated judicial actions, and dog-eat-dog economic warfare
- Understanding through information has been replaced with constant bombardment of brainwashing propaganda via reactionary media (think Fox News)

The Red Queen's Anti-Logic

At present, humankind is being programmed to progressively lose its reasoning capacity. It's difficult to realize what a basic assault on objectivity and rationality the Bush junta has launched. We can best get a sense of the fantasy-based thinking of the Bush cult from an article by Ron Suskind in the *New York Times*:

> In the summer of 2002, after I had written an article in Esquire that the White House didn't like about Bush's former communications director, Karen Hughes, I had a meeting with a senior adviser to Bush. He expressed the White House's displeasure, and then he told me something that at the time I didn't fully comprehend --but which I now believe gets to the very heart of the Bush presidency.

> The aide said that guys like me were "in what we call the reality-based community," which he defined as people who "believe that solutions emerge from your judicious study of discernible reality." I nodded and murmured something about enlightenment principles and empiricism. He cut me off. "That's not the way the world really works anymore," he continued. "We're an empire now, and when we act,

we create our own reality. And while you're studying that reality --judiciously, as you will -- we'll act again, creating other new realities, which you can study too, and that's how things will sort out. We're history's actors . . . and you, all of you, will be left to just study what we do."

You may think that only White House aides engage in this kind of delusional thinking. Think again. This kind of fantasizing begins with Dubya and runs throughout the entire Bush regime. Ron Suskind tells of another revealing experience he had in this regard.

Forty democratic senators were gathered for a lunch in March just off the Senate floor. I was there as a guest speaker. Joe Biden was telling a story, a story about the president. "I was in the Oval Office a few months after we swept into Baghdad," he began, "and I was telling the president of my many concerns"--concerns about growing problems winning the peace, the explosive mix of Shiite and Sunni, the disbanding of the Iraqi Army and problems securing the oil fields. Bush, Biden recalled, just looked at him, unflappably sure that the United States was on the right course and that all was well. "Mr. President," I finally said, "How can you be so sure when you know you don't know the facts?" Biden said that Bush stood up and put his hand on the senator's shoulder. "My instincts," he said. "My instincts." Biden paused and shook his head, recalling it all as the room grew quiet. I said, "Mr. President, your instincts aren't good enough!"

An indication of the deranged state of the mind of the Bush junta is their dismissal of Europe as the "old world." What they mean by this slur is that anyone--in Europe or elsewhere--who doesn't agree and cooperate with their policies of military imperialism is hopelessly out of step with current reality. As their spokesperson said: "We're an empire now, and when we act, we create our own reality."

In this book, the term "old world" refers to the current social disorder created by the criminal cabal and its Bush II puppet regime.

A New Culture to Stand Over Against the Old

In creating a new culture, we must build a foundation that will realize our goal of a commonwealth:

- An alliance founded on law and united by a compact with the people for the common good

- An alliance in which the supreme authority is vested in the people

We create a new culture to stand over against the old world by:

Recognizing that we have allowed America to be taken over by a gang of thugs

Most of us went to bed on November second, thinking we were all still Americans, only to discover when the sun came up on November third, that 48 percent of us were now "people without a country." Becoming stateless, overnight, is not something that anyone should take lightly. Cheney-Bush wants us to "come together," to heal the rifts within the nation – but they have never taken their own advice. It was in their formative phase under Newt Gingrich when they first issued a Contract on America – it was then that this plan was clearly laid. From that day to this, they have never wavered in their pursuit of the takeover of this nation, at the expense of anyone who was opposed. Do not heed the pre-selected one's advice: fight this takeover of your country as you would if they were wearing foreign uniforms, because they are the enemy of all that most people have come to expect.

—Jim Kirwan, "Resistance is Not Futile," *www.globalresearch.ca*, Center for Research on Globalisation, 11/4/2004

2. We must recognize that we have put ourselves into this terrible situation by our own ignorance.

Why have we let corporations into our polling places, locations so sacred to democracy that in many states even international election monitors and reporters are banned? Why are we allowing corporations to exclusively handle our vote, in a secret and totally invisible way? Particularly a private corporation founded, in one case, by a family that believes the Bible should replace the Constitution; in another case run by one of Ohio's top Republicans; and in another case partly owned by Saudi investors?

Of all the violations of the commons - all of the crimes against We The People and against democracy in our great and historic republic this is the greatest. Our vote is too important to outsource to private corporations.

It's time that the USA - like most of the rest of the world - returns to paper ballots, counted by hand by civil servants (our employees) under the watchful eye of the party faithful. Even if it takes two weeks to count the vote, and we have to just go, until then, with the exit polls of the news agencies. It worked just fine for nearly 200 years in the USA, and it can work again . . .

As Thomas Paine wrote at this nation's founding, "The right of voting for representatives is the primary right by which all other rights are protected. To take away this right is to reduce a man to slavery."

Only when We The People reclaim the commons of our vote can we again be confident in the integrity of our electoral process in the world's oldest and most powerful democratic republic.

—Thom Hartmann. "The Ultimate Felony Against Democracy,"
CommonDreams.org, 11/4/04

Possession and Hysteria

3. But we must recognize that most of "the people" of the United States--and the old world in general--have lost the capabilities required for self-government. In realizing a new culture, we must create new people. And the first step in that process is to recognize to what a deplorable state "the people" have allowed themselves to fall.

Progressive **awareness**[5], critical thinking, and self-awareness are essential capabilities which humankind must now struggle to regain, since a great many have allowed their minds to be literally taken over by destructive personalities and ideologies. For most humans, the regaining of critical thinking, self-awareness, and critical consciousness must be the first priority, because there is the very real danger of the masses of humankind becoming totally possessed by the structures and ideologies of those few who now rule the world politically and economically.

Possession is the extreme lower point on a continuum in which the highest achievement is identification with a Higher Positive Power. Negative or lower possession refers to:

- domination by something (as a negative spirit, a passion, an obsession, an addiction, or a fixed idea)

- a psychological state in which an individual's normal personality is replaced by another

Humans can allow other entities--personalities or ideas--to control them to varying degrees. If they allow other persons or concepts to take dominant control of their thoughts and actions, they lose the ability to think or act autonomously. As a personality or an ideology takes progressive control of them, they become possessed (an obsessive, a bigot, an ideologue) and finally end in hysteria--the manifestation of self-limiting or self-destructive tendencies.

In psychology, hysteria refers to the loss of sensory or motor function without organic pathology. The person suddenly cannot hear, see, or feel, or his arm or leg may be paralyzed, or he may be unable to speak--even though the bodily organs are completely functional.

Currently, possession and hysteria are present in much of the world's population. We see these phenomena most clearly in the fixed ideas and obsessive belief-systems of masses of people world-wide who are oblivious to the destruction of their lives by politicians and corporations. The phenomena of possession and hysteria are most evident in the American masses who have lost the ability to see what is happening in America and the world.

---

[5] See the co-author's (NL) recently published book, *Progressive Awareness*.

As humans become progressively possessed by destructive personalities and ideologies, they ultimately end in suicidal behavior: voting for and supporting people who are deliberately destroying them, volunteering to fight and die in senseless wars.

The technology of mind-control is a mature science. Those who work to manipulate the masses have the most sophisticated tools available in human history. Propaganda and brainwashing take place continually in all forms of mass media, most significantly in television. The masses have been rendered brain-dead by the purveyors of lies and inanity.

> Experiments conducted by researcher Herbert Krugman reveal that, when a person watches television, brain activity switches from the left to the right hemisphere. The left hemisphere is the seat of logical thought. Here, information is broken down into its component parts and critically analyzed. The right brain, however, treats incoming data uncritically, processing information in wholes, leading to emotional, rather than logical, responses. The shift from left to rightbrain activity also causes the release of endorphins, the body's own naturalopiates--thus, it is possible to become physically addicted to watching television, a hypothesis borne out by numerous studies which have shown that very few people are able to kick the television habit.
>
> —Peter Russell, "Dehypnosis - Breaking the Trance," *Waking Up in Time*

The horror of possession and hysteria is that the victims--average citizens—aren't aware of their debilitated state. Their brainwashing makes them believe--in the face of overwhelming evidence to the contrary--that they're still in control of their minds and that their situation is acceptable.

The major question currently staring people in the face is whether the world masses who've become "possessed" by such reactionary ideologies as "compassionate conservatism," fundamentalist Christianity, or fundamentalist Islam, will wake up enough to be able to *see* what's being done to them—they've lost jobs, pensions, and health insurance; their taxes are higher; they're sent to fight wars that burden the poor and middle class for the benefit of rich individuals and corporations—and create a new culture with which to take back their political and economic systems for their own betterment.

> (America is) the new model for the new concentration camp where the camp has been built by the inmates themselves and the inmates are the guards and they have this pride in this thing they've built. They've built their own prison and so they exist in a state of schizophrenia where they are both guards and prisoners. And as a result, having been lobotomized, they no longer have the capacity to leave the prison they've made or to even see it as a prison.
>
> —*My Dinner With Andre,* a film by Wallace Shawn and Andre Gregory

Cultural Trance

As Peter Russell makes clear, we're the victims of a cultural trance. Whereas in hypnotism, we're aware that someone is trying to influence us, with our cultural conditioning the situation is the opposite.

- Our consensus trance is not voluntary; it begins at birth without our conscious agreement.

- All authority is surrendered to the parents, family members and other caretakers, who initially are regarded as omniscient and omnipotent.

- Induction is not limited to short sessions; it involves years of repeated reinforcement.

- Clinical therapists would consider it highly unethical to use force, but our cultural hypnotists often do --a slap on the wrist, or severe reprimand for misbehaving. Or perhaps more subtle, but equally powerful, emotional pressures --'I will only love you if you think and behave as I tell you.'

- Finally, and most significantly, the conditioning is intended to be permanent. It may come from the very best of intentions, but it is, nevertheless, meant to have a lasting effect on our personalities and the way we evaluate the world.

This is why awakening from our cultural trance entails far more than a simple snapping of the fingers. There is a lifetime's worth of extremely powerful induction to be overcome.

We would seem to be firmly stuck with our conditioning. Indeed, for most of the time we are. Yet there are occasions when we do wake up, and see things in a different light. In those moments we are given a glimpse of what is possible.

Charles Tart maintains that "we are indeed, as a matter of verifiable fact, like zombies most of the time but we have a possibility of becoming conscious." He believes that "normal" consciousness is indeed a zombie-like state of greatly constricted and distorted, if not absent, awareness. Tart gives such ordinary consciousness the technical name of "consensus consciousness" in a purely descriptive sense and "consensus trance" when someone is focusing on it as a restricted state.

The Requisite Capabilities of the New Culture

4. In realizing a new culture, we must develop persons who possess essential new capabilities:

- Skills in democratic decision-making

- Both social and spiritual awareness

- The capability of working in the spiritual world to bring about effects in the material world

- The ability to commune with kindred souls

- An awareness and a participation in the struggle between the old culture and the new culture

- The understanding of our past in order to build a new culture

Imagine if you can a world in which truth is one general and something we will call blindness is the opposing general. These two simple factors one must choose between. There are no neutrals. We are frankly for or against and hold our positions by the force of the effort we put forth. The great struggle is not only to conquer our opposing forces, but to reclaim and form them into fighters for the truth. It is more of a game than the mere overcoming, for we are after the plunder of human souls to salvage.

—Stewart Edward White, *Across the Unknown*

The struggle of the people in opposition to the privileged class that controls the state, is the dynamic factor in our national development, the theme and meaning of our history.

We cannot understand the role of the people in history unless we also understand the historical illusions which misrepresent history in order to serve the interests of privileged classes. Thus culture must be studied as a weapon in the struggle of classes.

Cultural history emerges in its truth and grandeur when it is seen as an unceasing struggle between the oppressor and the oppressed. This is also the link between the present and the past. The long battle against the oppressor is not ended. Man has not yet become the full master of his own life, of the conditions of his social existence.

—John Howard Lawson, *The Hidden Heritage, 1950*

Realizing the Sovereignty of the Higher Realm

Much of our discussion above places us squarely in the muddle of the old culture: its recent takeover by the Bush junta and our allowing our voting system in 2000, 2002, and 2004 to be seized by reactionary corporations. We've seen that we must realize a new culture by developing a new kind of person--with exceptional capabilities. This latter discussion makes it clear that our creating a new culture is for the purpose of long-range development of new ideas, practices, and requisite capabilities. In part, we're realizing the invincible power of higher knowledge and higher consciousness.

To understand the most fundamental aspects of this new culture that we're realizing, we must consider the teachings of a Perennialist savant named Jesus of Nazareth who proclaimed the sovereignty of a higher realm (mistranslated "kingdom of heaven"). The Greek words referring to this new world are:

- *basileia*, denoting sovereignty, royal power, dominion, a rule or reign, an exercise of authority

- *ouranos*: the realm of Higher Being

As we examine Jesus' life and teachings, it is unmistakable that he was a sage within the Perennial Tradition proclaiming the sovereignty of the Higher Realm. Authentic wisdom is adapted by a Perennialist teacher relative to the needs of the people in a particular culture and time. Teachings are organic nutrients to be assimilated not meant to remain in unaltered, undigested form for curiosity seekers, theoreticians, or autocrats to pick over and "elucidate."

Inevitably, every Perennialist teacher's ideas and methodologies undergo two totally divergent modes of treatment:

- A group of genuine followers retains the original message and passes it on to the next generation of students and initiates

- A group of followers who did not understand the original teaching recast the authentic teachings into distorted dogmas; these ecclesiastical and philosophical deformities are then used to build despotic establishments over which the new tyrants rule

Both things happened to Jesus' teachings. Within a short time after Jesus' death, there came into being a tyrannical ecclesiastical system which developed a congeries of contradictory and disparate doctrines and writings. In this morass of confusion, a number of interpretations of Jesus' teachings vied for acceptance, having been created by the processes of excluding ideas thought to be unacceptable, accentuating personally selected doctrines, and organizing material into what was thought to be a coherent whole.

Thus in the early church a number of factions had arisen, with Peter and some of the other original apostles preaching a Judaized, sacerdotal Christianity requiring no more than belief, while Paul insisted that Jesus' teaching was about a spiritual rebirth such as he had himself experienced.

Both Jesus and Paul taught that religion is not mere belief in doctrines but a practical knowledge of the way to live within the sovereignty of the Higher Realm. The original teaching of Jesus was thus passed on through Paul and those whom he and his immediate companions taught in the many cities they visited.

If you watch a TV history of Christianity or read a Protestant or Roman Catholic account of the early church, Christianity's becoming the official religion of the Roman state during Constantine's reign is considered a great victory. The only measure of success for these moderns is whether or not a tradition triumphed over all its competitors. Never mind what distorting of the original message had taken place. If a particular religion came out on top, it's to be considered the best.

On the contrary, the formal religion that became known as the Holy Roman Church was and is nothing but a vast repository of false teachings and practices. At the present time, what is called Christianity, in all its Catholic, Orthodox, and Protestant guises, is a horrible deformity of Jesus' original teachings. It is only in such an anarchy of falsehood and deception that Mel Gibson's snuff film *The Passion of the Christ* could have any appeal.

Jesus' teaching says that man is capable of a second birth into the sovereignty of the higher realm. However, this re-birth or second birth belongs to the inner aspect of man, not to man as he seems to be in himself, a materialistic body living on earth.

To experience rebirth means to evolve to a higher level of understanding, to a higher being. This can only be achieved by new knowledge, gnosis, and by practicing this new understanding. The gnosis or knowledge which gives man this possibility of evolving is sometimes called Truth and at other times called the Word (Logos). It is not ordinary truth or knowledge; it is knowledge about this further evolutionary step which man can take as he realizes the new world of the brotherhood of man, the infinite value of the individual soul, and the ethic of love.

The new culture we're realizing is in large part within those who are members of it. As the new culture was earlier termed "the sovereignty of Higher Being" it is now also referred to as "the spiritual domain" and "the new commonwealth."

Chapter One

The Demonic Cabal

By Norman D. Livergood

From all available evidence it's clear that the most compelling hypothesis explaining the interconnected crimes, lies, and human slaughter occurring in our modern world is that a demonic cabal took control of the United States in the early part of the twentieth century and is now methodically destroying American and world institutions and values. The main goal of the cabal has been to consolidate political, economic, and social power in its hands while obliterating the minds of the masses to establish a militaristic, totalitarian dictatorship.

By designating this cabal as "demonic," I do not imply that there is need for hatred, anxiety, or hopelessness. It's simply the situation that this cabal has seized control and we need to face it and get on with the business of creating a new culture. On the other hand we should not simply sit about idly theorizing or smiling at the devastation of human beings in this debased culture. Something must be done!

The purpose of this chapter is to help American and world citizens see who and what is controlling events from behind the scenes, to assist in making clear just what kind of demonic forces are bringing about the destruction of American and world ideas and traditions.

It's clear that many people are so possessed by the current reactionary brainwashing that they will be unable to consider any of these ideas. But some people throughout the world are waking up to what's going on and they need to see behind the curtains to the real, criminal powers that manipulate human minds and destroy human liberties. We need to see the real face of our enemy.

I've chosen to use the word "demonic" because it seems most descriptive of the nature of this depraved coterie that has seized power illegitimately. They are certainly criminals in that they commit outrages continually (e.g. the holocausts of Hiroshima and Nagasaki, the assassination of JFK, the Iran-Contra gun-running/drug smuggling assault, the savings and loan felonies, the wars of Vietnam, Kosovo, Afghanistan, and Iraq, and the 9/11 atrocity). But their misdeeds are more base than that; they are evil and wicked in the truest sense and therefore are best described as demonic.

This chapter will deal with the broader aspects of the demonic cabal, referring as well to incriminating details. We'll first review how cabals have operated throughout history, seizing power and manipulating the populace. Reviewing the American experience, we'll see how a wealthy plutocracy during the American struggle for independence from Britain devolved into a criminal cabal. Next, we'll examine Plato's concept of an intelligent, beneficent elite and how this relates to our American experience. Finally, we'll explore ways in which this current demonic cabal is being overcome as its brittle strength weakens to the point of defeat.

Not Just an Elite but a Cabal

Though it is historically common for a small elite to lead any group, it's decidedly not "natural" or commendable for an elite to form into a cabal, a group of persons secretly united to bring about an overturn or usurpation in public affairs.

A cabal is a number of persons united in some close design, usually to promote their private views and interests in church or state by intrigue. Cabals are secret organizations composed of a few designing persons; a political cabal is often called a junta. The term also holds a general meaning of intrigue and conspiracy. Its usage carries strong connotations of shadowy corners and occult influence; a cabal is more evil and selective than, say, a faction, which is simply selfish.

The term cabal derives from Kabbalah (which has numerous spelling variations), the mystical interpretation of the Hebrew scripture, and originally meant either an occult doctrine or a secret society.

The term took on its present insidious meaning from a group of ministers chosen in 1667 by King Charles II of England.

A cabal, then is any small criminal group who seizes power illegitimately to benefit its members only, manipulating and impoverishing all other people within the nation. The very foundation of the capitalist system is based on the ideology of the cabal.

> Civil government, so far as it is instituted for the security of property, is in reality instituted for the defence of the rich against the poor, or of those who have some property against those who have none at all.

—Adam Smith, *Wealth of Nations,* 1776

The Destructive Cabal

The destruction of the American mind and American institutions is now so far advanced that the demonic cabal has been able to establish a police state without the people rising up against them.

The cabal has taken great pains to avoid publicity and recognition, to the point that most people are blind to its existence. It requires advanced powers of discernment to even see its presence, so hidden has been its subversive activity. Anyone who speaks of a cabal is immediately dismissed as a paranoid conspiracy theorist, lumped with extremists of all stripes, and made *persona non grata* in any professional field.

> For more than a century, ideological extremists at either end of the political spectrum have seized upon well-publicized incidents to attack the Rockefeller family for the inordinate influence they claim we wield over American political and economic institutions. Some even believe we are part of a secret cabal working against the best interests of the United States, characterizing my family and me as "internationalists" and of conspiring with others around the world to build a more integrated global political and economic structure—one world, if you will. If that's the charge, I stand guilty, and I am proud of it.

—David Rockefeller, *Memoirs*, 2002

At present, Americans are faced with an illegal junta which is repeating a vile era in American history: the seizure of all governmental powers by a single party during John Adams' presidency from 1797-1801. America is following in exact detail the monopolization of power practiced by the Federalist-Adams dictatorship.

Having illegally seized the presidency--with the criminal assistance of Jeb Bush and the U.S. Supreme Court in 2000 and stealing the 2002 and 2004 elections, gaining the majority in both houses of Congress--the puppet Bush II regime is privatizing public resources, crippling local, state, and federal governments by spending only for militarism (domestic and foreign), creating a huge federal debt that later generations will have to repay, and creating tax cuts and subsidies for the rich. Criminal, self-serving corruption runs rampant throughout the Bush II administration, as it did in his father's Iran-Contra and savings-and-loan crime sprees. The legal and moral degeneracy of the Bush junta is clearly seen in Karl Rove's outing of a CIA agent as political payback--and Rove experiencing no negative repercussions.

The horrible tyranny that is being created by the Bush junta is a threat to the entire world. For the first time in its history, Western Civilization as a whole is in danger of being destroyed by an international, demonic cabal centered around the Rockefeller interests, which include elements from the Morgan, Brown, Rothschild, Du Pont, Harriman, Kuhn-Loeb, and other groupings as well. This junta took control of the political, financial, and cultural life of America in the first two decades of the twentieth century.

Members of the Bush family, beginning with Prescott Bush, have served as satraps of the Rockefeller, Brown, and Harriman interests. Bush II is simply a puppet of this powerful cabal, and their schemes will be carried out by whatever next president comes to power unless we the people deflect them from this insane, murderous plot for global dominance.

The Modern Demonic Cabal

Winston Churchill was quoted by wartime associates as making reference to the "High Cabal," the international power elite. Since Churchill was a part of what we're referring to as the demonic cabal, we can understand why he would use the term "high" to describe it, while acknowledging its existence nonetheless. The "Demonic Cabal" includes: The American, British, Saudi, and Dutch ruling elites:

- In the U.S. the cabal revolves around the Rockefeller, Brown, Harriman, and Morgan family dynasties with their "thinktanks" such as the Council on Foreign Relations, Trilateral Commission, Bilderberg Group, and other pretentious enclaves of pseudointellectuals.

- The cabal includes the British royal family and the financial and political circles connected with it. The current cabal began in Britain with the Royal Institute of International Affairs and the Round Table group.

- Major players in the demonic cabal include the Saudi royal family and The Big Three--the bin Laden family, the al Ahmoudi family, and the Mahfouz family--the richest clans in that medieval kingdom. The Saudi brand of Islam is Wahabism, which enjoins its adherents to destroy all infidels in a holy war. Many of the "Iraqi insurgents" now killing Iraqis and American service personnel are trained in Saudi Arabia.

- The current cabal includes the Dutch royal family and related circles.

- The European arm of the cabal centers in the Rothschild empire and its many tentacles reaching into all European nations. The Rothschilds were active in financing the southern states during the American Civil War. In the early part of the twentieth century, the Rothschilds have formed an international banking dynasty, with a presence in 40 countries worldwide.

- A large number of financial, military, and political leaders in America and throughout the world provide support and cover for the demonic cabal.

    - The Republican party and its phony "culture of life"

    - The corporations that bribe and control politicians in both parties

    - Those in the Democratic party who are conspiring with the Bush junta by saying nothing and agreeing to everything

The Kennedy "assassination has demonstrated that most of the major events of world significance are masterfully planned and orchestrated by an elite coterie of enormously powerful people who are not of one nation, one ethnic grouping, or one overridingly important business group. They are a power unto themselves for whom those others work. Neither is this power elite of recent origin. Its roots go deep into the past."

—Colonel L. Fletcher Prouty, *JFK: The CIA, Vietnam, and the Plot to Assassinate John F. Kennedy,* 1992

In 1937, William E. Dodd, U.S. Ambassador to Germany, made this startling statement (as reported in George Seldes, *Facts and Fascism* (1943), p. 122: "A clique of U.S. industrialists is hell-bent to bring a fascist state to supplant our democratic government . . ."

Carroll Quigley, Georgetown University history professor (deceased), in *Tragedy and Hope: A History of the World in Our Time* (1966), made this claim:

There does exist and has existed for a generation, an international Anglophile network which operates, to some extent, in the way the radical Right believes the Communists act. In fact, this network, which we may identify as the Round Table groups, has no aversion to cooperating with the Communists, or any other groups, and frequently does so. I know of the operations of this network because I have studied it for 20 years and was permitted for two years, in the early 1960s, to examine its papers and secret record.

In addition to these pragmatic goals, the powers of financial capitalism had another far-reaching aim, nothing less than to create a world system of financial control in private hands able to dominate the political system of each country and the economy of the world as a whole. This system was to be controlled in a feudalist fashion by the central banks of the world acting in concert, by secret agreements arrived at in frequent private meetings and conferences. The apex of the system was the Bank for International Settlements in Basle, Switzerland, a private bank owned and controlled by the world's central banks which were themselves private corporations. The growth of financial capitalism made possible a centralization of world economic control and use of this power for the direct benefit of financiers and the indirect injury of all other economic groups.' pp. 950 and 324.

There exists in our world today a powerful and dangerous secret cult. This cult is patronized and protected by the highest level government officials in the world. Its membership is composed of those in the power centers of government, industry, commerce, finance, and labor. It manipulates individuals in areas of important public influence - including the academic world and the mass media. The Secret Cult is a global fraternity of a political aristocracy whose purpose is to further the political policies of persons or agencies unknown. It acts covertly and illegally.

—Victor Marchetti, *The CIA and the Cult of Intelligence*, 1975

In his 1913 book, *The New Freedom*, President Woodrow Wilson stated:

Since I entered politics, I have chiefly had men's views confided to me privately. Some of the biggest men in the United States, in the field of commerce and manufacture, are afraid of something. They know that there is a power somewhere so organized, so subtle, so watchful, so interlocked, so complete, so pervasive, that they had better not speak above their breath when they speak in condemnation of it.

After years of studying the present cabal, Arthur S. Miller, George Washington University law professor asserted:

Those who formally rule take their signals and commands not from the electorate as a body, but from a small group of men (plus a few women). . . . It exists even though that existence is stoutly denied. It is one of the secrets of the American social order. . . . A second secret is the fact that the existence of the Establishment --the ruling class --is not supposed to be discussed.

Out of this modern civilization economic royalists carved new dynasties. New kingdoms were built upon concentration of control over material things. Through new uses of corporations, banks and securities, new machinery of industry and agriculture, of labor and capital -all undreamed of by the Fathers -the whole structure of modern life was impressed into this royal service.

—Franklin Delano Roosevelt speech in Philadelphia on June 27, 1936

Understanding Brings Power and Hope

This expose of the demonic cabal is part of a larger effort on the part of this book and a number of other progressive voices to help citizens around the globe become aware of what's happening in the world. Far from this information about the cabal being a harbinger of doom or cause for hopelessness, it can be and is being used by many people to gain understanding and act to remove this cabal from power. The 2006 elections in the U.S. revealed unmistakably that this group of megalomaniacs can and does "misunderstimate" American and world citizens. Through continuing efforts to inform ourselves and act decisively and intelligently, we will overthrow this demonic cabal and institute governments of, by, and for the people.

Chapter Two

The New Totalitarianism

By Norman D. Livergood

The depraved international cabal that has a stranglehold on American and British political and financial power constitutes a new type of *Totalitarianism*, pillaging the world through *barbaric annihilation* and creating a World Police State.

American and world citizens have not fully awakened to the monstrous, diabolical nature of this totalitarian regime; they assume it must have some modicum of concern for its people, its nation, and human decency. Wrong! Unless we arouse ourselves from this deadly self-imposed stupor of ignorance, these homicidal maniacs will destroy us and the world.

Previously, imperialism had been the underlying policy of the cabal when it seized Puerto Rico, Hawaii, Cuba, the Philippines and the Mariana Islands and set up the German regimes that led to World War I and World War II.

Totalitarianism:

Absolutistic dominion through imposing the force of one power over others through armed violence; fascistic dictatorship A regime based on subordination of the individual to the state and strict control of all coercive measures such as censorship and state terrorism (think Patriot Act) The political concept that the citizen should be totally subject to an absolute state authority

Barbarism:

Characteristic of a cultural level more complex than primitive savagery but less advanced than civilization; marked by cruelty and lack of restraint; offending against contemporary standards of good taste or acceptability; backward

But British and American imperialism involved a certain amount of concern for the possessed territory and the people, if no more than pride in having control over the holdings of the empire. The new totalitarianism has absolutely no such concern; its only interest is imposing the diabolic policy of barbaric annihilation on the world, thereby reaping huge profits from its energy, financial, and "defense" industries and turning all countries into militarized police states whose peoples will be forced to become their "cannon fodder."

Although war is "used" as an instrument of national and social policy, the fact that a society is organized for any degree of readiness for war supersedes its political and economic structure. War itself is the basic social system, within which other secondary modes of social organization conflict or conspire. It is the system which has governed most human societies of record, as it is today.

—Leonard Lewin, "Report From Iron Mountain on the Possibility and Desirability of Peace," 1967

People throughout the world must become aware that this new totalitarianism is completely unlike any previous geopolitical power structure. Its very essence is annihilation; it possesses no redeeming or mitigating feature. To allow yourself to think of these people as *simply* foolish, incompetent, irrational, or wrong-headed is as mistaken and misinformed as thinking that Hitler was merely a well-meaning but mistaken leader of his people.

Uninformed people will say: "The Bush administration surely doesn't want to let the United States go to ruin, they have too much at stake. They must realize they're not winning in Iraq."

The cabal and its Bush puppet junta don't care a straw for what happens to American workers or the U.S. infrastructure; *they gain power and wealth through annihilation.* We must get that fixed in our minds! The more America becomes a drug-ridden war zone with a blasted economy and escalating crime (street crime and white collar crime), the more young people are forced to become "cannon fodder" for the cabal wars; they have no other jobs to go to. The cabal is not losing the war in Iraq, it's winning, as you can see from their realization of their goals.

The cabal junta's goals in invading Iraq involved much more than most people are aware of. Among the more obvious goals were:

- The theft of Iraqi oil through privatization (piratization)–that's proceeding apace

- The funneling of oil and no-bid contracts into Halliburton's maw—a huge success

- The installation of multiple U.S military bases in the region--advancing well

- The installation of a cabal puppet in control of Iraq (as in Afghanistan)—one stooge had to be replaced and now Maliki may have to go as well

Some of the hidden reasons the cabal invaded and occupied Iraq are:

- To reconfigure the Middle East geopolitically (think invasion of Lebanon in July 2006, Iran and Syria)

- To gain strategic control over Iraq's--and the surrounding territory's--hydrocarbon reserves to establish a cabal-based energy market to replace OPEC

- To maintain the U.S. dollar as the monopoly currency for the critical international oil market

- To dominate all nations of the world through the threat of military invasion and "regime change"

Those who can make you believe absurdities can make you commit atrocities.

—Voltaire

Taking Them At Their Word

Throughout much of the twentieth century, the cabal amassed wealth through the ownership and control of a variety of industries--as, for example, computers, automobiles, and transportation--even though their primary profits derived from the energy, financial, and "defense" sectors. Following the cabal's assassination of President John F. Kennedy, their primary strategy turned from corruption to outright criminality. They destroyed the basic structure of American democracy in 2000 when they seized the presidency through the Jeb Bush-Katherine Harris-Supreme Court *coup d'etat.* In terms of foreign policy, they have now publicly declared that their mode of operation will be the seizure of power and profits through the amassing of military might beyond challenge from other nations or the rule of law.

Three years ago, the Bush administration brushed aside the United Nations and all existing international legal restraints and began its illegal war. In so doing, it made clear that it no longer felt restrained by contracts, agreements and international law, but with its highly developed military strength based itself instead on the principle of 'might is right.' "In other words, the political system established on the rubble left by the Second World War, and which required that every country abide by international rules and laws, ceased to exist. The Iraq war and its extension to Lebanon and the Palestinian territories represents a return to imperialist politics in its most aggressive and brutal form.

—Ulrich Rippert, "Europe's inability to counter US-Israeli war policy," World Socialist Web Site, 7/21/06

Spokesmen for the criminal cabal have been blatantly outspoken about their primary goals; it's just that American and world citizens have found it difficult to believe that a group of people could be so ruthless, unjust, and cruel--so sub-human. It's time we took them at their word:

> We are an awesome revolutionary force. Creative destruction is our middle name. We tear down the old order every day . . . Seeing America undo old conventions, they [our enemies] fear us, for they do not wish to be undone . . . We wage total war because we fight in the name of an idea . . . Stability is for those older, burnt-out countries, not for the American dynamo.
>
> —Michael A. Ledeen, Freedom Chair holder at the American Enterprise Institute

> America has, and intends to keep, military strengths beyond challenge--thereby making the destabilizing arms races of other eras pointless . . .
>
> —Bush II, West Point, June 2, 2002

> The maximum amount of force can and should be used as quickly as possible for psychological impact-to demonstrate that the empire cannot be challenged with impunity. . . [W]e are in the business of bringing down hostile governments and creating governments favorable to us.
>
> —Harvard Professor Stephen P. Rosen, "The Future of War and the American Military: Demography, technology, and the politics of modern empire," *Harvard Magazine,* May-June 2002

> There is only one step from fanaticism to barbarism.
>
> —Denis Diderot, 18th century Enlightenment leader

The cabal has made it clear that it will maintain an overpowering military force to deter any future *military or economic* challenge and discourage rival coalitions of any type. Whereas previous cabal strategy involved vulture capitalism, the new totalitarianism--suffering an ever-weakening economy--now uses its military super-power status to extort, intimidate, and destroy its economic rivals.

Tod Lindberg, a columnist for the Reverend Moon's *Washington Times,* elaborated upon Bush's West Point policy announcement: "What Mr. Bush is saying here is that the United States will never allow a 'peer competitor' to arise. We will never again be in a position of 'superpower rivalry,' let alone a cog in a multilateral balance of power."

The cabal strategy of pre-emptive strikes against any nation or group it brands as terrorist, imposing "regime change" on the recalcitrant country, and setting up military bases and puppet-regimes, has been clearly outlined by cabal toadies. The right-wing British historian Paul Johnson kicked off the justification for the new totalitarianism with a 2001 article in the *Wall Street Journal* entitled "The Answer to Terrorism? Colonialism."

America and her allies may find themselves . . . not just occupying with troops but administering obdurate terrorist states. These may eventually include not only Afghanistan but Iraq, Sudan, Libya, Iran and Syria. Democratic regimes willing to abide by international law will be implanted where possible, but a Western political presence seems unavoidable in some cases.

Unending War For Unending Peace

We find it difficult to believe that a regime--such as that which controls the United States--could adopt barbaric annihilation through unending war as its primary operating principle. Yet, if we examine the history of the last century with a critical eye, we discover that to be the case.

The improvement of the lot of the working class under the Franklin D. Roosevelt, Dwight Eisenhower, and John Kennedy administrations must be seen as bright exceptions to the prevailing ideology and practice of exploiting and "grinding" workers through vulture capitalism.

Once we recognize that the current ruling elite has no interest whatsoever in anything other than amassing wealth and power, we must ask: What is it about this strategy of ceaseless war that fulfills so well the goals of this totalitarian cabal?

Modern industrial societies, such as America, Britain, Japan, Russia, China, and the European nations, develop the capacity to produce more than is required for their economic survival. A ruling faction that has no interest in improving the lot of the working class must find the most profitable and efficient way to "use up" this surplus production of goods, services, and people. Perpetual armed conflict provides the criminal rulers with a "balance wheel," a most effective technique of destroying the surplus. Only through this constant production-and-destruction cycle can the rulers maintain their industrial empires.

In previous decades, weaponry was amassed by the cabal for the purpose of not being used--merely to have on hand in case of emergency and to threaten the cabal's enemies in the ongoing "arms race." That former policy has now been scrapped; the new totalitarianism's primary strategy is unending annihilation through unending war.

The new totalitarianism doesn't maintain even the pretense of democratic rule; it's established an unabashed dictatorship (think domestic spying, warrantless arrests, and seizure of all three branches of the federal government). Without ongoing warfare, a totalitarian regime is unable to obtain acquiescence in its "legitimacy" or right to rule the nation. The possibility and actuality of war provide the sense of external necessity which dictatorships require to remain in power. Thus the Reichstag syndrome: the deliberate orchestration of attacks against the nation by the ruling faction which are "spun" into external aggression by a foreign power: the 1933 Reichstag fire, 9/11, the Spanish and British railway bombs, and stay tuned for another cabal-orchestrated "terrorist attack" in a theater of operation near you.

A totalitarian autocracy finds war to be a very effective ideological clarifier. People are either for the junta or against it. During armed conflict, there are, to put it simply, only two sides to a question because there cannot be more than two sides to a war. You are either "for" the brave soldiers fighting in Iraq (or Iran, or ?) or you are "for" the evil terrorists.

The wars of totalitarian regimes are, therefore, not "caused" by international conflicts of interest. A war-making dictatorship requires--and *thus brings about*--such conflicts. With the only goals the amassing of wealth and power by the ruling elite, the capacity of a nation to make war expresses the greatest social power it can exercise.

In July 2006, Israel, the fourth most powerful military power in the world, found an excuse to put into operation its long-standing, carefully constructed plan to invade Lebanon and escalate the Middle-East "conflict" into threats against Iran and Syria. This attack by Israel--sanctioned by the international cabal--wasn't about Lebanon, Gaza, Hamas, or Hezbollah. It was about Iran and Syria, the only countries in the region able and determined to challenge Israel and the U.S. As *The Times* (London) reported on 5/11/02, Israeli leader Sharon called for the U.S. to attack Iran the moment the invasion of Iraq was complete.

Israeli intelligence pointed the finger at Iran and Syria for supplying weapons and funds to Lebanon and the Palestinians; as if the Bush junta wasn't doing the same for Israel in a far more massive way. As Americans tuned into their favorite cabal-owned and controlled TV or radio "news" program during that time period, they found an American representative of the Israeli lobby working overtime to target Iran and Syria.

The totalitarian regime's war against Iran and Syria has been underway for several years, with covert military and financial actions against both countries an ongoing operation on the part of both America and Israel. America now has at least fourteen military bases in Iraq to boost its ability to carry out military strikes against Iran's nuclear sites from Iraq. But those bases also expose the American forces to a possible Iranian retaliation. Israeli military and intelligence forces have been operating out of Iraq--with incursions into northern Iran--for several years.

The July, 2006 "excuse" for cabal escalation of violence in the Middle East began with the Hamas rise to power in Palestine and Hezbollah gaining seats in the administrative council of Lebanon. Israel and the United States immediately announced that they would, sooner or later, punish the people of Palestine and Lebanon for voting the wrong way in free elections. Hezbollah was the de facto government in southern Lebanon as well as part of the coalition government in Beirut. When the Israelis contrived the excuse in the capture of Corporal Gilad Shalit by Palestinian forces--while for the past decade they had captured and killed hundreds of Palestinians--the genocidal punishment was severe indeed.

The actual "cause" of the July, 2006 incursion of Israeli forces into Lebanon appears to have been the June 24 Israeli abduction of two Gaza civilians, a doctor and his brother. They were reported to have been taken to Israel, presumably; nobody knows their fate. On June 25, "militants" in Gaza, probably Islamic Jihad, abducted an Israeli soldier across the border. The abduction of Corporal Shalit was the only thing American TV "commentators" talked about; Israel's original abduction was not even mentioned. Israel used the abduction of Shalit as the excuse for the escalation of Israeli attacks on Gaza. It now appears that a Palestinian-Israeli peace agreement was in the works and that the Israeli Shin Bet internal Security Service vetoed the settlement because it interfered with their prior plans to invade, destroy, and occupy Lebanon.

The Israeli abduction of the two Gaza civilians was actually part of Acting Prime Minister Ehud Olmert's West Bank annexation operation—what was "spun" as "convergence" and described in the U.S. as a "withdrawal." In fact it was a continuation of the ongoing Israeli annexation of the valuable lands and resources--including water--of the West Bank and the Jordan Valley and the decades-long, non-ending Israeli attacks on civilian and military groups among the Lebanese and the Palestinians.

> The way to break this cycle is for all actors to negotiate a political solution that responds to their legitimate grievances and demands. Everyone involved seems prepared to do this, except for Israel and the US, who rely on military force, prolonged occupations, and diplomatic sanctions and threats. What will Israel and the US do when there are no more Arab airports, bridges and power stations to destroy? The futility of such policies should be clear by now, and therefore a diplomatic solution should be sought seriously for the first time.
>
> —Editor-at-Large Rami G. Khouri, "The 4 pairs in the Middle East's death dance," The Lebanese *Daily Star*, Saturday, July 15, 2006

The Totalitarian "Force Projection"

The demonic cabal's new brand of totalitarianism doesn't need foreign colonies the way the Romans did; its only requirement is control of resources, territories, and peoples through the placing of strategic military bases throughout the world, allowing it to deploy forces almost anywhere on the planet at lightning speed. In line with their overall policy of barbaric annihilation, it invades a country and sets about to destroy its government, its infrastructure, and its people.

The cabal has done this in El Salvador, Panama, Haiti, Afghanistan, and Iraq. If you want to understand what kind of world the cabal has in store for us, you have only to look at Afghanistan. This country has essentially been decimated, reduced to a barbaric anarchy of warlords, drug-running Taliban gangs, roving bands of pillaging marauders, and a blasted economy propped up by a heroin industry which supplies 60% of the heroin consumed in the world. Meanwhile the military installations are used to guard the region's gas and oil wells and pipelines while an American puppet sits in Kabul. If you look carefully, you can see that this same pattern of planned chaos is rapidly overtaking America.

This insane scorched earth cabal strategy even has an official name: the "Salvador Option." This secret strategy was initiated under Jimmy Carter and subsequently used during the Reagan administration's fight against the leftist guerrilla insurgency in El Salvador in the early 1980s, supporting "nationalist" gangs that also included death squads, with money, equipment and military training. In 2006, *Newsweek* published an article about this barbaric policy, which the military admitted it was "considering."

> According to military insiders familiar with the discussions inside the Pentagon, using the 'The Salvador Option' in Iraq involved sending Special Forces teams to train Iraqi squads, most likely Kurdish Peshmerga fighters and Shia armed groups to attack Iraqi Sunnis inside the country and at its border with Syria.

> But it hadn't been agreed whether this would be a policy of assassination or so called 'snatch' operations, where targets are sent to secret facilities for interrogation, officials told *Newsweek*, whose article was circulated among various media outlets and strongly rejected by Secretary of Defense Donald Rumsfeld.

They also stated that during the talks, officials recommended that while U.S. Special Forces would lead operations in Syria, activities inside Iraq itself would be carried out by Iraqi militias.

In a January 10 [2006] interview, retired General Wayne Downing, former head of all U.S. special operations forces, stated that U.S.-backed death squads had been plotting and did actually carry out attacks against leaders of the so-called insurgency since March 2003.

But in the mainstream press, Donald Rumsfeld, and General Downing all refused to admit that the Salvador Option was underway in Iraq.

> —"For the U.S., the 'Salvador Option' seemed the best to use in Iraq,"
> *Aljazeera.com,* 5/9/2006

The "Salvador Option" policy of annihilation was used in Iraq from the time the cabal invaded it. Naive people the world over wonder how the Bush junta could have allowed itself to have failed so miserably in Iraq. Relative to its goals, the cabal has not failed in Iraq at all. It has destroyed the infrastructure, the government, and the people, while establishing at least fourteen military bases with which it guards the privatized Iraqi energy resources and provides a "force projection" to threaten and intimidate the surrounding nations, especially Iran and Syria and even including Saudi Arabia. The cabal policy of deliberately encouraging civil war between Sunni, Shia, and Kurd factions has been successful in bringing full destruction to Iraq.

As Harvard Professor Stephen P. Rosen explains:

> We are in the business of bringing down hostile governments and creating governments favorable to us. Conventional international wars end and troops are brought back home. Imperial wars end, but imperial garrisons must be left in place for decades to ensure order and stability. This is, in fact, what we are beginning to see, first in the Balkans and now in Central Asia. In addition to advanced-technology weaponry, an imperial position requires a large but lightly armed ground force for garrison purposes and as reassurance for allies who want American forces on their soil as symbols of our commitment to their defense.

> —Stephen Peter Rosen, "The Future of War and the American Military:
> Demography, technology, and the politics of modern empire," *Harvard*
> *Magazine,* May-June 2002

The new totalitarian regime has taken a page from the Roman handbook: to rule the world it's not enough to have overpowering military might--the rest of the world must be fully aware of that might and fear it. Totalitarianism requires propaganda such as 24-hour news coverage of Israeli attacks on Lebanon in 2006. Other nations get the message: the demonic cabal's military superiority will annihilate anyone or anything that gets in its way.

Freedom Through Knowing the Truth

The reason we must focus on the deadly nature of this new totalitarianism is to protect ourselves from being taken in by the false "culture" it's creating. We're in a battle not merely for whether this or that particular puppet regime of the demonic cabal starts this pre-emptive war or that, but whether or not our very being will be subverted by their lies and false values. A depraved culture--such as we now face--can destroy a person's soul, because the disorder of society is a disease in the psyche of its members. We must guard our souls against the degradations of the surrounding cabal culture which presses on us. It's necessary for us to diagnose the health and disease in our individual souls and at the same time examine disorder in the deranged new totalitarianism.

In 2003, UK Defence Minister Geoff Hoon declared in Parliament that the Iraqi mothers of innocent children killed by American-British cluster-bombs would one day be "grateful" for sacrificing the fruit of their wombs to the invaders.

Our resistance to a barbaric culture depends for its success on a precise comprehension of those against whom we struggle. One of the requirements for discerning the true essence of our antagonists is to describe their beliefs and actions in a straightforward manner. We must, in other words, identify the demonic cabal's new operating principle by its true designation: the new totalitarianism of barbaric annihilation--not mindlessly dismissing it as a merely incompetent but well-intentioned regime. Our search for understanding and truth arises out of the resistance of our souls to their destruction by a perverted culture. The situation we now face is the life-or-death of our very being.

> To be deceived or uninformed in the soul about true being means that "the lie itself" has taken possession of "the highest part of himself" and steeped it into "ignorance of the soul."

—Plato, *Gorgias* (382a-b)

Not working to discover the truth and not forming reasoned opinions about what's happening in the world is a way of being complicit in the new totalitarianism. We must be engaged in social-political analysis--as well as activities of struggle and dissent--because the order or disorder of a culture shapes its citizens' minds and souls. All persons who want to safeguard themselves must search assiduously for the truth: what's really happening in the world and with themselves.

People worldwide must resist the mind-manipulation of a Karl Rove or any of the other members of the demonic cabal. By making the effort to inform themselves, persons anywhere in the world can thwart the attempt by the culture of untruth to corrupt their minds and psyches. Any genuine struggle against the new totalitarianism must expose and fight against the "culture of untruth" created by the criminal cabal. If you read something by a so-called contemporary thinker that isn't battling against the new form of totalitarianism, then you know that he or she is not a genuine participant in the battle for truth.

One of the major onslaughts by the cabal against the minds of citizens worldwide is their scam of "moral rearmament of totalitarianism." This swindle began with the first Gulf War, when the "coalition forces" were cast in the light of "champion" of the Kurds and Kuwaitis, who had pleaded for Western intervention against the satanic Saddam Hussein. For cabal fellow-travelers, the Gulf War vindicated the West. Forget about the cabal incursions in Suez, Algeria, and Vietnam; totalitarian invasion had been legitimate all along. Bush I included mention of Korea and Vietnam in his 1992 State of the Union address, pretending that even the defeat of Vietnam could be reconverted into a triumph through morally regenerating totalitarianism.

Part of the cabal pretence in this scheme of barbaric annihilation is "Democracy by force," trying to make the world believe the lie that it's maintaining democratic principles in America and exporting this way of life to other nations. When thinking people the world over examine carefully what's happening, they see the cabal's client states--Britain, Israel, Pakistan, Afghanistan, Iraq, Saudi Arabia, India, Egypt--as nothing more than dictatorships controlled by the cabal--with not a scintilla of true democracy in the lot. Fortunately, even some leaders of other nations see through the cabal lies and subterfuge--such as the duly elected president of Venezuela, Hugo Chavez.

In a 2006 visit to Britain, Chavez was asked by a BBC journalist whether he was behaving a bit like his arch-enemy George W. Bush by taking a "you're with us or against us" attitude. President Chavez, aghast at such a question, replied, "It is the first time I have been offended this way in public--to be compared to the biggest perpetrator of genocide the world has known. To be compared to an assassin, someone who has committed genocide, an immoral man who should be put in jail by an international court. What exactly are these attitudes?

"Have we invaded any country?" he asked to great applause from the people surrounding him. Chavez's response electrified the audience.

Chavez is the only leader of a foreign nation who called the July, 2006 Israeli invasion and occupation of Lebanon what it really was: a new holocaust.

Getting the Language--and the Understanding—Right

In struggling against this new form of totalitarianism, we must use the correct terms to keep things straight in our minds. It's necessary to describe things accurately to understand them in the correct manner. For example, we can no longer use such phrases as "America attacked Iraq." "America" didn't attack Iraq, the demonic cabal that controls America carried out the invasion, occupation, and decimation of Iraq. We must distinguish ourselves--Americans--from our noxious rulers--and encourage citizens worldwide to separate in their minds the criminal activities of the cabal from the American people.

We must see the cabal wars for what they are: *destructive* military "defense" spending as merely a contrived means for diverting tax money from social programs--hidden ways for rulers to amass power and wealth, and eliminate human populations. When we call the cabal wars "wasteful," we're speaking from our perspective: we see the "waste" of human and technological resources. From the junta's perspective wars aren't "wasteful," but "strategically effective" in destroying armaments that American tax dollars pay the "defense industry" corporations to manufacture, "strategically necessary" in ridding the American rulers of unnecessary people to support through Social Security and other "wasteful" social programs.

If we're to comprehend what's happening in the world, we must understand how the cabal views events as well as how we perceive those same events. For example, decent American citizens see the failure of "reconstruction" in Iraq and New Orleans (following the Katrina disaster) as evidence of sheer "incompetence," wondering how American leaders can allow such blatant ineptitude to occur. Dubya wasn't facetious when he said to FEMA director Michael Brown he had done "a heck of a job" and when he awarded L. Paul Bremer the Presidential Medal of Freedom.

As head of the Coalition Provisional Authority in Iraq, Bremer had done a superb job of seeing that no-bid contracts went almost exclusively to cabal cronies, plus allowing the outright theft of billions of dollars by selected fellow-criminals. (Forget about the fact that Iraq is still a stricken war zone with almost none of the infrastructure rebuilt.)

FEMA Chief Michael Brown *had* done a heck of a job for the cabal: he had made sure that a troublesome section of New Orleans was laid waste and poor white and black people were left homeless and without food or medical supplies for days. Brown's successor did an even more outstanding job of seeing that most of the Katrina "reconstruction" no-bid contracts went to Halliburton and other crony corporations.

One final example puts a clincher to this. 9/11 has been seen by most of the world as perhaps the worst intelligence failure in U.S. history. So why did ex-CIA Director George "Slam-dunk" Tenet join Bremer in the line to receive the Presidential Medal of Freedom? My best guess would be because he was complicit in 9/11, that he saw that no one in the CIA blew the whistle to make it evident that Bush II was lying about weapons of mass destruction, and that the compromising and degrading of the CIA continued apace under his term of service as was initiated under Bush I and other CIA directors.

We must think outside the box if we're to understand this new form of totalitarianism. We can put nothing past them; they're capable of the most inhuman and unthinkable acts of depravity. The best hypothesis we have to explain 9/11 is that the cabal was complicit in its planning and execution.

As we look at Afghanistan, Iraq, the 2006 violence aimed at Lebanon, and the threats against Iran and Syria, we have to come up with a hypothesis that best explains all these variables. Deprived of the all-purpose cold-war Soviet threat since 1991, the cabal has sought for credible new candidates to play the role of world villain. In a January, 1991 article in *International Affairs* titled "Christianity and Islam," Edward Mortimer noted that in the neo-conservative camp "many even felt the need to discover a new threat to replace the Soviet one" and for this purpose Islam "lay ready to hand." The totalitarian cabal appears to have decided that Islam possesses all the right ingredients to provide a pretext for invading, destroying, and "occupying" the Middle-East--and the world.

Why And How We Must Fight

In struggling against this new form of barbaric totalitarianism, we first need to realize that what we face is not just a somewhat incompetent, defective government, but a demonic force against which we must engage in a life-or-death battle for survival. Totalitarian regimes destroy their own people and their own nation in the same way they annihilate other nations and peoples.

We must not ignore or downplay the vital threat this totalitarian regime presents to us as individuals and as a nation. Other people have ignored just this kind of buildup of totalitarian power and have found themselves the victims of torture, imprisonment, and murder.

It should be clear to any thinking person that we must engage in this struggle against the new totalitarianism--to save ourselves and our nation from this "foreign" cabal animated by their demonic, alien ideology of barbaric annihilation.

Chapter Three

We Can No Longer Afford Vulture Capitalism

By Norman D. Livergood

Vulture Capitalism's cost in terms of human death and human misery has become so unbearable that we must now abandon it and establish a life-affirming Commonwealth social system.

The political, economic, and general social structures of our society must now be repudiated and a new culture realized to ensure the preservation and betterment of all human beings, not just the privileged few.

In this chapter, we'll use the term "vulture capitalism" to refer to the specific economic structures and practices of the demonic cabal which took economic and political control of the United States in the early part of the twentieth century.

The term "capitalism," like any generic term, must be tied down to a particular application and practice. In theory, "capitalism" refers to a socioeconomic system in which the means of production are predominantly privately owned and operated for profit through the employment of labor. The prices of goods, services, and labor are affected by the forces of supply and demand in a market. Decisions regarding investment are made privately, and production and distribution are primarily controlled by companies all acting in their own interest. Although most developed countries are regarded as capitalist, some of them have been called "mixed economies," due to government-owned means of production and economic interventionism.

As a general theory and practice, private ownership of the means of production, can be either positive or negative in its outcome, depending on those who are in control of the processes. When we refer to vulture capitalism, therefore, we're not speaking of the general, world-wide practice of the private ownership of the means of production.

That's too vague a reference to have any real meaning. The destruction of human life and well-being that results from capitalism in today's world is predominantly that practiced by the capitalist syndicate currently dominating the American and British political, economic, and social structures.

Humankind Has Outgrown Vulture Capitalism

The human race is sufficiently intelligent and aware enough to take control of its own destiny, refusing to be deceived any longer by the death-dealing capitalist myths:

- "The invisible hand of the market works for the good of all"

- "Free trade is the only way to order international commerce"

- "Capitalists should pay little or no tax because they are the engine of the economy"

- "Unemployment and poverty are natural, inevitable afflictions in any economic system"

- "The United States has the right to attack any nation which threatens its national economy"

- "Economic efficiency is only possible under capitalism"

- "All manufacturing, public utilities, and commodities should be privately owned"

- "Capitalists ought to be able to make as much money as they can, no matter what the plight of the workers"

- "All things are working together for the best in this best of all capitalist worlds"

The Need to "Unemploy" Vulture Capitalism

The displacement of predatory capitalism with a new social structure for the well-being of all citizens will certainly not happen overnight, but we must begin now planning and working for this pro-human framework for society. This movement toward a people centered economic system must work in solidarity with the development of a citizen-based form of government. Our first need is to see clearly what our present situation truly is--and why we desperately need to rid ourselves of vulture capitalism and institute a new social order.

- For too long, people worldwide have been suffering under the dead hand of vulture capitalist oppression: humans reduced to the status of mere pawns and commodities within an inhuman system of obscene privilege for the predatory capitalist class.

- The vulture capitalist ideology has become so ingrained in people's minds that they consider economic favoritism a "fact of nature," the only possible way to order society. Questioning it seems to many the rankest form of subversion of incontestable principles, an attack on the very fundaments of the American way of life.

Most people are unaware of the historical fact that predatory capitalist oppression merely replaced earlier forms of despotism: the Roman Catholic Church, the Protestant Churches, and the tyrants and dictators at the head of empires and nation states. That vulture capitalism helped to remove people from earlier forms of tyranny makes no difference whatsoever, because it immediately enslaved those same persons in an equally despotic form of economic oppression.

America As a Preeminent Example

The transcendent value of our American experience is its demonstration that a people can take their destiny in their own hands and improve their life situation. The American colonists didn't merely wring their hands over their misfortune of suffering under British monarchy and colonialism. They threw off the chains of British imperialism --political and economic oppression.

Our situation is now different--for example, it would be foolish to oppose the cabal capitalists with violence, because they hold a monopoly on weapons which kill masses.

Nonetheless, we should take courage from the example of the American colonists who won their independence and begin planning now to take back our economic and political power as a people by realizing a new culture.

Out of this modern civilization economic royalists carved new dynasties. New kingdoms were built upon concentration of control over material things. Through new uses of corporations, banks and securities, new machinery of industry and agriculture, of labor and capital -all undreamed of by the Fathers the whole structure of modern life was impressed into this royal service.

—Franklin Delano Roosevelt, speech in Philadelphia on June 27, 1936

Even though in these and other instances Americans improved their circumstances only by degrees--and the lot of only some within the population--these were tremendous steps forward for humankind. Those and similar advances in human well-being still possess such tremendous power by their example that even the demonic cabal we currently suffer under must pay lip service to their principles of freedom and economic fairness.

Human social and spiritual evolution moves forward in starts and jumps. The American Declaration of Independence, the Bill of Rights, the Preamble to the Constitution, civil rights legislation, Social Security, and women's right to vote were watersheds in humankind's progression toward true freedom and justice.

The fact that the American Constitution was created as a plutocratic instrument--through the *coup d'etat* of the Constitutional Convention--means that this document possesses fatal flaws. These defects are revealing themselves in this era when the criminal cabal has seized power unlawfully and has undercut numerous constitutional rights and privileges.

The Necessity for New Political and Economic Structures

As we've discovered, it's necessary to realize an entirely new culture, though we'll be able to utilize some of the fundamental American political principles, such as the Bill of Rights. In the economic sphere, we must adopt an entirely new framework wholesale. The cabal capitalist system contains so much that is not only wrong but positively malignant that we must realize a totally different system of economic principles and practices.

We learned from FDR's New Deal and Lyndon Johnson's "Great Society" that when predatory capitalism's power is threatened by pressure from the populace, it will grudgingly--and temporarily--move in the direction of providing some regulation of its cutthroat practices and some social safety nets for workers to take the worst sting out of vulture capitalism's crises and offenses.

These steps are taken to save looter capitalism from the rising power of the working class. In such cases, new regulations are enacted to curb the most obvious and hated aspects of vulture capitalism and these are then trumpeted as a total and final solution to the problems. Unthinking people fall for this flimflam and support its con artists and snake oil salesmen. The supposed "final" solutions to predatory capitalism's "exuberances" and "irregularities" are held up as great victories by co-conspirator labor leaders and political hacks.

For thinking Americans it's important not to fall for these scams and con jobs. Propagandistic illusions of vulture capitalism's rectification and regulation are merely fantasy solutions to the problems facing human society and our planet. While predatory capitalists have pretended to tinker with their system, they've subjected the world to two world wars, the bestial conflagrations of Hiroshima and Nagasaki, unremitting general warfare (Korea, Vietnam, Iraq, Afghanistan), poverty, unemployment, and general human misery. Fake cosmetic surgery won't solve our critical social problems. We must adopt an entirely new and different system of economic thought and practice--one based on the principle that human life is the ultimate value to be served in our personal, commercial and industrial interactions.

Vulture Capitalism Is Fascism

Just as the flawed U.S. Constitution led inevitably to the dictatorial seizure of all branches of government--under both the John Adams administration (1796-1800) and again now under the Bush II junta--so the unsound, defective principles of predatory capitalism lead inexorably to fascism.

Fascism is the economic system in which a criminal cabal--termed an oligarchy, plutocracy, or ruling class--seizes and misappropriates the powers of the state to enforce the economic domination of privately owned cartels and corporations.

As militaristic imperialism is the guise vulture capitalism assumes as it plunders other countries, fascism is predatory capitalism's mode of ordering the entire society to maintain unequal distribution of economic and social power, substituting mechanistic for human values as the basis for civilized order.

In its early days, when predatory capitalism faced a world of untapped human and raw material resources, it could for a time allow some amount of monetary and social reward to accrue to workers, without in the least reducing its obscene amassing of profits and power.

Thus, the United States experienced relative economic and social expansion after the second world war. But the day inevitably comes when the world markets begin to dry up--due to pesky competitors, mindless waste and destruction of natural resources, and the inescapable exigencies of too many goods chasing too few consumers.

At that point, the only recourse for vulture capitalism is to adopt barbaric annihilation as its basic operating procedure, imposing dictatorial, police-state measures on the domestic population, and plunging the world into a "never-ending war" framework (read "war on terrorism").

The inevitable crisis point in the cabal capitalist system now engulfs all nations of the earth. The various major "capitalist" competitors--the demonic cabal that rules America, the dictatorial regimes of China, Russia, the European Union, Japan, and India--are engaged in a deadly struggle for dominance and survival. The criminal American cabal has brazenly announced its policy of attacking any nation it considers to be a threat to its economic or military power--whether that nation has carried out overt acts of aggression or not.

A Rerun of Predatory Capitalism's Inevitable "Crisis Points"

Predatory capitalism faced a similar crisis point in 1870. The cutthroat world competition for profits began to result in a change in the economic relations between the major capitalist powers. Previously a system of relatively "free trade" had predominated, but now corporations sought protection for their home markets from their international rivals. The replacement of the free trade system by tariff protection created the era of colonial acquisition.

In the face of reduced markets because of global competition, cabal capitalists began to adopt the policy of militaristic imperialism to ensure colonial markets for their products and provide access to raw materials. Each capitalist country's security was threatened by the protectionist policies of the other capitalist countries.

By tariffs and other protectionist methods, each capitalist state tried to close its home and colonial markets against its rivals. Each capitalist nation found it necessary to stake out its own "sphere of influence" to protect its own trade and industry, to ensure profits to its traders, manufacturers and financiers, and to prevent other predatory and hostile capitalist states from seizing reservoirs of raw materials and markets.

The inevitable result of this world capitalist struggle was World War I, followed in short order by World War II. The American capitalist cabal imposed dollar imperialism on the rest of the world, forcing all nations to deal in American dollars in all their financial and industrial transactions. The vulture capitalists had discovered what they considered to be a way out of their crises: perpetual war. After earlier world struggles, the victors had enjoyed a short period of profit-making as the defeated nations (for example, Japan, Germany and other European nations after World War II) required new outputs of goods and services.

The Degenerate Capitalist

Among many reasons why we can no longer tolerate vulture capitalism is that the members of this class are becoming increasingly soulless, ruthless and murderous. There have been isolated moments in our history when a few persons within the capitalist camp have attempted to create somewhat salutary human conditions within society, because those few capitalists leaders possessed some sense of decency, propriety, and fellow feeling. But that situation no longer exists in the twenty-first century: the new breed of vulture capitalists is composed of the most debased and corrupt persons imaginable.

When the President of the United States is the grandson of a war criminal, proven to have been complicit in the rise to power of Adolf Hitler, that's as bad as it can get. When that degenerate who seized the presidency through a coup d'etat lies to start a war that kills thousands of American soldiers, things are horrendous indeed.

Make no mistake about it, the depraved, murderous rulers we now suffer under are themselves leaders within the predatory capitalist class and have been created in their very persons by the diabolic ideology of vulture capitalism.

The rise of the Progressive Movement during the Great Depression somewhat concerned the cabal capitalists, because it represented the working class rising up against capitalist oppression in general. So the vulture capitalists allowed for some improvement in the lot of the workers after the second world war, as exemplified in the GI bill provision for education. But during the latter part of the twentieth—and now the twenty-first--centuries, the members of the cabal have become totally indifferent to human suffering and have no interest in justice or equality of opportunity in society.

Instead of feeling a need to improve the lot of the workers, they now consider it to be to their benefit if conditions for workers are as bad as possible--to force them into the military as cannon fodder for their imperialist wars. They are quite content to see America devolve into devastated war-zone cities wracked by drugs and crime. They no longer see a need to provide workers even the bare necessities of life. They are deliberately creating a two class society: the obscenely wealthy class and the destitute peasant class.

As they see it, they now have the means of amassing fortunes without having to be the least concerned about workers--after all there are billions of laborers in Asia and other parts of the world who are willing to work for the lowest possible pay--serving either as chattel or wage slaves. And it's no longer good policy, as they see it, to "reconstruct" a nation once they've attacked and plundered it--such as Afghanistan or Iraq. After all, their experience with helping to reconstruct Germany and Japan after World War II resulted in those countries having the impertinence to become economic competitors!

So now their practice is to leave a country like Afghanistan or Iraq to sink into a hell hole of warlordism and drug cartels. They say they're "reconstructing" Iraq, but the millions of dollars in "misplaced" reconstruction fees that wind up in the pockets of Halliburton or other Republican-supporting corporations is moot testimony that they're lying--as usual.

The Vulture Capitalist Attack on American Citizens

You may feel that none of this matters very much as long as the insane capitalists just don't hassle you too much and leave you alone with your two part-time jobs and the opportunity to watch NFL and NBA games and sit-coms on television. That's what the German people in the 1930s thought, too. But fascist governments don't just attack foreign countries; they also destroy their own people.

The slaughter of Americans began with the 1992 FBI raid on the cabin of Randy Weaver in Idaho, in which Weaver's wife and son were killed. The Waco, Texas atrocity followed in 1993, with the ATF and the FBI ruthlessly killing American citizens, then the 1995 Oklahoma City bombing perpetrated by a U.S. military trained insurgency team.

Beginning in 2001, Americans have experienced attacks on our constitutional freedoms--domestic spying, betrayal of CIA agents out of spite, and the criminal rigging of the 2000, 2002, and 2004 national elections--among dozens of other outrages perpetrated by this capitalist cabal.

> The open attack on the Geneva Conventions by the President of the United States and his defense of torture . . . has the most profound and ominous implications for the democratic rights of the American people. There is no iron wall between foreign and domestic policy. A regime that employs torture as part of its foreign policy will sooner or later employ the same methods against its political opponents at home.

> —Joe Kay and Barry Grey, "The Bush administration and the CIA prisons: a new campaign of lies," Word Socialist Website (*www.wsws.org*), 9/18/2006

The attacks on our constitutional freedoms and the uncontrolled corruption which besets Washington is bad enough, but we must awaken to the stark fact that cabal capitalists are killing American citizens. If you stand idly by--you're going to be murdered.

If we carefully study two of the most blatant instances of the murder of American citizens--the Oklahoma City bombing and the 9/11 horror--the most reasonable hypothesis appears to be that the criminal cabal planned and carried out these atrocities. The second most viable hypothesis is that they were complicit in their occurrence--by design or through incompetence. Either way, the capitalist cabal is killing Americans outright.

What Perspective Should We Take?

We certainly don't want to attack these unfortunate vulture capitalist rogues through violence of any kind. That would undercut the very principles we're working to implement. We begin by examining our present situation in all its stark reality--no matter how disturbing the spectacle. We must not mince words and call these monsters "well intentioned" or "fearless" leaders. We must see them in all their hideousness if we're to grasp the critical necessity to realize an entirely new economic-political culture.

The fact that America at present enjoys more freedom than most other countries in the world is not because of the capitalist cabal, BUT IN SPITE OF IT. From the beginning of our country the predatory capitalist elite has endeavored to degrade American freedom and subjugate labor.

Vulture capitalists--and their academic lap-dogs pretend that American freedom has only been made possible by its policies and practices. Quite the opposite is the truth. What freedoms we have been able to gain have been wrested from their hands through long struggle by the working class.

The ravages of predatory capitalism are becoming clear for all Americans to see and feel. We either overthrow this form of economic slavery or we'll end up actual chattel slaves to a new capitalist class of criminal thugs. To regain our constitutional freedoms, we must establish equitable economic principles. We can begin by working for the realization of the Second Bill of Rights as presented by President Franklin D. Roosevelt in his State of the Union Address in January, 1944.

In his State of the Union Address, Roosevelt declared that the nation had come to recognize, and should now implement, a second bill of rights. Roosevelt did not argue for any change to the United States Constitution; he believed that the second bill of rights should be implemented politically, not by federal judges. Roosevelt's stated justification was that the "political rights" granted by the Constitution and the Bill of Rights had "proved inadequate to assure us equality in the pursuit of happiness." Roosevelt's remedy was to create an "economic bill of rights" which would guarantee:

- "The right to a useful and remunerative job"

- "The right to earn enough to provide adequate food and clothing and recreation"

- "The right of every family to a decent home"

- "The right to adequate medical care and opportunity to enjoy and achieve good health"

- "The right to adequate protection from the economic fears of old age, sickness, accident, and unemployment"

- "The right to a good education"

Roosevelt stated that having these rights would guarantee American security, and that America's place in the world depended upon how far these and similar rights were carried into practice.

Our efforts toward a commonwealth social system--involving a new economic structure and a revised governmental format--must begin with clear awareness of our present situation, as outlined above.

Critical examinations of the predatory capitalist system by such thinkers as Karl Marx, Friedrich Engels, Rosa Luxemburg, and Leon Trotsky help us see its glaring defects. Writing my Ph.D. dissertation on Karl Marx's early thought, I came to see that he and the other socialist thinkers saw clearly how the ideology of capitalism reduces humans to "commodities" within a mechanistic system. Their vision of a society in which humans would be the primary value offered a viable alternative to vulture capitalism.

However, when it comes to the implementation of such a "new society," there the socialists seem to me to trail off into vague nostrums ("withering away of the state") or propound absolutistic dogmas ("dictatorship of the proletariat") that have little if any merit. The movement away from predatory capitalism to a new, humanistic economic system will not occur "automatically" as the workers of the world magically unite, telling themselves they have nothing to lose but their chains.

Most of the advocates of "gradualism," such as Gar Alperovitz's *America Beyond Capitalism*, are largely palliatives and propaganda placebos meant to make the unthinking masses believe that predatory capitalism is magically changing its stripes and becoming beneficent. Nearly all the scholastic studies of capitalism, such as J. A. Schumpeter's 1911 *The Theory of Economic Development*, of R. H. Tawney's 1922 *Religion and the Rise of Capitalism*, offer no genuine insights or solutions whatsoever.

The Public Service Economy

Historically, federal, state, and local governments have managed certain businesses and industries which American citizens thought best kept in public hands: prisons, schools, forests, parks, military bases, retirement funds, utilities, etc. And American citizens have also wanted their government to regulate certain businesses and industries which the citizens felt could only be scrutinized by public agencies, not privately-owned enterprises.

Beginning in the 1960s the capitalist cabal's front organizations--Cato, Heritage Foundation, American Enterprise Institute (AEI), Committee on the Present Danger, Free Congress Foundation, Council for Inter-American Security, Council for National Policy, etc.--began to raise a loud outcry that governmental regulatory agencies had been "captured" by the industries under regulation.

Of course, the allegations were largely true--their political puppets had made sure that the public regulatory agencies such as OSHA (Occupational Safety and Health Administration), EPA (Environmental Protection Agency), and EEOC (Equal Employment Opportunity Commission), were either crippled or co-opted.

But many Americans, made indifferent and ignorant by the demonic cabal's subversion of American education beginning in the early decades of the twentieth century, can't see that the groups claiming to be watching out for citizens' interests are actually fronts for the American vulture capitalist group. The mind-robots eat up the catch slogans of: "get the government off the backs of the people" and "consumer choice." So they stand still when the elite's political puppets put through legislation which creates deregulation and privatization of public institutions.

The cabal's political puppets broke up some of their large competitors, such as AT&T, IBM, savings and loan institutions, and airlines, so the cartel could increase its holdings in the telecommunication, computer, banking, and air travel industries. Then, the cabal began its deregulatory experiments with the opening of access to networks. Under this approach, the physical infrastructures of the networks (such as airports, cables, pipelines) remained regulated natural monopolies, but access to these networks was opened so that the remaining elements could be submitted to competition: airline traffic, telecommunication services, gas and electricity production, etc.

Americans know that historically, the U.S. was created on the principle that citizens own public land, highways, schools, ports, airports, parks, the airwaves, government buildings and other assets. Under the present criminal regime, public assets such as energy production plants, water resources, prisons, and many others, have been seized by members of the cabal under the guise of "privatization." Americans must create a government that will serve as the protector of the citizenry, and champion their cause when confronted with the predatory greed of profit-motivated corporations and individuals. Americans don't see anyone in the federal or state government doing anything but assuring that the big corporations' profits skyrocket even more. So Americans are beginning to inform themselves--primarily through the Internet and progressive books.

Our economic situation at present--a very few obscenely rich people owning companies and corporations and having illegally seized state and federal political power--is one which we can and must change. Our current economic and political circumstances are not written in stone; humans have lived under very different political and economic conditions throughout our history.

We must begin to overthrow this present state of affairs where most of us suffer under wage-slavery. The political system and the economic situation should be directed toward the welfare of all Americans, not just a few. Since the vulture capitalists have rigged the 2000, 2002, and 2004 national elections, for us to have any chance of creating positive change in America, we'll first need to make certain that our election process is reclaimed by the people.

We must first make all Americans aware of our present plight and then begin in all possible ways to overthrow the tyranny of cabal capitalism, producing material changes leading to political freedom and economic equality of opportunity. In some instances this may involve the public ownership of the means of production: companies, factories, businesses, institutions, etc. We can bring about these changes by joining with thinking citizens worldwide in specific initiatives such as boycotting and in citizen action groups available through progressive Internet sites.

To be able to direct publicly-held institutions effectively, workers must be sufficiently intelligent to know how to plan and carry out short-and long-term projects, avoid being taken in by manipulative persons, and evaluate and maintain all essential operations. Such intelligent administration of public enterprises will require an effectual educational system to produce efficient leaders. In today's world, the most proficient means of educating large numbers of people is through those Internet sites not dominated and controlled by the capitalist cabal.

All thinking persons must join in this effort to throw off the lethal vulture capitalist shackles that bind the minds and bodies of workers worldwide. Humankind has overthrown tyrannies and tyrants throughout its history. We can no longer afford not to throw off the malignancy of vulture capitalism.

Chapter Four

Dollar Imperialism

By Norman D. Livergood

An imperialistic regime extends its power and dominion over other nations through military, economic, and cultural means. This involves the military acquisition of territory, gaining control over the political and economic life of subject groups, *and imposing its monetary system on conquered nations.*

The Assyrian, Egyptian, Chinese, Roman, and British Empires all established a single currency standard for the regions over which they ruled. The British forced their colonies and most other nations of the world to use the British pound sterling as the international monetary standard during its world rule in the eighteenth, nineteenth and early twentieth centuries.

The Rule of the Yankee Dollar

When America emerged from the second world war as the most powerful nation in the world, both economically and militarily, the demonic cabal that had seized political, economic, and social control of the United States in the first decades of the twentieth century was able to impose the American dollar on the world as the standard currency. In 1944, even before the war was over, the Western nations met at Bretton Woods, New Hampshire, to agree on the American dollar as the world currency. Bretton Woods established a dollar standard to replace the gold standard.

The value of the dollar was fixed to gold at $35 an ounce, and the world's currencies were fixed to the dollar. Following World War II, the international cabal wanted to make sure its dollar would be the international currency standard, so it created, among other processes, the Marshall Plan, named after Truman's secretary of state, George Marshall. The plan lent American dollars to all the nations of Europe to "assist in the return of normal economic health in the world."

The cabal propaganda promised that as the European economies improved, their currencies would stabilize and there would be a return to European economic prosperity. The real reason for the Marshall Plan was that once these countries had been put back on their feet by American aid, their currencies would be tied to the American dollar and they would be forced to buy American products, benefiting the economy of the United States.

Also, the Marshall Plan forced any European country wanting aid to denounce communism and socialism. Even Britain had to renounce its ties to earlier socialist policies.

The Marshall Plan offer of financial help to European countries had an underlying catch: it involved establishing the Organisation for European Economic Co-operation (OEEC) that controlled how the money was spent. All countries requesting aid had to join the OEEC, meaning they had to trade with each other, accept capitalism as their economic system, and agree that their currencies would be tied to the American dollar.

Eventually, sixteen European countries accepted Marshall Aid and by 1953 the United States had provided $17 billion in relief. It was offered to all the nations of Europe even those in the east, but understandably Stalin refused to allow them to accept it. The Soviets forbade countries under their control from accepting Marshall Aid. Stalin quite correctly saw the Plan as "dollar imperialism." He believed that the United States was trying to bribe countries to join the American side in the developing Cold War and the global currency war of the American dollar versus the Soviet ruble.

In response to the Marshall Plan, the Soviets established Comecon which was Stalin's attempt to thwart dollar imperialism. The East and West were now tied into two economic blocs, which had entirely different political, economic, and social aims. Marshall Aid further increased tension between the two sides and led to each bloc consolidating its hold over its European allies. The Iron Curtain had slammed shut across eastern Europe.

The cardinal purpose of the imperialist camp is to strengthen imperialism, to hatch a new imperialist war, to combat socialism and democracy.

> —Andrei Zhdanov, Politburo member and Leningrad party boss, September 22, 1947, a report to the first conference of Cominform, the international communist information bureau

The United States adopted what was called the Truman Doctrine, a policy of "containment" against the Soviet Union, attempting to stop the spread of communist regimes--and the Soviet ruble. The Truman Doctrine was given the cabal's imprimatur by George Kennan in an article under the pseudonym "Mr. X" in the *Foreign Affairs* quarterly.

The international cabal upheld the Bretton Woods agreement until August of 1971, when Nixon declared US bankruptcy--the US would no longer redeem dollars in gold. This occurred because the costly Vietnam war, beginning in the 1960s, had drained US gold reserves. By 1968 the redemption of US dollars for gold had reached crisis levels, since foreign central banks holding dollars feared that US deficits would make their dollars worthless, preferring gold instead. Nixon reneged on the Bretton Woods agreement, refusing to redeem dollars for gold. After 1971, the dollar was no longer fixed to an ounce of gold, something measurable, it was fixed only to the printing press of the cabal's Federal Reserve System.

Dollar Imperialism's Cat's Paws: EuroDollar, PetroDollar, and IFI

Two cabal extortion schemes--Eurodollars and Petrodollars--continue to impose the American dollar on the world, forcing other nations to trade in the U.S. currency and support the dollar by buying American treasury bonds. After World War II, the dollar became the only global reserve currency. This meant that other nations' central banks had to hold dollars in reserve to guarantee against currency crises, to back their export trade, and to finance imports of oil and other goods and services. Today, some 67% of all central bank reserves are in dollars, with only about 15% in Euros. Until the creation of the Euro, there had not even been a theoretical rival to the dollar reserve currency role.

Dollar imperialism is based on global extortion: you either use dollars and follow cabal directives or your economy goes into the toilet and you're branded a terrorist nation. With nothing to control the cabal's creation of U.S. dollars, it prints more bills than the American economy justifies. It buys foreign goods and services with dollars that cost almost nothing to print. When the US was still on the Bretton Woods gold standard, between 1945 and 1965, total supply of dollars increased only some 55%. The world experienced low inflation and stable growth. After Nixon's break with gold, dollars expanded by more than 2,000% between 1970 and 2001!

Since most commodities are tied to dollars, this means that if you want to buy a barrel of Saudi oil, a German auto, or an American computer, you must have dollars. In 1972-73, the cabal made an iron-clad arrangement with Saudi Arabia to support the power of the House of Saud in exchange for their accepting only U.S. dollars for its oil. The rest of OPEC was to follow suit and also accept only dollars. Because the world had to buy oil from the Arab oil countries, it had this additional incentive to hold dollars as payment for oil. The cabal's "trade partners" [dollar imperialism victims] throughout the world hold so many dollars that they're afraid to create a dollar crisis. Other nations, fearing a global collapse, inflate or deflate their own currencies relative to the U.S. dollar, actually weakening their own economies, to support the Dollar Syndicate.

As nations throughout the world began to use the U.S. dollar as reserves for their own currencies, two large pools of dollars in foreign hands were created: Eurodollars and petrodollars. It works like this: a German company, say BMW, sells its cars in the U.S. for dollars. BMW exchanges those dollars for marks or Euros through currency transfer with the Bundesbank or European Central Bank (ECB). The ECB thus builds up its dollar currency reserves: Eurodollars. Those nations that supply or purchase energy commodities amass the same kind of dollar pool and the result is the petrodollar.

Since the oil shocks of the 1970's, when the price of oil increased by 400%, nations have felt the need to have large reserves of dollars to pay for oil. Since that energy scare, creating a large U.S. dollar reserve has become a national security policy for many countries. Boosting export sales denominated in dollars is a national priority. But the Bundesbank or the ECB can no longer receive gold for their dollars, so they have to decide what to do with the mountain of dollars their trade is earning. Most nations have decided to at least earn interest on their dollars by buying supposedly safe, secure U.S. Treasury bonds. The cabal thugs are certain that foreign "trade partners" will be forced to continually buy more U.S. debt to prevent the global monetary system from collapsing, as threatened to happen in 1998 with the Russian default and the LTCM hedge fund crisis.

Nations throughout the world now hold an estimated $1 trillion to $1.5 trillion in U.S. Government debt. If we look at the essence of this process, we can recognize it as global coercion, pure and simple. In effect, the cabal has become addicted to foreign borrowing. They're able to spend as much as they want on military adventures--putting huge sums into the hands of their Republican supporters--because they don't have to use savings to finance their consumption. The cabal lives off creating by fiat the U.S. dollars that the rest of the world is forced to use.

The difference between what a nation sells to the U.S. and what the U.S. sells to that nation is called the trade deficit. The country today with the largest trade deficit with the U.S. is China.

The Chinese yuan is fixed to the dollar. The U.S. is being flooded with cheap Chinese goods, often outsourced by U.S. multinational corporations such as Wal-Mart. As of 2003, China's trade surplus with the U.S. was more than $100 billion a year, Japan $70 billion, Canada $48 billion, Mexico $37 billion, and Germany $36 billion; a total deficit of almost $300 billion of the colossal $480 billion deficit.

The total U.S. debt--public and private--has more than doubled since 1995. It is now officially over $34 trillion. It was just over $16 trillion in 1995, and "only" $7 trillion in 1985. Most alarmingly, it has grown faster than income to service it, as indicated by U.S. gross domestic product (GDP). The U.S. economy--as subverted by the cabal--now requires a daily fix of $2.5 billion to stay afloat.

All this huge trade surplus with foreign nations benefits only the wealthy upper 1% in the U.S.--the members and supporters of the demonic cabal. American workers are losing jobs and retirement funds, their income is decreasing rapidly, and their standard of living is deteriorating alarmingly. Globalization is just a euphemism for dollar imperialism.

Dollar Imperialism Is Beginning to Crack

Within the last fifteen years, dollar imperialism has faced new challenges and dangers. The cabal's impoverishment of Third World states through its international financial institutions (IFI) such as the World Bank (WB) and the International Monetary Fund (IMF) has drained the wealth of local economies. The IFI structural adjustment policies, free trade doctrines, and privatization directives fragment and weaken the client states, causing widespread corruption as politicians and private sector elites, such as Enron, pillage the treasuries of the victim nations.

This crisis situation now requires a "new imperialism," as journalist Martin Wolf made clear in an October 10, 2001 propaganda piece in the *Financial Times*. Wolf argued that bombs and marines must supplement IMF and WB functionaries [debt-masters] in "restructuring" economies and ensuring the subordination of Third World States. He asserted: "To tackle the challenge of the failed [pillaged and depleted] state what is needed is not pious aspirations but an honest and organized coercive force."

In other words, dollar imperialist wars throughout the world, which have left nations in debt-slavery to the IMF, must now be supplemented by new military conquests such as those in Afghanistan and Iraq. Recolonization through pre-emptive invasion of "bad countries" is the new dollar imperialism strategy, a process already underway in the Middle East and Latin America.

All of this dollar imperialism will be masked as the "spread of democracy," as Bush's 2005 inaugural speech made clear. Robert Kagan used his column in the *Washington Post* to praise Bush's inaugural speech as a new U.S. foreign policy break-through. Kagan wrote: "The goal of American foreign policy is now to spread democracy, for its own sake, for reasons that transcend specific threats. In short, Bush has unmoored his foreign policy from the war on terrorism."

Dollar Imperialism: Petrodollar Warfare and Oil Depletion Warfare

Dollar Imperialism's "center of gravity" is the rising depletion of oil supplies throughout the world and the military, political, and economic struggles that accompany this global flash point. One of the ways the U.S. keeps control over Europe and Japan is by having a stranglehold on their energy supply.

According to the Department of Energy, oil consumption by the developing world will increase by 96% between 2001 and 2025, while consumption of natural gas will rise by 103%. For China and India, the rate of growth is even more dramatic: China's oil consumption is projected to jump by 156% over this period and India's by 152%.

It's highly unlikely that energy-exporting countries will actually be able to deliver such increased quantities of oil and gas in the coming decades, whether for political, economic, or geological reasons--no matter what nations such as

Saudi Arabia claim. Dollar imperialism energy corporations have deliberately reduced their refinery resources, causing shortages in gasoline and oil, resulting in oil and gas prices skyrocketing all over the world--bringing windfall profits to the cabal energy conglomerates.

Since 1950, worldwide oil consumption has grown eightfold, from approximately 10 to 80 million barrels per day. Gas consumption, which began from a smaller base, has grown even more dramatically. Hydrocarbons now satisfy 62% of the world's total energy demand, approximately 250 quadrillion BTUs out of a total supply of 404 quads. But no matter how important they may be today, hydrocarbons are sure to prove even more critical in the future. According to the Department of Energy, oil and gas will account for 65% of world energy in 2025, a larger share than at present; and because no other source of energy is currently available to replace them, the future health of the global economy rests on our ability to discover and harness more and more of these hydrocarbons.

To understand the crisis in world oil supply, we must define precisely what is meant by "peak oil." Peak oil occurs when half the oil in the ground around the world has been pumped out. From that moment on the remaining oil is harder to extract, so you must pump water and natural gas into the oil field to maintain pressure as the production in barrels per day declines. Using more energy to pump it out and less of an outflow means oil is more expensive to produce and there's increasingly less of it to go around. Peak oil is a simple geological fact: there's no more cheap oil.

America has long since hit the peak of oil production and is now in decline. World oil production will hit that same peak within the next few years. According to oil industry experts and independent geologists, peak oil has possibly already arrived, with a plateau in global oil production in 2005, midpoint peak by 2008 and terminal decline setting in from 2010 on.

With the onset of Peak Oil, the world has entered the end-game phase of the industrial revolution. The dollar imperialists are trying to grab a stranglehold on world resource streams, so that China--now the world's largest consumer of steel, grain, meat, and coal--will be left out in the cold--literally. But China is steadily securing long-term oil contracts with Saudi Arabia, Iran, Venezuela, and Nigeria; the Chinese are even seeking a sizeable portion of Canadian oil production, and in 2005 attempted to buy an American oil company, Unocal.

While on the surface the U.S. and China seem to be trading politely--Americans buy cheap Chinese goods, the Chinese invest their earnings in U.S. Treasury Bills to enable Americans to purchase even more Chinese imports--beneath the surface both are angling for a superior position in the ongoing dollar imperialism conflict. If China were to decide to declare open war against the dollar imperialists, it would sell off its dollar holdings, tie its currency to the Euro, co-operate with other countries in forming a coalition to oppose the dollar imperialists, and the American economy might be destroyed, with America landing on the ash heap of failed empires. However, to maintain control of global resource flows, the dollar imperialists have clearly demonstrated that they're willing to play their most monstrous card--their spectacularly lethal weapons of mass death and destruction.

Dollar imperialist hired gun Secretary of State Condoleezza Rice now has the job of going around the world threatening other nations with first-strike, unprovoked retaliation against their going up against the Bush junta in competing for oil and gas reserves or in trying to use any other currency than the American dollar.

In March, 2005, Condy tried to intimidate Indian Foreign Minister Natwar Singh in New Delhi to back away from India's plan to import natural gas by pipeline from Iran, claiming that any such endeavor would frustrate U.S. efforts to isolate the hard-line clerical regime in Tehran. Indian leaders let it be known that their desire for additional energy supplies trumped Washington's ideological opposition to the Iranian regime. Declaring that the proposed pipeline will be necessary to meet India's soaring energy needs, Foreign Minister Singh told reporters, "We have no problem of any kind with Iran."

Following her attempt at extortion in New Delhi, Rice flew to Moscow and demanded of President Vladimir Putin that he cease his crackdown on the privately-owned energy giant, Yukos, and allow increased investment by American firms in Russia's energy industry. She threatened that the Bush junta would stop "collaborating" in the development of Russia's vast oil reserves. While embracing Rice's call for enhanced U.S.-Russian relations, Putin showed no inclination to back away from his plans to increase state control over Russian energy companies and to use this authority to advance Moscow's geopolitical objectives. Condi's animosity toward Putin really stems from the fact that he's been moving against the handful of billionaire plutocrats in Russia (many of whom also hold Israeli citizenship) who grabbed control of the Russian economy with the open connivance of then-Russian leader Boris Yeltsin, following the collapse of the old Soviet Union.

The Hidden Reasons for the Invasion and Occupation of Iraq

The entire misadventures of the Bush junta in Afghanistan and Iraq can best be understood as Eurasian salvos in the cabal's ongoing dollar imperialism. The international cabal was not responding to the trumped-up threat from Saddam's non-existent WMD program and certainly was not fighting international terrorism. The junta's invasion of Iraq involved much more than most people are aware of. Among the more obvious purposes were:

- the neo-colonial theft of Iraqi oil
- the funneling of oil and no-bid contracts into Halliburton's maw
- the installation of multiple U.S military bases in the region
- the installation of a cabal puppet in control of Iraq

Some of the hidden reasons the demonic cabal invaded and occupied Iraq are:

- to reconfigure the Middle East geopolitically
- to gain strategic control over Iraq's--and the surrounding territory's--hydrocarbon reserves to establish a cabal-based energy market to replace OPEC
- to maintain the U.S. dollar as the monopoly currency for the critical international oil market

Saddam Hussein's cardinal sin had been to tie Iraq's oil sales to the Euro. Saddam announced in September 2000 that Iraq was no longer going to accept dollars for oil being sold under the UN's Oil-for-Food program, and the switch to the Euro as Iraq's oil export currency. This was one of several dangerous steps towards establishing the Euro as an alternative oil transaction currency--the "petroEuro"--that nations--including those within OPEC--had begun to contemplate seriously. The international cabal felt it had to show the world--through pre-emptive invasion of a sovereign nation without provocation or reason--that it would not tolerate any attempt to displace the U.S. dollar as the sole oil transaction currency. A *Financial Times* article dated June 5, 2003, confirmed that Iraqi oil sales had returned to the international markets and were once again denominated in U.S. dollars--not Euros.

The Bush junta implemented this currency transition despite the adverse impact it had on profits from Iraq's export oil sales. In mid-2003 the Euro was valued approximately 13% higher than the dollar. The conversion from the Euro to the dollar negatively impacted the ability of future oil proceeds to rebuild Iraq's infrastructure. This sabotaging of Iraqi oil revenues was never mentioned by the five U.S. major media conglomerates who control 90% of information flow in the U.S. Surprise, surprise.

The PetroEuro Coalition

In January 1999, members of the European Union introduced a single currency, the Euro, a new basis for European and world trade. In 2002, the Euro replaced national European currencies. The Euro was now a de facto competitor with the American dollar for world trade--including energy transactions. Momentum is building toward at least the dual use of Euro and dollar pricing.

The European Union has a bigger share of global trade than the U.S. and, while the U.S. has a huge current account deficit, the EU has a more balanced external accounts position. The EU enlarged in May 2004 with ten new members. It has a population of 450 million and an oil consuming-purchasing population 33 percent larger than the U.S. Over half of OPEC crude oil was sold to the EU as of mid-2004.

In order to reduce currency risks, Europeans will sooner or later pressure OPEC to trade oil in Euros. Countries such as Algeria, Iran, Iraq, and Russia export oil and natural gas to European countries and in turn import goods and services from them. OPEC member countries and the Euro-zone have strong trade links, with more than 45 percent of total merchandise imports of OPEC member countries coming from the countries of the Euro-zone, while OPEC members are the main suppliers of oil and crude oil products to Europe.

Not a single government in Europe was, or is, prepared to oppose American militarist aggression. The disastrous polices of US imperialism in Iraq have also accelerated the decline and crisis in Europe . . .

The European Union (EU) is in severe crisis. Apart from the expansion of police powers, the process of unification has experienced one setback after another. The European constitution failed because of differences between the various European governments, and in the face of widespread opposition from French and Dutch voters. There is no trace of a common foreign policy today. Militarily, the US domi-nated NATO calls the tune in Europe. Britain will not join the Euro-zone in the foreseeable future. And in the absence of any common financial and tax policy, the Euro is increasingly less credible.

The US has used its powerful position in Europe to encourage intra-European conflicts.

—Uli Rippert, "The dead-end of European capitalism and the tasks of the working class," World Socialist Web Site, 3/15/06

A powerful new coalition is forming to struggle against the cabal's dollar imperialism. This coalition includes na-tions that possess economic and military might. Venezuelan leader Hugo Chavez established barter deals for trading its oil with twelve Latin American countries as well as Cuba. The cabal's hit man Rumsfeld immediately began threatening this coalition with U.S. military action.

These new coalition partners--as much concerned with geostrategic issues as purely economic issues--are also being joined by nations such as Japan, Pakistan, North Korea, and the OPEC and European Union countries in combating dol-lar imperialism. The coalition and its supporting nations all have good reason to be fed up with the cabal's imperialistic offensives. Many of them had legitimate energy and manufacturing contracts with Iraq totaling trillions of dollars. The cabal brazenly nullified all those contracts when it invaded Iraq and took control of the country. The ongoing assaults on their economies by the cabal's dollar imperialism leaves all of them working toward a way to get out from under the American puppet junta's thumb. They are forming agreements and joint ventures among themselves to achieve their goal of independence from the cabal.

The OPEC countries know that the cabal has set up its Caspian Sea pipelines in an effort to undercut it, and the European Union countries have experienced continual threats and assaults on their economies from the cabal. The U.S. Treasury Secretary, for example, threatens to weaken the dollar whenever the European Union nations are perceived to be getting out of line with cabal policy. A weaker dollar is a direct attack on the other economies of the world.

Many regimes throughout the world are equally fascistic and dictatorial in the treatment of their people. However, in numerous ways average Americans are far worse off than our European counterparts in this age of dollar imperial-ism. Though there have been recent cutbacks, most Europeans still have free health care, free education through the university level, adequate retirement for the elderly, an average of five weeks paid vacation, and sick leave and parental leave. Spending for social programs in Europe runs about 50 percent above that in the United States. Alternate energy development (wind, hydro, tidal and hydrogen cell power), food safety, organic and anti-GM laws, and labor laws are already in place--the envy of ecology activists in the U.S.

Many of the ways in which Europe is forging ahead of America, in this era of the Bush junta, have been described by Steven Hill in a January 2006 essay titled "Europe Leaves the U.S. Behind" on the Common Dreams Website:

In the political realm, Europe utilizes full representation electoral systems that gives representation to voters across the political spectrum, public financing of elections that fosters debate, universal voter registration, voting on a weekend or on a holiday, and national electoral commissions that establish na-tionwide standards and practices. Women and third parties have far greater representation at all levels of government. In the U.S., we are still stuck with our 18th-century winner-take-all system, privately financed elections, poor voter participation, poll-tested sound bites aimed at undecided swing voters, voting on a busy work day, and haywire decentralized election administration left to over 3000 counties scattered across the country.

In the media realm, Europe boasts a robust public broadcasting sector (radio and TV) and subsidized daily newspapers, leading to more media pluralism, a better informed citizenry, more people reading newspapers, and a higher level of what political scientist Henry Milner calls "civic literacy." In the U.S., we are still stuck with corporate media gatekeepers, media monopolies, an astonishing loss of political ideas and a poorly informed citizenry.

In the economic realm, Europeans have developed practices such as codetermination,' which provides meaningful worker representation on corporate boards of directors, and powerful works councils in the workplaces. There is more of a balance of stockholder and stakeholder rights, forcing business leaders to confer more extensively with their workers and labor unions. There also are continent wide minimum labor and environmental standards, including more union-friendly laws.

Taken together, these fulcrum institutions work coherently to form the basis of a 'European Way' that is distinctly different from the 'American Way.' This provides a rough blueprint of where institutional development in the United States needs to go in the 21st century. Those who care about the future of our country should take their cues from Europe.

Coalition Energy and Military Might

These coalition nations wield political and economic clout because of their vast energy reserves and their growing military might. In 2006 Russia is likely to surpass Saudi Arabia as the world's largest oil exporter. Both Japan and China are trying to negotiate with Russia to build a pipeline that would serve their energy needs.

Iran is currently producing about 4 million barrels per day, but is thought to be capable of boosting its output by another 3 million barrels or so. According to *Oil and Gas Journal,* Iran has an estimated 940 trillion cubic feet of gas, or approximately 16% of total world reserves. Only Russia, with 1,680 trillion cubic feet, has a larger supply.

As it takes approximately 6,000 cubic feet of gas to equal the energy content of 1 barrel of oil, Iran's gas reserves represent the equivalent of about 155 billion barrels of oil. This, in turn, means that its combined hydrocarbon reserves are the equivalent of some 280 billion barrels of oil, just slightly behind Saudi Arabia's combined supply. At present, Iran is producing only a small share of its gas reserves, about 2.7 trillion cubic feet per year. This means that Iran is one of the few countries capable of supplying much larger amounts of natural gas in the future.

China's is aggressively pursuing oil and gas supplies, and has already signed delivery contracts with Angola, Canada, Indonesia, Iran, Kazakhstan, Nigeria, Saudi Arabia, Sudan and Venezuela. In November 2004, a mega-gas deal between Beijing and Tehran worth $100 billion was finalized. Billed as the "deal of the century" by various analysts, this agreement is likely to increase by another $50 to $100 billion, bringing the total close to $200 billion, when a similar oil agreement, currently being negotiated, is completed.

The gas deal between China and Iran entails the annual export of some 10 million tons of Iranian liquefied natural gas (LNG) for a 25-year period, as well as the participation, by China's state oil company, in such projects as exploration and drilling, petrochemical and gas industries, pipelines, services and the like. The export of LNG requires special cargo ships, however, so Iran is currently investing several billion dollars in adding to its small LNG-equipped fleet.

Putin is now contemplating the possibility of being supplanted by China if Russia loses the confidence of Tehran and appears willing to trade favors with Washington over Iran. Russia's Gazprom may now finally set aside its stubborn resistance to the idea of entering major joint ventures with Iran.

China is also using some of its new trade income to purchase relatively modern arms from Russia, including fighter planes, diesel-electric submarines and destroyers. China is also expanding its arsenal of short-range ballistic missiles, many capable of striking Taiwan and Japan. None of these systems compare to the most advanced weaponry in the American arsenal, but the cabal is making loud noises about neutralizing Chinese military capabilities.

In January, 2005, Russian President Vladimir Putin announced that Russia is fitting its strategic bombers with cruise missiles capable of delivering a massive precision strike thousands of miles away. These are hypersonic intercontinental missiles that use cruise missile technology to zigzag and avoid being shot down once they re-enter the earth's atmosphere.

Petro-Euros and The Dreaded Bourse

The idea of Russia and other countries breaking away from the stranglehold of the U.S. dollar and adopting the Euro as a reserve currency in place of the dollar was endorsed by Putin as early as 2004.

President Vladimir Putin has stated both publicly and privately that invoicing Russia's crude-oil and gas exports to the European Union in euros instead of in dollars makes very good sense for both Russia and the EU. Putin is known to have very close relations with "old Europe", primarily Germany and France. His statements and those of German and French leaders have even on occasion drawn attention to the fact that US global dominance fundamentally rests on the fact that the dollar is the international currency, and that if an exit from the dollar were to occur in the sphere of global petro-transactions, the effect would be seriously to undermine that global dominance.

Furthermore, a number of oil-exporting countries have already gone on public record as to their preference to make an exit from petro-dollars in favor of petroeuros. They have indicated that if Russia begins such a move to petro-euros, they will rapidly follow Russia's lead. The net effect would be a rapid international abandonment of the dollar as the international currency, which would in turn bring down the towers' of the heavily debt-ridden US economy.

—W. Joseph Stroupe, "Crisis Towers Over the Dollar,"
Asia Times Online, Nov 25, 2004

The first coalition member nation to actually announce plans to break away from the dollar death-grip is Iran. The Tehran government announced that beginning in March 2006, it would start competing with New York's NYMEX and London's IPE with respect to international oil trades, using a Euro-based international oil-trading mechanism. As of December 2006, the proposed Iranian oil bourse has not been launched. Iran's bourse plans portend that without some sort of U.S. intervention, the Euro will become a major competitor with the U.S. dollar in the international oil trade. A bourse is a stock exchange for securities trading; the word is derived from the French stock exchange in Paris, the Federation Internationale des Bourses de Valeurs.

The reason Iran has chosen to make this bold move is undoubtedly the cabal's ongoing clandestine war against its civilian and military infrastructure. In January 2005, Seymour Hersh reported in the *New Yorker* that the Central Intelligence Agency and U.S. Special Operations Forces (SOF) had begun in 2004 flying unmanned "Predator" spy planes over Iran and sending small reconnaissance teams directly into Iranian territory.

These invasions of a sovereign territory, are supposedly intended to pinpoint the location of hidden Iranian weapons facilities for possible attack by U.S. air and ground forces. "The goal," Hersh explained, "is to identify and isolate three dozen, and perhaps more, such targets that could be destroyed by precision [air] strikes and short-term commando raids."

Military analyst William Arkin, believes it highly probable that CENTCOM is probing Iran's air and shore defenses by sending electronic surveillance planes and submarines into--or just to the edge of--Iranian coastal areas. "I would be greatly surprised if they're not doing this," he said in an interview. "The intent would be to 'light up' Iranian radars and command/control facilities, so as to pinpoint their location and gauge their effectiveness." It was precisely this sort of aggressive probing that led to the collision between a U.S. EP-3E electronic spy plane and a Chinese fighter over the South China Sea in April 2001.

This notion that the United States is getting ready to attack Iran is simply ridiculous . . . Having said that, all options are on the table.

—President George W. Bush, February 2005

The next offensive in the cabal's dollar imperialism war will thus most likely be the unprovoked attack of Iran. The hidden reason for this attack is Iran's huge energy reserves--and its daring to threaten an oil bourse linked to the Euro. The international cabal's attack on Iran is almost inevitable, because Iran is threatening to commit a far more unforgivable "offense" than Saddam Hussein's conversion of Iraq's oil exports to the Euro in the fall of 2000; Iran is also encouraging other nations of the world to join them in setting up an international energy market linked to the Euro.

Iran's Shiite theocracy is certainly a questionable factor in the Middle East, and the cabal's destruction of Iraq's Sunni power has somewhat played into Iran's hands. That an attack by the cabal on Iran would be insane, does not seem to make any real difference to the Neanderthal reactionaries who create cabal policy.

Many Middle-Eastern leaders have said that they would stand by Iran if the American puppet junta attacks it. On December 18, 2005, Pakistani Foreign Minister Khursheed Kasuri said his nation strictly opposed any U.S. attack on Iran and would stand by Iran if this extreme step were taken by Washington. Japan has indicated its solidarity with Iran--most likely because Japan obtains about fifteen percent of its oil from Iran and has few easy alternative sources to make up the difference in the event of a cabal offensive.

In February, 2006, France, Germany, Russia, and China allowed themselves to be bullied by the cabal into voting in the International Atomic Energy Agency (IAEA) to report Tehran to the UN Security Council. This act lays the basis for sanctions and future military action against Iran. On February 15, 2006, Secretary of State Condoleezza Rice, speaking to the Senate Foreign Relations Committee, declared that the US would "actively confront" Iran and called for $85 million to fund anti-Tehran propaganda and to support opposition groups inside and outside the country.

However, on February 13th, Syria announced that it is switching the primary hard currency it uses for foreign goods and services from the U.S. dollar to the Euro in a bid to make it less vulnerable to pressure from Washington. This appears to be an act of solidarity with Iran in response to the caving in of other nations to the Bush junta's pressure.

Iran has spent the past few years cementing economic and military ties with Russia, China, and the EU. The leaders of China, Russia--and to a lesser extent even those of the EU--would be acting in self-defense by drawing a line in the sand around Iran. In fact, both China and Russia seem to be doing just that. In February, 2006, Russia thumbed its nose at Washington by announcing it would go ahead and honor a $700 million contract to arm Iran with surface-to-air missiles, slated to guard Iran's nuclear facilities. In 2005 Russia sold some of its more advanced missiles to Syria, Venezuela, and Iran, just as the cabal amped up its rhetoric against these countries. Russia is also continuing to negotiate with Iran concerning its nuclear program, in an effort to avoid UN sanctions. Even as late as February, 2006, China is announcing that it intends to finalize its energy contracts with Iran worth more than $100 billion. National Developmental Reform Commission chief Ma Kai will lead a delegation to Tehran as early as March to sign agreements for massive exports from the Yadavaran oil fields.

The cabal has been engaged in a clandestine war against Iran for a number of years--as Seymour Hersh's 2005 *New Yorker* articles documented. With the threat of the Iranian bourse establishing the Euro as a competing energy currency, the cabal has begun planning for a horrifying new offensive against Iran. Recent reports reveal active Pentagon planning for operations against Iran's suspected nuclear facilities. The publicly stated reasons for any such overt action will be masked as a consequence of Iran's nuclear ambitions.

Most frightening of the cabal's plans were those announced in August, 2005 by intelligence analyst Philip Giraldi in an article in the *American Conservative*: "In Case of Emergency, Nuke Iran." Giraldi reported the resurrection of active U.S. military planning against Iran, including the shocking disclosure that in the event of another 9/11-type terrorist attack on U.S. soil, Vice President Dick Cheney's office wants the Pentagon to be prepared to launch a potential tactical nuclear attack on Iran--even if the Iranian government was not involved with any such terrorist attack against the U.S.

> The Pentagon, acting under instructions from Vice President Dick Cheney's office, has tasked the United States Strategic Command (STRATCOM) with drawing up a contingency plan to be employed in response to another 9/11-type terrorist attack on the United States. The plan includes a large-scale air assault on Iran employing both conventional and tactical nuclear weapons. Within Iran there are more than 450 major strategic targets, including numerous suspected nuclear-weapons-program development sites. Many of the targets are hardened or are deep underground and could not be taken out by conventional weapons, hence the nuclear option. As in the case of Iraq, the response is not conditional on Iran actually being involved in the act of terrorism directed against the United States. Several senior Air Force officers involved in the planning are reportedly appalled at the implications of what they are

doing -that Iran is being set up for an unprovoked nuclear attack -but no one is prepared to damage his career by posing any objections.

—Philip Giraldi, "In Case of Emergency, Nuke Iran," *American Conservative*, August 1, 2005

Tehran possesses a real arsenal of modern, destructive weapons, unlike Saddam Hussein's illusory WMD concocted by rabid right extremists such as Wolfowitz and Cheney. Iran has purchased the Russian-made Sunburn cruise missile, specifically designed to defeat the US Aegis radar defense system and said to be the most lethal antiship weapon in the world.

If attacked, Iran would likely stir up increased Shi'ite rebellion in Iraq against U.S. occupation forces, an insurgency that might far surpass in extent and deadliness the current Sunni-led resistance. Tehran might also unleash its 300 North Korean-engineered Shahab-3 ballistic missiles on U.S. bases in Qatar, Saudi Arabia, Uzbekistan, Afghanistan, and Iraq. If the cabal invades it, Iran's response would be to wage a guerilla war similar to that undertaken by the Sunni-led resistance in Iraq. Tehran has already announced efforts to increase the size of its seven-million-strong "Basiji" militia forces, which were deployed in human wave attacks against Iraq during the 1980s. Recent news reports from Iran indicate that tens of thousands of rifles are currently being handed out.

Even if the Iranian regime were to abandon all nuclear programs and completely demolish its nuclear facilities, Washington would invent another pretext for its provocative actions, which are aimed at establishing US ascendancy in the region over America's European and Asian rivals.

—Editorial Board of the World Socialist Web Site, 1/21/06

A possible scenario in this cabal assault on Iran is that an American city might be attacked from within by "terrorists," with Tehran again being assigned the guilt, and Israel allowed to "retaliate" against Iran. In a replay of 9/11, the Iranian mullahs would be blamed for the terrorist bombing of an American city. Throughout 2006, cabal planners have been concocting various "strategic concepts" and "strike packages" for possible action against Iran. International press reports confirm that Pentagon officials met with their Israeli counterparts to discuss the possible participation of Israeli aircraft in some of these scenarios. Vice President Dick Cheney declared in January 2005 that "the Israelis might well decide to act first" if Iran proceeded with the development of nuclear weapons--obviously hinting that Washington would look with favor upon such a move.

In 1981, the Israeli Air Force destroyed Iraq's Osirak reactor, setting its nuclear program back several years. But the situation in Iran is now both more complex and more dangerous, according to Shahram Chubin, an Iranian scholar who is the director of research at the Geneva Centre for Security Policy. The Osirak bombing "drove the Iranian nuclear-weapons program underground, to hardened, dispersed sites," Chubin told Seymour Hersh. "You can't be sure after an attack that you'll get away with it. The U.S. and Israel would not be certain whether all the sites had been hit, or how quickly they'd be rebuilt. Meanwhile, they'd be waiting for an Iranian counter-attack that could be military or terrorist or diplomatic. Iran has long-range missiles and ties to Hezbollah, which has drones—you can't begin to think of what they'd do in response."

Ominously, in June 2005, Israel ordered nearly 5,000 "smart bombs" from the United States that can penetrate six-foot concrete walls such as those that might encase Iranian nuclear sites. The deranged cabal strategists may decide that the only way to take out Iran's hardened nuclear sites is to use nuclear bombs. If so, Christian fundamentalists in many parts of the world may experience "rapture" before they expected it.

Whatever the nature of a strike against Iran by the cabal, Iran might retaliate with missile strikes on oil tankers in the Persian Gulf, provide covert aid to the insurgency in Iraq, or even launch an attack on Israel's main installations at Dimona that house a large arsenal of around 200 nuclear missiles. At that point, the world's biggest nuclear power, the U.S. forces commanded by cabal puppets, would move in strength against an Iran painted as an enemy beyond the pale.

It seems insane for Iran to continue it nuclear program, but we have to remember that in today's world only those nations with already-established nuclear weapon capability are somewhat less vulnerable to attack from the demonic cabal.

The cabal has already begun its counterattack against ideas such as those expressed in this chapter. The first of these attacks was fired off by a Professor Robert Looney, professor at the Naval Postgraduate School in a paper published in the *Middle East Policy* journal. Note that Professor Looney is a member of a military installation and that his paper was not published in an economics journal but in a foreign policy journal.

Loney offers no genuine argument against the four major claims made in this chapter:

1. That the hegemony of the dollar is essentially a monetary and political extortion scheme

2. That the dollar is kept in its position as sole world exchange currency through military threat by the cabal

3. That the cabal attacked Iraq because Saddam was moving to the Euro (among other reasons)

4. That Iran is now being diplomatically and politically attacked (likely soon to escalate to military attack) because it is planning to move to the Euro through its international bourse

Professor Looney can only offer this feeble rebuttal:

> Even though the United States may derive some economic benefit from having its currency serve as the dominant international reserve currency, the gains are not nearly as great as is often assumed--around 0.5 percent of GDP at best, much of which is offset by lost manufacturing exports and jobs associated with the strong dollar.

> It follows that the notion that the United States undertook the Iraq war over its concern with the consequences of Saddam Hussein's denominating Iraq oil sales in Euros (and the direction that might lead other producing countries) is little more than another web-based conspiracy theory.

Note that Professor Looney does not explain what is meant by his unsupported claim that the gain for the U.S. in having the dollar remain the sole transactional currency is only 0.5 percent of GDP. How is that figure arrived at? Who is the beneficiary of that amount of gain--the people or the politicians? This is clearly a phony statistic created to befuddle those ignorant enough to swallow it. Having failed to disprove any of the claims of this and similar reports, Looney reverts to the mere assertion that this is a vast web-based conspiracy theory--and pretends that he has proven his claims.

In this chapter, I'm exposing the imperialistic machinations of the demonic cabal in the sphere of currency warfare. The dollar imperialistic cabal perpetually struggles against enemy regimes. But, even more importantly, dollar imperialism involves the cabal's continual warfare against the interests of American workers--and working people throughout the world.

As Americans, we must be aware of what the cabal is doing to us and to others throughout the world. They're exposing Americans to extreme danger from other nations because of their militaristic, economic despotism. Americans are placed in a terrible bind in which we have to dissent from the thugs who run our government, while at the same time try to preserve our nation's heritage. The best way to be loyal to our American values is to struggle against the un-American, extremist junta trying to destroy our nation.

In our discussion of dollar imperialism, it's incorrect to say that the United States or America is attacking the world economically. It's not the U.S. as a nation that is perpetrating these imperialistic horrors, but the demonic cabal that controls the American federal government. The American people are not at war economically with the rest of the world, only the international cabal and its puppet figures such as the Bush junta and Tony Blair's administration.

The common people in all nations must jointly rise up against this international cabal and take back our rights and liberties--our countries, realizing a new culture.

Chapter Five

How American Elections Became a Criminal Enterprise

By Michelle Mairesse

Every day we hear laments about the state of the state or the nation or the world. The twenty-first century seems to be a powder keg rolling downhill. We have already witnessed enough chicanery, bad faith, fecklessness, and desecration to make us wary of the future.

Yet we hope.

But hope, be it wan or fervent, is not enough. Most Americans are by nature pragmatists. For us, remedies begin in action.

What can I do to heal a sick planet? we ask. What can I do to feed the hungry? What can I do to stop wars? What can I do to bring wise leaders to the fore?

Very often we are told we can make the most lasting changes, the most powerful statements, the largest contributions to the health and happiness of the state by pondering all the possibilities and exercising our franchise. Participating in free elections is at the same time a duty and a privilege.

We have grown complacent about our elections. We like to think that someone is in charge of the orderly ritual of designing, allotting, and counting the ballots. There are officials whose job it is to keep the roll of voters and supervise the count. There are bound to be a few errors and a few lost votes, but on the whole, our elections are well-conducted and honest.

In this chapter, I hope to convince you that the entire electoral process is in grave danger, has been insidiously subverted, and will continue to erode unless we intervene. We can hope, but hope is not enough.

This is a call to action!

What Happened in 2000?

Who was elected president in 2000, Democrat Al Gore or Republican George W. Bush? For 36 hectic days after the 2000 election, most Americans were distracted by the circus in Florida. While wrangling reporters, politicians, lawyers, and judges argued about counting or not counting punch card ballots, Florida Governor Jeb Bush, George W. Bush's brother, was orchestrating the last act of the radical Republican plan to send the eldest Bush boy to Washington.

The first act began after Jeb's election in 1998. Jeb and his cohorts let special interests know that they expected political donations of $2 for every $1 donated to Democrats or defaulters would lose access to the governor and the legislative leadership, and their businesses would tank. As they say in lobbyist circles, "Pay to play." No sooner had he taken the oath of office than Jeb Bush began ferreting out and replacing Democrats throughout Florida state government, his first purge of Democratic voters. According to Lance deHaven-Smith, in his book entitled *The Battle for Florida*,

> Top Republicans used the powers of their offices to inject partisanship and instill fear down through the ranks of the state bureaucracy. In 1998 political operatives working for the Speaker of the House secretly examined voter registration records to learn the party affiliations of specific state employees and to identify agencies with high concentrations of Democrats. After it was determined that the most Democratic agency in the state government was the Florida Department of Education, the department was restructured and the positions of many of its employees were eliminated. Florida law forbids any consideration of partisan orientations in state hiring, firing, and contracting, but it fails to contemplate the more sinister possibility that highly partisan elected officials might purge the state bureaucracy indirectly by reorganization and privatization.

Lance deHaven-Smith describes how education took another hit in 1999:

Following the lead of state representative John Thrasher, who was the House Speaker that year and the year before, the Legislature eliminated the Florida Board of Regents, which had been responsible for overseeing the State University System. The board was replaced by separate boards of trustees at all ten of the state universities, and the governor was given the power to make all the trustee appointments. This created an enormous source of new patronage and also undermined the political neutrality of the state universities. With the Board of Regents out of the way, Republicans quickly replaced many of the university presidents with political insiders.

Jeb ultimately appointed staunch Republicans to control Florida's educational system: state senator Jim Horne as Florida's first Secretary of Education and most of the individual university presidents.

With their troops in place and their coffers filling up, the Florida Republican Party systematically began to disenfranchise Democratic voters. Secretary of State Sandra Mortham paid a private company $5700 per annum to purge the voter registry of all ex-felons. Although Florida courts twice ruled that ex-felons whose civil rights had been restored before they came to Florida were entitled to vote, in 1999 newly-elected Secretary of State Katherine Harris and Director of the Division of Elections Clay Roberts ignored the courts and continued the drive to disenfranchise black Democratic voters, felons or not. Harris hired Data Base Technologies (DBT, now a division of Choicepoint) and paid them $4.3 million to compile the most extensive scrub list possible. Race was a big factor in compiling matches for the list. Blacks make up less than 15% of Florida's population and 90% of them vote Democratic, so targeted blacks made up more than 50% of the ex-felon list.

After the election, the vice-president of Choicepoint testified before a congressional committee that Florida state officials had ordered DBT to eliminate voters by making incorrect matches. Choicepoint gathered its information from the Internet and did not make a single verifying telephone call.

Were the errors minor? No, they were outrageous. Here are two typical examples: *Randall* Higginbotham, *age 41*, was scrubbed from the voting roster because he was identified as *Sean* Higginbotham, *age 30*; and David Butler, *Jr.* of *Florida* was scrubbed from the voting roster because he was misidentified as convict David Butler of *Ohio*. Five months before the election, Harris circulated the hit list of 57,700 names to all the precincts with instructions to remove those voters from the rolls.

On Election Day 2000, rich white Republican voters stood in short lines and used up-to-date equipment, including electronic machines that let them correct their ballots. Things were different in black districts. Some voters were flagged down at a roadblock, where highway patrol officers checked their drivers' licenses. Others waited in long lines for an inadequate number of booths and ancient recording equipment. All too often, innocent citizens whose names appeared on the ex-felons list were informed for the first time that they could not vote when they showed up at the polling place.

Greg Palast, an award-winning American reporter based in England, broke the story of the scrub list and documented its sleazy origins in *The Observer*, London, November 26, 2000. Updates, as well as each edition of Palast's *The Best Democracy Money Can Buy* have added irrefutable, hard evidence of fraud. (Palast's most recent estimate of *all* qualified Florida voters barred from casting a ballot in Election 2000 stands at 90,000.)

The story was big in Europe, but the American press ignored it completely. Massive civil rights violations that subverted an election just didn't resonate with the mainstream press. On January 10, 2001, lawyers acting for the NAACP sued and won their case against ChoicePoint's DBT, Secretary of State Katherine Harris (who coincidentally was enthusiastically co-chairing the Bush campaign), and Bush loyalist Clay Roberts, Director of the Division of Elections. In July 2002, to atone for its staggering error rate of 95%, DBT agreed to remove innocent voters from the now infamous list of purported ex-felons. (In 2002, the purge list hadn't been corrected. In 2004, another suspicious list appeared.)

Radical Republicans found other ingenious ways of disenfranchising opposition voters. Two-page ballots with misleading directions were printed in Austin, Texas (the center of the George W. Bush presidential campaign), returned to Florida, and distributed in black districts. Some really strange-looking ballots appeared in other Democratic districts. The most notorious of all was the butterfly ballot, which had punch holes running along the center, flanked by the candidates' names. Palm Beach, election supervisor and lifelong Republican Theresa LePore became a Democrat shortly before the election, when she designed the ballot that confused more than 3,000 Jewish voters into casting presidential ballots for Christian Reform Party candidate Pat Buchanan.

Beginning early on Election Day, Democratic poll watchers phoned complaints to LePore's office about the difficulties voters were having with the ballot. Between noon and one, she responded to the precincts with a memo: "Please remind all voters coming in that they are to vote only for one (1) presidential candidate and that they are to punch the hole next to the arrow next to the number next to the candidate they wish to vote for." LePore registered as an Independent after the election.

Some votes were simply later trashed by ballot handlers. In Duval County, 27,000 ballots were discarded, over half of them from black precincts in Jacksonville. No official challenges were filed within the 72-hour time limit, so thousands of mostly Democratic votes were lost. Sixteen-thousand votes for Gore disappeared overnight from the ongoing Volusia County tally and were reinstated only when an election supervisor questioned the subtraction of already registered votes. No voting machine company representative or election official was able to explain what happened.

Around 8 p.m. on Election Day, a consortium consisting of ABC, CBS, CNN, Fox, NBC, and AP consulted their exit polls from Voter News Service and projected a Gore victory. The Bush camp immediately went into action. Jeb Bush telephoned his first cousin John Ellis at the Fox News decision desk for information. Another call came from the Bush campaign in Austin, Texas. Ellis claims he spoke with cousin George W. Bush five times on Election Night without revealing any confidential exit poll information. It's difficult to believe that no campaign strategizing was going on, for Ellis told the *New Yorker* later, "Me with numbers, one of them a governor, the other the president-elect. Now, *that* was cool."

Bev Harris, author of *Black Box Voting: Ballot Tampering in the 21st Century*, says she uncovered an 87-page CBS news report that contained a shocker: the erroneous subtraction of Gore's votes in Volusia caused the election to be called for Bush. Claiming that the Voter News Service numbers from one Democratic county were flawed, the Bush election team called a press conference at the governor's mansion in Austin. The Bush spokesman declared that the race was too close to call in both Pennsylvania and Florida. Between 8:00 and 9:00 p.m., according to Ellis, Bush pulled ahead. Between 9:00 and 9:30, the other television networks agreed that the race was too close to call. But shortly after midnight, Bush's numbers plunged rapidly by thousands of votes and Gore jumped into the lead. Despite Gore's soaring numbers, at 2:16 a.m. Fox News announced that Texas Governor George W. Bush had won Florida, with its 271 electoral votes. Within minutes, the other television networks repeated Fox's false information.

When Gore heard the fake news of his defeat, he phoned his congratulations to Bush and headed for the Knoxville War Memorial to deliver his concession speech to the nation. Gore's chief deputy in Florida advised him to hold off. After all, there were still 360,000 uncounted votes. It was much too early to concede formally.

Out of six million votes cast in Florida, Bush's lead was reported to be a mere 537 votes. The Florida Constitution had no provisions for a statewide recount, so Gore asked for a partial recount in four southern counties where glaring irregularities had shown up. The last thing the Bush team wanted was a fair recount. They complained to the press that Gore was a sore loser, and the press largely agreed.

On December 8, the Florida Supreme Court overturned a circuit court decision and ordered a manual recount. Based on findings in the circuit court trial, Gore was awarded 393 votes, reducing Bush's lead to 154 votes. That's when the Bush camp went ballistic.

Tom DeLay and the national party sent hordes of out-of-state operatives to intimidate and rampage. They bullied Republican county clerks to amend overvotes in Republican counties, to amend incomplete absentee ballot applications, and to accept late-arriving military ballots lacking signatures. These operatives increased their numbers with real berserkers when the recount began. They charged into the county administration building, threatened violence to the mild county canvassers, and halted the recount of Miami-Dade ballots. (Despite court orders, eighteen counties never even attempted a recount. Secretary of State Katherine Harris certainly wasn't insisting on it.)

The Bush campaign team and lawyers diligently circulated misinformation--misinformation about Florida's election laws, about the reliability of manual recounts (both Jeb and George W. claimed that only machines could count accurately), and about the likelihood of a constitutional crisis.

As for Florida's election laws, they were quite clear. After a series of fierce, close contests, the legislature had carefully laid out legal procedures for contesting elections and conducting recounts. The Florida Constitution specifies that the intent of the voter be paramount during ballot recounting. Because electronic machines had repeatedly failed to read, discern intent, and count ballots accurately, manual recounting is mandated.

As for a constitutional crisis, none was imminent. That inconvenient fact did not stop the Bush camp from flogging the issue, for they wanted the U.S. Supreme Court to intervene and prevent the recount.

Normally the legislature wouldn't have been involved in the election controversy until after December 12, when they could have taken whatever actions were necessary until

December 18. Hastily, the Republican leadership called the legislature into special session while the judiciary branch still addressed election issues, an extraordinary move.

Speaker of the House Tom Feeney, Jeb's bosom political buddy, took the podium and, with a little help from his friends on the Bush legal team, criticized the Florida Supreme Court decisions. He warned that if the dispute continued to December 12, Florida's electoral slate would be excluded from the Electoral College vote. Since Florida had submitted its election results as they were certified, the electoral slate was never in danger. Nevertheless, on November 22, Speaker Feeney declaimed, "Yesterday, if the Court had merely enforced firm and clear statutory deadlines, the Florida Supreme Court could have given us a resolution. Indeed, I fear it has given us a potential constitutional crisis." Right on cue, the sheep-like press corps took up the rallying cry, "constitutional crisis!" If one reporter had telephoned an expert in Florida constitutional law, the "crisis" myth would have died a natural death.

When it looked as though the election would be settled in the courts, Jeb Bush's Florida legal staff warned the state's major law firms not to represent Gore. As with the "pay to play" threats the radical Republicans had used to extract political donations, the risk to law firms aiding the Gore camp was financial--they could be denied access to state contracts and to the governor, dispenser of patronage plums to the party faithful.

In the meantime, Bush family attorney Jim Baker worked the legal front. The Bush legal team, determined to delay or stop the recount, appealed to the U.S. District Court of Appeals, the Florida Supreme Court, and the U.S. Supreme Court. The first two courts denied the appeal. Then the U.S. Supreme Court gave them the nod. From that moment, the fix was in.

The justices had no business interfering in the election. The U.S. Constitution authorizes Congress to settle election disputes, not the Supreme Court. Justices Antonin Scalia and Clarence Thomas, who had close relatives working with and for Republican organizations, should have recused themselves, but they, along with the three other rightwing judges on the court, issued a complex ruling instructing the Florida courts to find a recount method that would apply "equal standards." The decision came down at 10 p.m. on December 12, 2000, two hours before the deadline to submit voting results. In short, the

U.S. Supreme Court ran the clock out on American voters and handed Florida's electoral votes and the presidency to George W. Bush.

Somewhat belatedly, eight major news organizations paid the University of Chicago's National Opinion Research Center (NORC) almost $900,000 to do a recount of the disputed ballots in Florida. NORC concluded that Gore won the most votes throughout the state, no matter what tabulating method was used. After sitting on the report for nine months, the mainstream media released the results with misleading headlines ("Supreme Court Did Not Decide Outcome") and buried NORC's astounding conclusion on the inside pages almost as an afterthought.

Reviewing the actual results of the statewide examination of 175,010 disputed ballots, on November 12, 2001 Robert Parry, www.consortiumnews.com, cleared away the media fog:

> So Al Gore was the choice of Florida's voters -- whether one counts hanging chads or dimpled chads. That was the core finding of the eight news organizations that conducted a review of disputed Florida ballots. By any chad measure, Gore won. Gore won even if one doesn't count the 15,000-25,000 votes that USA Today estimated Gore lost because of illegally designed 'butterfly ballots,' or the hundreds of predominantly African-American voters who were falsely identified by the state as felons and turned away from the polls. Gore won even if there's no adjustment for George W. Bush's windfall of about 290 votes from improperly counted military absentee ballots where lax standards were applied to Republican counties and strict standards to Democratic ones, a violation of fairness reported earlier by the Washington Post and the New York Times. Put differently, George W. Bush was not the choice of Florida's voters anymore than he was the choice of the American people who cast a half million more ballots for Gore than Bush nationwide.

> 'Full Review Favors Gore,' the Washington Post said in a box on page 10, showing that under all standards applied to the ballots, Gore came out on top. The New York Times' graphic revealed the same outcome. Earlier, less comprehensive ballot studies by the Miami Herald and USA Today had found that Bush and Gore split the four categories of disputed ballots depending on what standard was applied

to assessing the ballots' punched-through chads, hanging chads, etc. Bush won under two standards and Gore under two standards.

The new, fuller study found that Gore won regardless of which standard was applied and even when varying county judgments were factored in. Counting fully punched chads and limited marks on optical ballots, Gore won by 115 votes. With any dimple or optical mark, Gore won by 107 votes. With one corner of a chad detached or any optical mark, Gore won by 60 votes. Applying the standards set by each county, Gore won by 171 votes. This core finding of Gore's Florida victory in the unofficial ballot recount might surprise many readers who skimmed only the headlines and the top paragraphs of the articles. The headlines and leads highlighted hypothetical, partial recounts that supposedly favored Bush. Buried deeper in the stories or referenced in subheads was the fact that the new recount determined that Gore was the winner statewide, even ignoring the 'butterfly ballot' and other irregularities that cost him thousands of ballots. The news organizations opted for the pro-Bush leads by focusing on two partial recounts that were proposed, but not completed, in the chaotic, often ugly environment of last November and December.

The articles about the new recount tallies make much of the two hypothetical cases in which Bush supposedly would have prevailed: the limited recounts of the four southern Florida counties by 225 votes and the state Supreme Court's order by 430 votes. Those hypothetical cases dominated the news stories, while Gore's statewide recount victory was played down.

Parry concludes, "In its coverage of the latest recount numbers, the national news media also showed little regard for the fundamental principle of democracy: that leaders derive their just powers from the consent of the governed, not from legalistic tricks, physical intimidation and public-relations maneuvers. It is that understanding that is most missing in the news accounts of the latest recount figures."

The HAVA Shell Game

In 2000, the Department of Defense spent $6.2 million on a small Internet voting experiment for a few members of the military. On June 2, 2003, the DoD announced that the Secure Electronic Registration and Voting Experiment, or SERVE, would allow military personnel and Americans overseas to cast their votes over the Internet during the 2004 election.

The Federal Voting Assistance Program, under the umbrella of the DoD, paid Bermuda-based Accenture $22 million to conduct its Internet voting project. Strange to say, Accenture had recently acquired election.com from Osan Ltd., a Saudi investment group that owned 51% of the company.

In February 2004, two weeks after a panel of scientists determined that the Accenture system was extremely vulnerable to tampering and lacked any way for voters to verify that their ballots were cast or counted, the DoD canceled the program. Accenture, surprised by the announcement, first denied that the program had been canceled, but later backed down. Spokeswoman Meg T. McLaughlin said the decision to continue testing SERVE would allow Accenture to study Internet voting further.

When the voting machine companies took a drubbing after the 2000 election, the Information Technology Association of America (ITAA), a high-powered lobbying group, launched a task force that included Accenture, Northop-Grumman, and Lockheed-Martin. Their focus: replacing punch card and lever systems with brand new electronic voting machines.

Here we have the Pentagon, offshore companies, and foreign proprietors mucking about in our elections. Quietly, stealthily, the full-scale takeover of our national election process occurred when the voting machine companies entered the mix with money laundering and bribes operating at the highest levels of government (think Jack Abramoff). In their wake came the orchestrated obfuscation and confusion that has characterized every national election since 2000.

In December 2003, ITAA launched a second group, the Election Technology Council. Its membership included Advanced Voting Systems, Diebold, Election Systems and Software (ES&S), Hart InterCivic, Sequoia, and Unilect. These electronic voting machine firms successfully lobbied Congress to pass and fund the Help America Vote Act (HAVA).

Congress agreed to funnel $3.9 billion to the states, and hence into the coffers of the voting machine companies to provide touch-screen machines lacking any paper trail or receipt.

Although Representative Bob Ney (R) of Ohio and Representative Steny Hoyer (D) of Maryland jointly sponsored (HAVA), its prime mover was Representative Ney who, as House Administration Committee chairman, held hearings on voting irregularities in Ohio.

Only one voting rights group testified before his committee: the American Center for Voting Rights. The Brad Blog exposed them as a phony GOP front group founded by two Bush/Cheney operatives shortly before the hearings.

The hearings often focused on voting rights for the disabled. Since Diebold contributed one million dollars to the National Federation for the Blind and at least $26,000 to the American Association of People with Disabilities, we should not be surprised that spokesmen for those organizations testified that their members badly needed electronic voting machines *without a paper trail.*

Congressional members made several attempts to amend HAVA so that the voting machines would have a paper trail--voter verified paper ballots--but Ney stalled all of them. Just before the 2002 election, he and the other HAVA co-sponsors sent a letter to their colleagues arguing against amending HAVA to include paper records with touch screen voting machines lest they disenfranchise the disabled. (Did anyone ask how the disabled voted *before* the advent of electronic voting machines?) The twisted logic prevailed. HAVA does not mandate electronic voting machines, contrary to popular belief, but HAVA does mandate that a single disabled-accessible device, a paperless, direct recording electronic machine (like Diebold's), be installed in every precinct in the United States.

The act also contains some really dandy suggestions for improving our elections. Voter IDs, for example, called an unofficial poll tax in some quarters, and "ineligible voters" lists--think Jeb Bush's purge lists--to ensure that only the right voters do the voting.

Unlike the Indian tribes dealing with Jack Abramoff, the voting machine companies got their money's worth.

Ney's former employee, DiStefano and his partner Roy C. Coffee received at least $180,000 from Diebold to lobby for HAVA and "election reform." Beginning in 2002, DiStefano and Coffee contributed $20,000 to Ney's campaigns. Diebold paid at least $275,000 lobbying fees to Greenberg Traurig, Jack Abramoff's firm, to influence members of Congress.

Super lobbyist Jack Abramoff accommodated Ney with stadium skyboxes, expensive restaurant dinners, and campaign funds, and Ney participated in one of the now notorious Abramoff golfing junkets that jetted to Scotland in 2002.

The most succinct account of this can of worms or, better, this bucket of snakes, appears in the April 22, 2005 issue of *Executive Intelligence Review* concerning the August 2002 Trip.

> Abramoff, former DeLay aide Michael Scanlon, religion-manager Ralph Reed, Rep. Robert Ney (R-Ohio), and U.S. government procurement official David Safavian took a lavish golfing vacation to Scotland. The trip was sponsored by the NCPPR [National Center for Public Policy Research] and Abramoff's private charity, the Capital Athletic Foundation, with money taken from Indian tribes.

> Abramoff and his lobbying partner Scanlon are currently under investigation on allegations of looting over $60 million in fees and contributions from Indian tribes who owned gambling casinos. Representative Ney, the House Administration Committee chairman, was at the time of the trip working on a bold scheme by Abramoff. The Texas Tigua tribe's El Paso casino was closed down by state government action, because of an 'anti-gambling' crusade secretly organized by Abramoff, and paid for by rival casinos and run publicly through Reed and his Christian Coalition networks. Then Abramoff arranged for the Tiguas to pay him and Scanlon millions to campaign to reopen the casino.

After the Scotland junket, Ney met with the Tiguas and promised to amend his national election-reform bill to override the closing of their Texas casino. Abramoff had the Tiguas contribute $32,000 to Ney's campaign committee and a political action committee. But the tribe got stiffed, as was often the case when they dealt with or through Abramoff. Ney unsuccessfully attempted to insert their amendment into his national "election-reform" bill, and the Texas casino remains closed.

Ney cozied up closer to Abramoff when Abramoff and his partner-in-crime Adam Kidan were bullying Konstantinos "Gus" Boulis into selling them the SunCruz fleet of casino boats. Although Ney represents a rural Ohio district and had no business getting involved with the Florida negotiations, he inserted derogatory comments about Boulis into the Congressional Record, calling him "a bad apple." After the sale, Ney inserted a statement in the Record, lauding Kidan as "a solid individual and a respected member of the community" and as someone "who has a renowned reputation for honesty and integrity." After Boulis was gunned down in Fort Lauderdale on February 6, 2001, two associates of Kidan and one Gambino mob henchman were charged with the murder.

The U.S. Attorney's office in Florida charged Jack Abramoff and partner Adam Kidan of defrauding investors when they purchased the SunCruz fleet. Abramoff pled guilty January 4, 2006 to two counts: Conspiracy to Defraud the United States and Wire Fraud. Adam Kidan pled guilty December 15, 2005 to two counts: Conspiracy to Defraud the United States and Wire Fraud.

The Justice Department conducted the second prosecution against Abramoff and Michael Scanlon in the U.S. District Court for the District of Columbia. They are charged with bribing public officials and defrauding Abramoff's Indian clients. Abramoff pled guilty January 3, 2006 to three counts: Conspiracy to Defraud the United States, Mail Fraud, and Tax Evasion. Scanlon pled guilty November 21, 2005 to Conspiracy to Defraud the United States.

Former Representative Ney pled guilty to accepting bribes from Jack Abramoff and Michael Scanlon.

Now we come to Representative Tom Feeney (R-Fla.). Remember him? After inventing a "constitutional crisis" in 2000 when he was Speaker of the House in Florida, Feeney moved up to the U.S. congress.

In 2003, Abramoff's NCPPR paid for Feeney's Scottish golfing jaunt with Ralph Reed, who would be chairman of the 2004 Bush-Cheney campaign for the southeastern United States. Feeney strongly supported touch-screen voting installations in time for the 2004 election, perhaps relying on his expertise as an attorney and lobbyist for Yang Enterprises, Inc. (YEI), a position he occupied throughout his tenure as a Florida legislator.

Brad Friedman was way ahead of the pack in exposing Feeney's questionable entanglement as general counsel and registered lobbyist with client YEI:

> Curtis, a life-long Republican up until then, had been a programmer at YEI, which had several top-secret clearance contracts with the state, NASA and other government agencies. Curtis' understanding at the time was that the prototype he was being asked to create (built to the very precise specifications of Feeney) was to address Feeney's concerns that the Democrats might attempt to electronically rig the election and Feeney wanted to know what to look out for in that event. After informing YEI CEO Mrs. Li-Woan Yang that he would not be able to hide the vote flipping routines in the software source-code as Feeney had requested, Curtis testified that Mrs. Yang informed him that the program was needed to 'rig the vote in South Florida.'

> The story also concerns Curtis' long-standing and now-verified claims that YEI was employing a now-convicted Chinese spy and was also engaged in massively overcharging on contracts such as the one it had with the Florida Department of Transportation. As well, there is the startling tale of the untimely, and unexplained demise of the Florida Inspector General, Raymond Lemme, who had been investigating Curtis' charges against YEI and Feeney. Curtis has since passed a polygraph test concerning these charges.

Feeney has been more than casual and less than forthcoming about his extensive prepaid traveling at home and abroad. He was "misled" about his Scottish golf trip sponsored by Abramoff. He first reported that his $2000 trip to West Palm Beach in 2003 was sponsored by a lobbyist. When reporters pointed out that he had violated House rules, a year passed before he "updated" the identity of the sponsor as a conservative foundation. A charity registered as a foreign agent sponsored an Asian trip in 2003, a clear violation of House rules. The Korea-U.S. Exchange apologized for "their" mistake.

Feeney received $4000 from felon Abramoff and three of his clients, $5000 from felon "Duke" Cunningham, and is a key supporter of indicted Tom Delay. With friends like these, he doesn't need enemies to take him down.

Unclean Machines

Defense contractor SAIC has been charged with fraud and has a history of security breaches in its systems, but it still gets big contracts from the Pentagon and the CIA, where some of its executives have previously served. It is moving up fast in the field of electronic vote-counting.

Cleveland-based Diebold took a lot of heat for the antics of then CEO Wally O'Dell, a major fund-raiser for George W. Bush. O'Dell's widely publicized letter promising to deliver Ohio's votes to Bush seemed a bit over the top.

After firing O'Dell, Diebold announced that it was withdrawing from its contract with North Carolina. A barrage of complaints and lawsuits forced the firm to reorganize. You'll agree that they had a lot of reorganizing to do after you read Ann Ryder's account of Diebold's latest acquisition, Global Election Systems, which counted much of the vote in the Florida 2000 presidential election. Ryder's story, entitled, "Voting Machine Dirt and Then Some," appeared in North Carolina Conservative.com.

In 2002, Diebold bought Global Election Systems, which then became Diebold Election System. Global was founded by three men, one of whom spent a year in prison for fraud against the Canadian government and was part of the collapse of the Vancouver stock exchange. He was first convicted in 1974 for political corruption. Another of the founders was jailed for stock fraud, tax evasion, and money laundering. The last of the trio defrauded Chinese immigrants and sold the real estate that had been posted as bond to bail out one of the jailed partners.

The staffer who handled the ballot printing for Global was a convicted cocaine trafficker. He brought into the company a fellow former inmate who had been in the slammer for computer-aided embezzlement. This embezzler became the lead programmer for the Global Election Systems' vote-tally product that is still in use. By late 2000, Global's voting system contained the first double set of books problem where all votes are recorded twice internally and don't need to match. It appears to hide some forms of vote fraud. The guy quit when Diebold took over, but was then hired right back as a consultant.

One or two bad apples? Well, no. There are more.

Diebold's election division is headed by Bob Urosevich. Todd Urosevich, Bob's brother, is an executive at Elections Systems & Software, Inc. (ES&S), America's largest manufacturer of touch-screen voting machines. In his unjustly ignored book, *Fooled Again: How the Right Stole the 2004 Election & Why They'll Steal the Next One Too*, Mark Crispin Miller explains connections Senator Chuck Hagel (R. Nebraska) has with ES&S.

As American Information Industries (AIS), it [ES&S] had been variously chaired, coowned and directed by Chuck Hagel for several years before he quit in 1995 to run for senator from Nebraska the next year. (In 1997, AIS became ES&S, after merging with Business Records Corp.--a part of Cronus Industries, a holding company controlled by several wealthy hard-right activists, including Caroline Rose Hunt of the Hunt oil dynasty and other figures evidently interested in wielding quiet influence on government).

In 1996, Hagel defeated an incumbent Democratic governor, won every demographic group, including blacks who had never voted Republican before, and was the first Republican in 24 years to be elected to the Senate. His victory was considered the biggest upset in the nation. Did it help that he owned the voting machines or that his campaign finance manager was also owner and director of ES&S?

Criminal Connections

Daniel Hopsicker of MadCowMorningNews investigated the sorry background of the major vote machine companies and found evidence in the public record that Sequoia Pacific, a company counting one in three American votes, "has been run, perhaps for decades, as a Continuing Criminal Enterprise specializing in blatant and widespread bribery of public officials, with numerous felony convictions, Mob ties, and a history replete with stories of threats, coercion, and even murder."

Sequoia Pacific's transgressions, he says, are typical of all three major election services. In 2000, Louisiana newspapers bruited the story of Commissioner of elections Jerry Fowler, "convicted of taking as much as ten million dollars over a period of a decade from Sequoia's Southeast Representative, a man named Pasquale 'Rocco' Ricci, from Marlton, New Jersey." Fowler was sentenced to five years in prison.

Court documents from the case revealed that Sequoia Pacific and ES&S colluded to buy and sell voting machines to each other until they reached the figure they would ask the state of Louisiana to pay.

Hopsicker also discovered that Sequoia Pacific operates through a number of dummy front companies. Uni-lect, International Voting Machines, Garden State Elections, and Elec-tec were some of Sequoia Pacific's aliases. When it wasn't colluding with a competitor, it was colluding with itself. But in the voting machine business, shell companies and shell games are commonplace.

How are some of the smaller companies? Not so good.

Voting Fraud in the USA: A Tale of Two Brothers
By Angry Girl, November 3, 2004

Last year, two of Diebold's top executives, Howard Van Pelt and Larry Ensminger, moved over to Advanced Voting Solutions, which is the new name of the scandal ridden voting company Shoup Voting Solutions.

In 1971 Shoup Voting Machine Co. had been indicted for bribing politicians in Florida. In 1979 Ransom Shoup was convicted of conspiracy and obstruction of justice during an FBI inquiry into a Philadelphia election. Shoup got a mere three year suspended sentence.

In the meantime, Philadelphia bought new voting machines from a new voting machine company, Danaher-Guardian. But this company only sells voting machines formerly known as the 'Shouptronic.'

It's enough to make Luddites of us all. But before we rush the polling booths armed with sledgehammers, let's demand that Congress REPEAL HAVA and return to paper ballots.

The Many Miracles of 2002

If you believe in miracles, you will accept the results of the 2002 midterm elections as accurate. If you believe in extraordinary coincidences, you'll say it's a coincidence that all the election upsets occurred where there were electronic voting machines.

We've already mentioned that in 1994, Chuck Hagel, former CEO of ES&S, was the first Republican in 24 years to win a Senate seat in Nebraska. He ran again in 2000 and, according to his Web site, "was re-elected to his second term in the United States Senate on November 5, 2002 with 83% of the vote. That represents the biggest political victory in the history of Nebraska." It's probably a mere coincidence that Hagel was decidedly in bed with ES&S and owns a substantial share of the company that counts 80% of Nebraska's vote.

There were the usual problems in Florida. The sleazy "felons list" was still in circulation. Some voters were annoyed on seeing the touch-screen register for Jeb Bush instead of their preferred choice. One candidate sued to have the machines examined, but the judge ruled that the machine's innards were a trade secret. Doesn't that give "secret elections" a new meaning? After the election, supervisors in one county discovered 103,000 uncounted ballots. Oops. They're just a little slow to get organized in Florida, that's all.

In Minnesota, after unbeatable Paul Wellstone died in a plane crash days before the election, popular Democrat Walter Mondale replaced him on the ballot and led in the polls, Then a miracle happened. In the last *seconds* of machine vote-counting, a huge shift to the Republican candidate took place, and Norman Coleman unexpectedly defeated Mondale. How often does that happen? Probably a coincidence.

In Georgia, popular Democratic senator and Vietnam veteran Max Cleland, who lost three limbs in a grenade explosion, was defeated by Saxby Chambliss. During the election, Diebold applied uncertified patches for "malfunctioning machines", and, purely by coincidence, 60% of the electorate by county switched their party allegiance between the primaries and the general election. Yes, that's 60%. Probably a coincidence. It does seem arrogant of Diebold to have named its program patch "rob-georgia-zip." There were other curious results in Texas, Missouri, and Alabama, but surely the strange counts were mere happenstance, accidents, coincidence.

The Continuing Storm

In 2004, the first news about the presidential election was reassuring. Mainstream reporters, apparently sending their dispatches from lunar outposts, said the election had gone smoothly. Earth-dwellers experienced a very different reality. From coast to coast, came complaints of voter intimidation, erratic machines, and crazy numbers.

The morning after the 2004 presidential election was eerily similar to the morning after the 2000 presidential election. All the well-founded predictions that George W. Bush would lose went out the window, and he was once again, by some sleight-of-hand, installed in the office previously awarded to him by the Supreme Court. Something was seriously wrong. There were questions, not all of them from Democrats, but the American press ignored them.

What Had Happened?

Dissenters, subjected to the usual "get over it" routine, had to go to the International Press Service for a hearing. Ralph Nader described radical Republican tactics to the IPS, "What they 'do' is minorities, and make sure that there aren't enough voting machines for the minority areas. They have to wait in line ... for hours, and most of them don't. There are all kinds of ways, and that's why I was quoted as saying, 'this election was hijacked from A to Z.'"

> As far as I'm concerned, this election was clearly stolen. What they did in Ohio was systematically deny thousands of African Americans, and other suspected Democrats, the vote.

> It was like Mississippi in the fifties, and it was deliberate ... had there been enough (voting) machines, and had people equal access to the polls with a reliable vote count, there is no doubt that John Kerry would have carried Ohio.

> —Harvey Wasserman, author and lecturer, told the
> *International Press Service*

There was evidence to support Wasserman's claim, and then some. Not only were African-Americans often targeted, but many Democrats attempting to register were undermined by a peculiarly sinister program. A Republican consulting firm, Voters Outreach of America, is headed by Nathan Sproul, formerly head of the Arizona Republican Party and Arizona Christian Coalition. The Voters Outreach program, which conducted registration drives in Florida, Michigan, Minnesota, Nevada, Ohio, Pennsylvania, and West Virginia, was accused of ripping and discarding Democratic registrations. Former employee Eric Russell retrieved ballots from the trash and offered them to the FBI as evidence. Presumably, the FBI is still investigating.

Critics in Oregon charged the same company with using the same tactics, but in Oregon the firm called itself America Votes, which is actually the name of a non-partisan organization. The Republican National Committee acknowledges that it hired Voters Outreach of America to register voters, stating that it had zero tolerance for any kind of fraud. No formal severing of ties to Sproul's Voters Outreach Program, though. (Two months after the election they were still paying Sproul.) No apologies to the thousands of people who were cheated of their right to vote and were unaware of their disenfranchisement until they arrived at their polling place.

Outright Vote Fraud

Gradually, news about the not-so-smooth election seeped into the American press. The November 14, 2004 *Cleveland Plain Dealer* reported a voter hearing where, for three hours, voters offered sworn testimony about election day voter suppression and irregularities. A *Washington Post* article (December 15, 2004) reported dissatisfaction across Ohio.

The foul-ups appeared particularly acute in Democratic-leaning districts, according to interviews with voters, poll workers, election observers and election board and party officials, as well as an examination of precinct voting patterns in several cities.

In Cleveland, poll workers apparently gave faulty instructions to voters that led to the disqualification of thousands of provisional ballots and misdirected several hundred votes to third-party candidates. In Youngstown, 25 electronic machines transferred an unknown number of votes for Sen. John F. Kerry (D-Mass.) to the Bush column.

In Columbus, Cincinnati and Toledo, and on college campuses, election officials allocated far too few voting machines to busy precincts, with the result that voters stood in line as long as 10 hours--many leaving without voting. Some longtime voters discovered their registrations had been purged.

The *Post* reported that there had been protest marches and demands for a recount.

After the election, local political activists seeking a recount, analyzed how Franklin County officials distributed voting machines. They found that 27 of the 30 wards with the most machines per registered voter showed majorities for Bush. At the other end of the spectrum, 6 of the 7 wards with the fewest machines delivered large margins for Kerry.

In New Mexico, Hispanic voters were frequently given provisional ballots that never made the count. In North Carolina, machine malfunctions occurred throughout the day. They doubled votes and subtracted votes. In Carteret County, over 4500 votes were irretrievably lost. In Pennsylvania, inner-city voters and college students waited hours to vote. For them, there was a shortage of machines and even of ballots.

In New Jersey, the *Newark Star-Ledger reported*, "Hundreds, perhaps thousands, of new voters at Rutgers University reluctantly filled out paper provisional ballots or walked away from the polls when their names could not be found at polling locations."

Many more instances of sleazy and sometimes fraudulent tactics could be cited, and critics predicted that the whole nightmare scenario could repeat in 2006 and 2008. As Mark Crispin Miller declares in his book *Fooled Again* that:

the Republican Party did whatever it could do, throughout the nation and the world, to cut the Kerry vote and pad the Bush vote. Some of the methods were exceedingly sophisticated, like the various cyber-scams pulled off in a tight complicity with Diebold, ES&S, Sequoia, Triad and other corporate vendors of electoral infrastructure. Other methods were more bureaucratic: the disappearance of innumerable Democratic registration forms, countless absentee ballots and provisional ballots, as well as multitudes of would-be 'felonies' never committed or committed by somebody else, or for no given reason whatsoever.

There were vast logistical inequities in state after state. Democratic precincts got far too few machines, and those machines kept breaking down, or turning Kerry votes into Bush votes, with long, long lines of would-be voters stuck for hours (or, as often happened, giving up and not voting); while pro-Bush precincts tended to have plenty of machines, all working well, so that voting there was quick and easy. And were old-fashioned dirty tricks meant to scare people into staying home, or to send them to the wrong address, or to get them out to vote a day too late? There was also outright bullying, intimidation and harassment--the oldest methods of mass disenfranchisement, just as obvious in 2004 as they were in Dixie after Reconstruction, only now such methods were used nationwide (and the U.S. federal government, in this case, was behind them).

The preparations for chaos began before the election:

In April, 2005 Marion County Clerk Doris Anne Sadler revealed that Election Systems and Software, known as ES&S, which sold Marion County, Florida its voting system, installed illegal software before the November 2004 election.

In the late hours of July 2, 2004, persons unknown entered the offices of an Akron consulting firm for the Democratic Party and stole only two computers containing campaign related information. In October, a similar burglary occurred in the Lucas County Democratic Headquarters in Toledo. Only three computers containing sensitive campaign information were selected from an array of appliances and a cash box.

In Franklin County, Ohio, the Republican Party paid expenses for a group calling themselves "the Mighty Texas Strike Force." They were tasked to intimidate Democratic voters by phone and in person. Bands of them harassed and threatened Democrats on Election Day. (Shades of the berserkers unleashed in Florida in 2000.)

Some swing state precincts (Florida, Ohio, New Mexico, Colorado, Nevada and Iowa) saw long lines of minority voters and college students waiting for scarce or malfunctioning machines. (There were only three machines per 1400 people at some locations in Ohio.) An estimated one-third of them dropped out of line without voting. On December 20, 2004, Scripps Howard News Service reported that a review of election results in a ten-county sampling revealed that more than 12,000 ballots failed to record a vote for president, almost one in every ten ballots cast.

In Warren County, Republican operatives said a Homeland Security alert forced them to shut down the vote count, which they then removed to an unapproved, unsecured warehouse to count in secret. The FBI denied that any alert had been issued. The official Warren County tally gave Bush a third of his winning margin in Ohio.

The most vehement voter complaints concerned the tendency of some machines to switch their vote from Kerry to Bush. In Ohio's Mahoning County, election officials confirm that at least eighteen machines visibly shifted votes from Kerry to Bush throughout the day. Some voters tried repeatedly to have the machine verify their vote for Kerry, without success. Voters from Franklin County declared under oath that their vote for Kerry faded away and could not be retrieved. County canvassers attributed these malfunctions to computer "glitches," but when a computer consistently favors one candidate, a pre-inserted program, not a glitch, is responsible.

The Center of Republican Vote Fraud: Ohio

To repeat: elections were anything but smooth in Ohio. In their detailed and documented *How the GOP Stole America's 2004 Election & Is Rigging 2008, (published in 2005),* Bob Fitrakis & Harvey Wasserman describe the extraordinary circumstances surrounding the 2004 Ohio election. "In the lead-up to the 2004 elections, numerous and independent non-governmental organizations requested permission from Ohio election officials to gain access to polling stations for routine observation and monitoring, as in Iraq and Ukraine.

These requests were uniformly rejected. Without public explanation, Ohio Secretary of State J. Kenneth Blackwell [who simultaneously chaired the Bush-Cheney campaign in Ohio] refused all requests from non-partisan national and international organizations to establish impartial observation and monitoring procedures during the Ohio 2004 election.

Co-author and El Salvador election observer Bob Fitrakis was personally present in a meeting in which Matt Damschroder, former chair of the Franklin County Republican Party and Director of the Franklin County (Columbus) Board of Elections, denied international monitoring groups the right to observe the Ohio elections. Among other things, Damschroder warned that if they set foot within 100 feet of polling places in Franklin County, he would have them arrested.

Throughout the rest of the world, such an edict would be viewed as an admission of intent to steal an election. The United Nations and other election protection organizations would see Ohio's actions as the core definition of renegade dictatorship. The Bush administration made it clear in Ukraine that such behavior would not be tolerated.

With the denial of access to international monitors, Ohio's 2004 election would generally be considered a 'demonstration election,' a meaningless show for a repressive regime. By international standards, it had no more credibility in the eyes of history or the world than one in Castro's Cuba, the former Soviet Union or any of scores of dictatorships where elections, presidential and otherwise, are mere window dressings, with a predetermined outcome and an electorate deprived of its rights.

After Ohio's election, in further violation of internationally accepted procedure, and of American election law, Blackwell ordered that all tally sheets and other crucial documents pertaining to the presidential vote be locked down. As we write, public access to those records is still being denied.

Despite press complacency and self-congratulations of election officials, the situation in Florida was rough, not smooth. Staffers of the emergency hotline for the Kerry Campaign Headquarters in Broward County from late October through the 2004 election took calls from voters whose complaints sound suspiciously like those of Ohio voters. On November 7, 2004 they reported:

Many of the calls to our hotline were from voters who had pressed the 'Kerry' button on their electronic voting screen, only to have 'Bush' light up as the candidate they had chosen. In some cases, this would happen repeatedly until about the 5th or 6th time the voter pressed 'Kerry' and eventually his name would light up. In other cases, the voters pushed 'Kerry' but were later asked to confirm their 'Bush' vote.

We had calls about a road block, put up by the police at 7 a.m. on November 2, which blocked road access to two precinct locations in majority black districts. There was no justification for the road block --no accident or crime scene or construction.

We spoke with hundreds of voters who were certain they had registered to vote in the past six months, well before the October 18 deadline, but were not on the rolls. And those were just the people who had the information to contact us.

The local paper, citing the Supervisor of Elections office as its source, told all people voting by absentee ballot that they could turn in ballots by hand to any of its seven offices by 5 p.m. on Tuesday, November 2. Every single one of those offices except one was closed on Tuesday.

All of these problems do not even take into account the 58,000 absentee ballots that had been 'lost' by the Supervisor of Elections, in perhaps the most Democratic county in the state, disenfranchising thousands of people who were disabled, out of the country, or elderly and unable to get to the polls. These events, and many others, have been documented and also reported to lawyers, but we fear they will not get the attention they deserve. This is what we witnessed in just one county. We believe that these 'voting irregularities' raise serious concerns about the legitimacy of the results in Florida, and more broadly, about the health of democracy in this country. www.legitgov.org

A Repeat of the 2000 Florida Vote Fraud

Sam Parry of consortiumnews.com was also disturbed by the Florida count. On November 9, 2004, he wrote:

George W. Bush's vote tallies, especially in the key state of Florida, are so statistically stunning that they border on the unbelievable.

While it's extraordinary for a candidate to get a vote total that exceeds his party's registration in any voting jurisdiction---because of non-voters---Bush racked up more votes than registered Republicans in 47 out of 67 counties in Florida. In 15 of those counties, his vote total more than doubled the number of registered Republicans and in four counties, Bush more than tripled the number.

Statewide, Bush earned about 20,000 more votes than registered Republicans.

The exit polls show Bush winning about 14% of the Democratic votes statewide and losing Independent voters to Kerry by a 57% to 41% margin.

So where did all those extra votes come from? Were the exit polls wrong? Did Democrats and Independents lie to the exit pollsters?

The Astounding Significance of the Exit Polls

Up until about 12:30 a.m. immediately following Election Day, all the standard polls showed that John Kerry would win the presidency by around one and a half million votes. Consultants Edison Media Research and Mitofsky International had been hired to conduct exit polls for the National Election Pool, a consortium of the nation's five major broadcasters and the Associated Press. Edison/Mitofsky released the results of their large, nation-wide exit polls to their clients at 4 p.m. Election Day. Their data indicated that Kerry would win by 3%.

Exit pollers ask people emerging from the polling station how they actually voted. Before the tallying is complete, an exit poll sampling accurately indicates what the final vote count will be. Exit polls are so accurate that the variation between the final vote count and the sampling is plus or minus one tenth of one percent. To the consternation of Edison/Mitofsky, the discrepancy between the presidential exit polls and the final published vote tally was far beyond the margin for error, over two points. A two percent variation between exit polls and final tallies is simply mind-boggling to statisticians. Whenever such a variation occurs anywhere else in the world (say, Latin-America or Ukraine), election watchers immediately declare the vote count fraudulent.

When Edison/Mitofsky, the pollsters of record, and the other pollsters confronted the startling disparity, a strange thing happened. Rather than declare the vote tally corrupted, the other pollsters said it was their exit polls that were flawed, but refused to release their raw data for public inspection. Looking for some kind of pattern to explain the "failure" of the exit polls, the pollsters proposed that Bush supporters voted later in the day, after the exit poll results were in; that pollsters were unable to access some polling stations; that women voters were over-represented in the sampling; and that Kerry voters were more amenable to completing the poll questionnaire than Bush voters.

That last wistful rationalization sounds rather desperate, doesn't it? To date, not a single one of these rationalizations is supported by any credible evidence.
—*http://www.btinternet.com/~nlpwessex/Documents/WATvotefraud2004.htm*

A pattern does emerge from the first exit poll numbers, those released before the final vote tally was posted, those that were not "corrected for sampling errors." The pattern that emerges shows up in thirty-three of the fifty-one voting jurisdictions. In those thirty-three states, no matter who won, we find a big variation between six early exit polls and the final count. In every case, there is a 4% or 5% swing in Bush's favor in the final count. This swing shows up in all the close states, in Colorado, Florida, Iowa, Minnesota, New Hampshire, New Mexico, Ohio, Pennsylvania, and Wisconsin. With the exception of Wisconsin, discrepancies between exit polls and final vote counts all went in Bush's favor. (Exit polls showed Kerry winning by .4% in Wisconsin, which he did.)

In "The Unexplained Exit Poll Discrepancy," A Research Report from the University of Pennsylvania (December 29, 2004), Dr. Steven F. Freeman says the discrepancy between exit poll and vote tally is an anomaly even if one considers only the battleground states of Florida, Ohio, and Pennsylvania. "The likelihood of any two of these statistical anomalies occurring together is on the order of one-in-a-million. The odds against all three occurring together are 250 million to one."

In July 2005, the University of Illinois at Chicago's Institute of Government and Public Affairs Professor Ron Baiman and eleven colleagues from other universities issued a disturbing in-depth statistical study of the exit poll and final tally variance. Their methods and conclusions have withstood intense scrutiny.

Here is the unvarnished truth about the 2004 election from Professor Baiman's report: There have been several methods to estimate the probability that the national exit polls would be as different as they were from the national popular vote by random chance. These estimates range from one in 1,240 to one in 16.5 million. No matter how one calculates it, the discrepancy cannot be attributed to chance.

The executive summary concludes that, "the many anecdotal reports of voting irregularities create a context in which the possibility that the overall vote count was substantially corrupted must be taken seriously."

On November 5, 2004, Michael Keefer of Global Research approached the variance from another direction:

> One can surmise that instructions of two sorts were issued. The election-massagers working for Diebold, ES&S (Election Systems & Software) and the other suppliers of black-box voting machines may have been told to go easy on their manipulations of back-door 'Democrat-Delete' software: mere victory was what the Bush campaign wanted, not an implausible landslide. And the number crunchers at the National Election Pool may have been asked to fix up those awkward exit polls.

> But how do we know the fix was in? Because the exit poll data also included the total number of respondents. At 9:00 p.m. EST, this number was well over 13,000; by 1:36 a.m. EST on November 3 it had risen by less than three percent, to a final total of 13,531 respondents-but with a corresponding swing of three percent from Kerry to Bush in voters' reports of their choices. Given the increase in respondents, a swing of this size is a mathematical impossibility.

Steve Freeman and Josh Mitteldorf's article "A Corrupted Election: Despite What You May Have Heard, the Exit Polls Were Right" (February 15, 2005) concludes:

> The exit polls themselves are a strong indicator of a corrupted election. Moreover, the exit poll discrepancy must be interpreted in the context of more than 100,000 officially logged reports of irregularities during Election Day 2004. For many Americans, if not most, mass-scale fraud in a U.S. presidential election is an unthinkable possibility. But taken together, the allegations, the subsequently documented irregularities, systematic vulnerabilities, and implausible numbers suggest a coherent story of fraud and deceit.

> —*http://www.inthesetimes.com/site/main/article/1970*

GAO Confirms Voting Machine Risks

Immediately after Bush was proclaimed the winner of the 2004 election, the U.S. House Judiciary Committee received more than 57,000 complaints of irregularities and outright fraud. Many of the complainants presented their testimony under oath as sworn statements and affidavits in public hearings and investigations conducted by the Free Press and other voters' rights organizations. In Ohio and elsewhere, many of the complaints centered on the erratic performance of electronic voting machines.

Senior Judiciary Committee Democrat John Conyers, a strong supporter of voters' rights, asked the General Accountability Office to investigate electronic voting machines as used in the November 2, 2004 presidential election.

On October 20, 2005, the scrupulously nonpartisan Government Accountability Office released a 107-page report on the reliability and security of voting machines. Listed on the front page are the key findings of the report:

GAO Report Results in Brief

While electronic voting systems hold promise for a more accurate and efficient election process, numerous entities have raised concerns about their security and reliability, citing instances of weak security controls, system design flaws, inadequate system version control, inadequate security testing, incorrect system configuration, poor security management, and vague or incomplete voting system standards, among other issues. For example, studies found (1) some electronic voting systems did not encrypt cast ballots or system audit logs, and it was possible to alter both without being detected; (2) it was possible to alter the files that define how a ballot looks and works so that the votes for one candidate could be recorded for a different candidate; and (3) vendors installed uncertified versions of voting system software at the local level. It is important to note that many of the reported concerns were drawn from specific system makes and models or from a specific jurisdiction's election, and that there is a lack of consensus among election officials and other experts on the pervasiveness of the concerns. Nevertheless, some of these concerns were reported to have caused local problems in federal elections-resulting in the loss or miscount of votes-and therefore merit attention.

This document confirms our worst fears about voting machines. They are hackable, fragile, unreliable, and unworthy of our trust. There is more, much more, in the report. Problems looming on the horizon haven't even been addressed yet. One nightmare scenario: standards for federal and state voting machine certification could take years to formulate and might be unenforceable at the local level.

There is no longer any excuse for fatuous politicians to call election reform advocates conspiracy theorists. The evidence is in. Read it. Act on it. Take back our right to cast a straightforward vote and have it count.

Why should a functioning democracy allow private companies to conduct its elections? The seemingly generous offer of the federal Help America Vote Act (HAVA) to purchase the machines for the states is only fairy gold.

The bill for care, maintenance, security, inspection, certification, and replacement will be paid by the states. For the manufacturers and purveyors, voting machines are a cash cow to be milked in perpetuity. The continual battle against partisan tricks will create whole cadres of computer police--who themselves will need to be policed. At any stage of the process, ballots can vanish without a trace, and, within limits, can be created without a trace. (Such limits include reporting more votes than there are voters in a precinct, a report that surfaced more than once in 2004.)

A machine with a paper trail is no better. Machines can be programmed to register a vote for candidate X while issuing a paper receipt for candidate Y. Machines with paper rolls and printers are even worse, creating yet another way for machines to malfunction.

How Do We Explain the 2006 Election?

Long lines, power failures, voting machine crashes, false screen readings, questionable tallies, inaccurate voter rolls, paper ballot shortages, voter identity problems, and voter intimidation occurred in the midterm election after all.

On November 22 the *New York Times* reported, "Tens of thousands of voters, scattered across more than 25 states, encountered serious problems at the polls, including failures in sophisticated new voting machines and confusion over new identification rules.

"Voting experts say it is impossible to say how many votes were not counted that should have been."

Despite the vigilance of 850 federal marshals and thousands of poll watchers, 40,000 voters registered the same old complaints on hotlines provided by Common Cause and the Election Protection Coalition. Most of the complaints came from Florida, Maryland, Pennsylvania, and Ohio. Sound familiar?

Frustrated voters described the same outrageous machine vote flipping (Democratic votes registered as Republican on the summary screen) that turned up in Arkansas, Arizona, Florida, Illinois, Kentucky, and South Carolina, according to Voters Unite.

The Virginia State Board of Elections vowed to investigate complaints of intimidation, threats, and false information designed to suppress voting in black districts. And remember the butterfly ballot in Florida? On many ballots in Democratic districts, ballots printed in Austin, Texas, Democrat Jim Webb's name was cut off or split on two pages. Webb's last name had also been cut off on the electronic ballots used by voters in Alexandria, Falls Church, and Charlottesville, the only jurisdiction in Virginia that uses balloting machines manufactured by Hart Inter Civic of Austin. (Webb won the tight Virginia election, nevertheless).

With so much widespread cheating going on, how did the Democrats win?

The Election Defense Alliance (EDA) has the answer. Their careful analysis of national exit polls revealed a 4% bias, three million votes, favoring Republicans.

Jonathan Simon, co-founder of EDA, announced, "We see evidence of pervasive fraud, but apparently calibrated to political conditions existing before recent developments shifted the political landscape, so 'the fix' turned out not to be sufficient for the actual circumstances."

"When you set out to rig an election, you want to do just enough to win. The greater the shift from expectations, (from exit polling, pre-election polling, demographics) the greater the risk of exposure--of provoking investigation. What was plenty to win on October 1 fell short on November 7."

Sally Castleman, National Chair of EDA, explained, "The numbers tell us there absolutely was hacking going on, just not enough to overcome the size of the actual turnout. The tide turned so much in the last few weeks before the election. It looks for all the world that they'd already figured out the percentage they needed to rig, when the programming of the vote rigging software was distributed weeks before the election, and it wasn't enough."

Real Reform

Here is a solution to our voting problems: Federally mandate a printed paper ballot in a standardized format. No more butterfly ballots. No more hanging chads. No more electronic willies. These pencil-marked ballots must be hand-counted in plain view of press and public. This is the way the French, the Germans, the Japanese, the Canadians and other civilized democracies vote. Civil servants count the ballots in the presence of representatives of all the political parties on the ballot. If the counting takes a week, no one is agitated. The results of the exit polls, never more than a tenth of a percent off, have already determined the winners.

Optical scanners will not be used to count the vote. They are susceptible to hacking, and if the count is challenged, they are always bypassed in favor of the slower but more accurate public hand count.

Civil servants can certify the custodial trail of paper ballots and can be held responsible for them. Civil servants should register voters and maintain voter rolls. Every registering citizen will be issued a receipt or copy that will be recognized in the appropriate precinct. Secretaries of state and other partisan officials should have no role in the entire election process. They can be and have been bought, both in the initial vote and in the recount process.

Recounts will be conducted by civil servants in the same fashion as the general election.

Civil servants should maintain a bureau to process all provisional ballots and mailed ballots. Election fraud should be a federal crime subject to severe penalties.

Call to Action

We, the people, must insist on reform. We can expect nothing of our corrupt and spineless political masters. To all appearances, the press is content to sleep through the apocalypse. Today, this very day, is the time for all of us who care about our repressed democracy to speak out, organize, and be heard above the din of propaganda and commerce. Work for reform before the next election.

Chapter Six

The Bush/Saudi Connection

By Michelle Mairesse

In 1920, under a League of Nations mandate, officials from France and Great Britain carved up vast tracts of warlord-dominated territories in Arabia into what they imagined would be nation states devoid of the complex historical, cultural, and tribal realities of the Mideast.

Instead of establishing European-style nation states, the strongest warlords quickly entrenched themselves with the aid of standing armies and spy networks. In much of the Mideast, fealty is often accorded to tribal overlords and the Islamic sects they favor rather than to the territory and people within the boundaries of the nation state. Jonathan Rabin succinctly defines the reality, past and present, of the desert sheikdoms: "The systems of government that have evolved in Syria, Iraq and Saudi Arabia are paranoid family dictatorships with ancestral roots in a single city or village."

—Jonathan Raban, "Western conceit of nation-building ignores culture and history of Arabia,"
Seattle Times, November 24, 2002

Islamic fundamentalists like Osama bin Laden make their appeals to the nation or community of believers, not to any particular nation state, although the rich and powerful among the Muslims have founded Western-style businesses and formed corporations both inside and outside the boundaries of their native countries. Because Osama himself is a scion of a rich Saudi family with wide-ranging business interests throughout the world, the split Saudi personality is most evident in him and the bin Laden clan. Osama, who calls America "The Great Satan," has done business with the infidel Americans whenever it suited him.

Throughout the eighties, when the United States assisted the Saudis in a giant military buildup of airfields, ports, and bases throughout the kingdom, many of the contracts were awarded to the largest construction company in Saudi Arabia, the Saudi Binladen Group, founded by Osama bin Laden's father.

At the same time, the United States trained and armed troops in Afghanistan to fight the Soviets. The United States and Saudi Arabia spent about $40 billion on the war in Afghanistan, recruiting, supplying, and training nearly 100,000 radical mujahideen from forty Muslim countries, including Pakistan, Saudi Arabia, Iran, Algeria, and Afghanistan itself. Among the recruits were Osama bin Laden and his followers.

—Michael Parenti, *9-11 Terrorism Trap: September 11 and Beyond*
City Lights Books, San Francisco, 2000

With C.I.A. funding, Osama bin Laden imported engineers and equipment from his father's Saudi construction company to build tunnels for guerrilla training centers and hospitals, and for arms dumps near the Pakistan border. After the Soviets withdrew from Afghanistan, the C.I.A. and the Pakistani intelligence agency sponsored the Taliban organization, a government composed of the fanatic Wahhabi Islamic sect, the same sect that is the state religion in Saudi Arabia. Although followers of the Wahhabi sect do not refer to themselves as Wahhabis, the label is useful because it applies to a single Muslim group with a set of beliefs peculiar to them alone: Wahhabis maintain that Shi'ites and Sufis are not Muslims, and that Muslims should not visit shrines or celebrate Mohammed's birthday.

—Laura Secor, "*Which* Islam?," *Boston Daily Globe*, December 15, 2002

The Saudi sheiks have been Wahhabis since they intermarried with the family of a puritanical Muslim scholar, Mohammed ibn Abd al-Wahhab, in 1774. Supported first by Britain and later by the United States, the Saudis captured the Muslim holy cities of Mecca and Medina, easily gaining control of the entire Arabian peninsula.

Wherever they ruled, the Wahhabis imposed their medieval code on their hapless subjects, making public spectacles of stoning adulterers to death and maiming thieves, destroying decorated mosques and cemeteries, prohibiting music, sequestering women, and promoting war on infidels. The Saudi sheiks have lavished funds on anti-American and anti-Israeli terrorists-in-training while indoctrinating other Muslims through its worldwide network of religious schools, mosques, newspapers, and presses.

Jihad

The Wahhabi Taliban in Afghanistan had the blessings of the Saudi royal family and of The Big Three--the bin Laden family, the al Ahmoudi family, and the Mahfouz family--the richest clans in that medieval kingdom. (Khalid bin Mahfouz is bin Laden's brother-in-law, according to the C.I.A.). The desert oligarchs profited from world-wide investments as well as sleazy banking schemes such as the infamous Bank of Credit and Commerce International.

Salem bin Laden, Osama's brother, has conducted all his American affairs through James Bath, a Houston crony of the Bush family. Bath's former business partner Bill White testified in court that Bath had been a liaison for the C.I.A. In 1979 Bath invested $50,000 in Arbusto, George W. Bush's first business venture. Rumor had it that Bath was acting as Salem bin Laden's representative. "In conflicting statements, Bush at first denied ever knowing Bath, then acknowledged his stake in Arbusto and that he was aware Bath represented Saudi interests."

—Wayne Madsen, "Questionable Ties: Tracking bin Laden's
money flow leads back to Midland, Texas"

In addition to doing aviation business with Saudi sheiks, Bath was part owner of a Houston bank whose chief stockholder was Ghaith Pharaon, who represented the Bank of Commerce and Credit International (BCCI), a criminal global bank with branches in 73 countries. BCCI proceeded to defraud depositors of $10 billion during the '80s, while providing a money laundry conduit for the Medellin drug cartel, Asia's major heroin cartel, Manuel Noriega, Saddam Hussein, the C.I.A., and Islamist terrorist organizations worldwide.

—"The Press on the BCCI-bin Mahfouz-bin Laden Intelligence Nexus,"
Boston Herald, December 11, 2001

Big Three wheeler-dealer Khalid bin Mahfouz, one of the largest stockholders in the criminal bank, was indicted when the massive BCCI banking scandal blew apart in the early 1990s. The Saudi royal family placed him under house arrest after discovering that Mahfouz had used the royal bank to channel millions of dollars through fake charities into bin Laden's organizations, but Mahfouz was not so much punished as inconvenienced.

—Jonathan Beaty & S. C. Gwynne, *The Outlaw Bank: A Wild Ride Into the Secret Heart of BCCI*,
Random House, New York, 1993

Members of the Wahhabist Saudi oligarchy are driven by the sometimes conflicting emotions of power lust and religious fervor. Their support of radical Islamists follows from their ambition to dominate the Muslim world, but their fear that radical Islamists might overthrow the Saudi regime at home motivates them to fund and encourage holy warriors in countries other than their own.

As Daniel Pipes points out, jihad (holy war) is a central tenet of Muslim belief. According to one calculation, Muhammad himself engaged in 78 battles, of which just one (the Battle of the Ditch) was defensive. Within a century after the prophet's death in 632, Muslim armies had reached as far as India in the east and Spain in the west.

—Daniel Pipes, "Jihad: How Academics Have Camouflaged Its Real Meaning," December 2, 2002,
History News Network Website

Pipes traces the bloody advance of fundamentalist jihadists against their twentieth century co-religionists. "Islamists, besides adhering to the primary conception of jihad as armed warfare against infidels, have also adopted as their own Ibn Taymiya's call to target impious Muslims. This approach acquired increased salience through the 20th century as Islamist thinkers . . . promoted jihad against putatively Muslim rulers who failed to live up to or apply the laws of

Islam. The revolutionaries who overthrew the Shah of Iran in 1979 and the assassins who gunned down President Anwar Sadat of Egypt two years later overtly held to this doctrine. So does Osama bin Laden."

In 1989, bin Laden established al Qaeda (the Base) in Afghanistan to organize extremist Wahhabis and disperse their networks throughout the country. A year later, he returned to Saudi Arabia and founded a welfare agency for Arab-Afghan veterans. Bin Laden hoped to mobilize the veterans as a kind of religious-military army, but King Faud discouraged the venture. When King Faud invited 540,000 American troops to the kingdom to fight in the Gulf War, bin Laden lambasted the royal family and urged religious authorities to issue *fatwahs* (religious rulings) condemning the American infidels.

In 1991, Osama bin Laden and a band of Afghan veterans agitated in Sudan for a holy war against the enemies of Islam. In 1992, he claimed responsibility for the attack on American soldiers in Yemen, and again for attacks in Somalia in 1993. He was mum about the terrorist truck bombing of the World Trade Center in 1993, the explosion that killed six people and injured more than a thousand, but investigators knew bin Laden had donated heavily to the religious "charity" that financed the bombing operation.

Spiked Investigations

In February 1995, when he was appointed chief of the F.B.I.'s counter-terrorism section in Washington, John O'Neill immediately assembled and coordinated a team to capture Ramzi Yousef, who was en route from Pakistan to Afghanistan. Yousef was strongly suspected of planning and directing the World Trade Center bombing in 1993.

In three days, the kingpin of the World Trade Center bombing was in custody, and O'Neill went on to accumulate damning evidence against the 1993 World Trade bombers that led to their conviction in American courts. For the next six years, John O'Neill tirelessly investigated terrorist strikes against Americans and American interests in Saudi Arabia, East Africa, and Yemen, often encountering American officials' roadblocks on the way. Even in 1996, after Jamal Ahmed al-Fadl turned himself in at the American Embassy in Eritrea and divulged details of bin Laden's and al Qaeda's organization and operations, the State Department refused to list al Qaeda as a terrorist organization.

In February 1998, bin Laden assembled a number of terrorist groups, including Islamic Jihad, and issued a fierce fatwa calling for the deaths of all Americans. On August 7, 1998, 226 people died in the simultaneous bombing of American embassies in Tanzania and Kenya. Investigators blamed bin Laden for the attacks. On August 20, 1998, President Clinton amended Executive Order 12947 to add Osama bin Laden and his key associates to the list of terrorists, thus blocking their US assets--including property and bank accounts--and prohibiting all U.S. financial transactions with them. The United States conducted a missile attack against bin Laden's facilities in Afghanistan.

On October 12, 2000, two suicide bombers ignited their boatload of explosives next to the USS Cole, an American destroyer refueling in Aden, off the coast of Yemen. The blast killed seventeen sailors and wounded thirty-nine others. O'Neill and his crack investigating team were dispatched to Yemen and hit a stone wall. He had hoped satellite intercepts of phone calls between an al Qaeda operative in Aden and Osama bin Laden in Afghanistan would lead him to the mastermind of the Cole attack, but the American ambassador and the Yemeni officials blocked the investigation at every turn.

O'Neill resigned from the F.B.I. in July 2001 and signed on as security chief for the World Trade Center in September. He died in the WTC attack on September 11, 2001.

Oil Diplomacy

In *Forbidden Truth: U.S.-Taliban Secret Oil Diplomacy and the Failed Hunt for bin Laden*, two French intelligence analysts, Jean-Charles Brisard and Guillaume Dasquie, claim that the Clinton and Bush administrations impeded investigations of bin Laden and his al Qaeda terrorist group in order to maintain good relations with Saudi Arabia and to maintain the stability of the oil market. "As the late John O'Neill told one of the authors [Brisard] of this book, 'All of the answers, all of the clues allowing us to dismantle Osama bin Laden's organization, can be found in Saudi Arabia.'"

Jean-Charles Brisard and Guillaume Dasquie, *Forbidden Truth: U.S.-Taliban Secret Oil Diplomacy and the Failed Hunt for bin Laden* (2002) Thunder's Mouth Press/Nation Books, New York

In articles and interviews, Brisard has expanded on this statement, pronouncing the official story about bin Laden's exile from his native Saudi Arabia in 1994 and his frozen assets to be a canard. Not only did O'Neill and the F.B.I. have extensive information concerning the finances of bin Laden and al Qaeda, but the business connections between the bin Ladens, the Mahfouzes, the al Ahmoudis, the Saudi royal family, and the Bush family kept turning up in their investigations.

Mahfouz, who owns Nimir Petroleum, has conducted joint ventures with the al Amoudi family, which owns Delta Oil. Delta Oil and Unocal planned to build a pipeline through Afghanistan before the Taliban backed away. These Saudi companies are still partnered with bigger oil companies (such as Texaco and Unocal) in developing Central Asian oil projects.

Although Brisard's interpretation of events has been disputed, the documentation of *Forbidden Truth* is impeccable. Clearly, the finances and fortunes of the Saudi oligarchs and the Bush family have been intertwined for many years, and oil has been the lubricant of choice, even non-existent oil.

In *The Conspirators,* Al Martin describes an instance of the latter. He says that the Gulf Oil Drilling Supply, of New York, Miami, and Bahrain, was Jeb Bush's favorite artifice for oil and gas frauds:

> The fraud was rather simple. Richard Secord arranged through then Vice President George Bush Sr.'s old friend, Ghaith Pharaon, the then retired head of Saudi intelligence, for Gulf Oil and Drilling to purchase from the Saudi government oil and gas leases in the Gulf which were effectively worthless.

The leases would be embellished to appear extremely valuable and then used as loan collateral. Great American Bank and Trust of West Palm Beach subsequently failed under the weight of unpaid Iran-Contra loans.

> Also, in the case of Gulf Oil Drilling Supply, there was some moderately large international lending to that company. As you would suspect, it was principally out of the old George Bush friendly banks--Credit Lyonnais and Banque Paribas, which, combined lent $60 million dollars to Gulf Oil Drilling Supply, which, of course, was defaulted on later.

> —Al Martin, *The Conspirators: Secrets of an Iran-Contra Insider,* National Liberty Press, LLC, 2002

Special Saudis

Michael Springmann, formerly chief of the visa section at the US Embassy in Jeddah, Saudi Arabia, claims that he rejected hundreds of suspicious visa applications, but the

C.I.A. officer overruled him and ordered the visas to be issued. Springmann protested to the State Department, the Office of Diplomatic Security, the F.B.I., the Justice Department and congressional committees, but in vain.

> —Center for Cooperative Research, "Hijackers who were under surveillance before 9/11"

Springmann observed that 15 of the 19 people who allegedly flew airplanes into buildings in the United States got their visas from the same CIA-dominated consulate in Jeddah. As a special favor to residents of Saudi Arabia (including non-Saudi citizens), applicants for non-immigrant visas can apply at private travel agencies and receive their visa through the mail. During the months following the 9-11 attack, 102 applicants received their visas by mail, two more were interviewed, and none were rejected.

The Saudis always got special treatment. In a November 6, 2001 BBC broadcast Greg Palast revealed just how special that treatment was. Even after Pakistan expelled the World Association of Muslim Youth (WAMY) and India claimed that the organization was linked to terrorist bombings in Kashmir and the Philippines military accused WAMY of funding Muslim insurgency, the F.B.I. got orders to leave the "charitable association" alone.

After 9/11, investigators of the Islamic charities discovered overwhelming evidence that Saudis at all levels worked in tandem with the terrorists. David Kaplin reports, "At the Saudi High Commission in Bosnia, which coordinated local aid among Saudi charities, police found before-and-after photos of the World Trade Center, files on pesticides and crop dusters, and information on how to counterfeit State Department badges. At Manila's international airport, authorities stopped Agus Dwikarna, an al Haramain representative based in Indonesia. In his suitcase were C4 explosives." The interlocking charities make it difficult to follow the money trail. "Many share directors, office space, and cash flow. For two years, investigators have followed the money to offshore trusts and obscure charities which, according to court records, they believe are tied to Hamas, al Qaeda, and other terrorist groups." (*US News and World Report*, December 15, 2003).

"The White House official line is that the Bin Ladens are above suspicion --apart from Osama, the black sheep, who they say hijacked the family name. That's fortunate for the Bush family and the Saudi royal household, whose links with the Bin Ladens could otherwise prove embarrassing. But Newsnight has obtained evidence that the FBI was on the trail of other members of the Bin Laden family for links to terrorist organisations before and after September 11th."

—Greg Palast and David Pallister, "FBI and US Spy Agents Say Bush Spiked Bin Laden Probes Before 11 September," *The Guardian*, November 7, 2001

In the Boston Globe, March 11, 20004, Carl Unger, author of *House of Bush, House of Saud: The Secret Relationship Between the World's Two Most Powerful Dynasties*, states that the 9/11 commission should ask who authorized the evacuation of 140 Saudi nationals on at least eight aircraft making stops in 12 cities immediately following the attacks. "Many of the passengers were high-ranking members of the royal House of Saud. About 24 of them were members of the bin Laden family, which owned the Saudi Binladin Group, a multibillion dollar construction conglomerate." Unger obtained passenger lists for four of the flights, which are posted on his website: *www.houseofbush.com* and includes the name of Prince Ahmed bin Salman.

"As reported last year by Gerald Posner in 'Why America Slept,' Prince Ahmed not only had alleged ties to Al Qaeda, but may also have known in advance that there would be attacks on 9/11. According to Posner, Abu Zubaydah, an Al Qaeda operative who was part of Osama bin Laden's inner circle and was captured in 2002, made these assertions when he was interrogated by the CIA. The commission should ask Mueller about Zubaydah's interrogation. They should also ask whether the FBI interrogated Prince Ahmed before his departure.

"But Prince Ahmed will never be able to answer any questions because not long after the CIA interrogation, he died of a heart attack at the age of 43. Yet we do know that he was on one of the flights."

Unger believes that this episode "raises particularly sensitive questions for the administration. Never before in history has a president of the United States had such a close relationship with another foreign power as President Bush and his father have had with the Saudi royal family, the House of Saud. I have traced more than $1.4 billion in investments and contracts that went from the House of Saud over the past 20 years to companies in which the Bushes and their allies have had prominent positions --Harken Energy, Halliburton, and the Carlyle Group among them. Is it possible that President Bush himself played a role in authorizing the evacuation of the Saudis after 9/11? What did he know and when did he know it?"

—*www.boston.com/news/globe/ideas/articles/2004/04/11/unasked_questions?mode=PF*

In October 2001, the Treasury Department identified the Muwafaq Foundation, largely endowed by Khalid bin Mahfouz, as an al Qaeda front that had funneled millions of dollars to bin Laden. Some families of the 9/11 victims have named Mahfouz and dozens of prominent Saudis, including members of the royal family, in a lawsuit that accuses the Saudis of funding the 9/11 terrorists. Bush administration officials stated that they would seek to have the suit dismissed or delayed.

—Jeff Gerth and Judith Miller, "Saudis Called Slow to Help Stem Terror Finances," *New York Times*, November 28, 2002

Senators Bob Graham and Richard C. Shelby, leaders of the congressional panel ending an investigation of the 9/11 attacks, said the administration should declassify information concerning Saudi funding of terrorists.

"Citing 'their people and a lot of their leaders and probably even the royal family,' Shelby said: 'I believe [the Saudis] cannot support so-called charities that support terrorism on a big scale, and then pretend that they're our friends or our allies.

"'As we get into the money trail, it might be embarrassing, but the American people need to know; the victims and their families need to know,' he added. Shelby and Graham said avoiding embarrassment and maintaining good relations with Saudi Arabia are not legitimate reasons to withhold information from the public.

"'The question is,' Graham said after the news conference, 'will we get [the information declassified] in 30 years when the archives are open, or will we get it in time, before the next attack?'"

—Dana Priest and Susan Schmidt, "9/11 Panel Criticizes Secrecy on Saudi Links," Washington *Post*, December 12 2002

Doubtless one of the connections the senators referred to was the Princess Haifa, the wife of Prince Bandar, Saudi ambassador to the United States for the last twenty years, the longest serving ambassador in Washington. Princess Haifa had been making monthly transfers, $130,000 in all, from her Washington bank account to a needy woman who relayed some of the checks to her husband and another man who assisted and funded the two hijackers who were based in San Diego.

—Greg Miller, Greg Krikorian and H.G. Reza, "FBI Looks at Saudi's Links to 9/11," *Los Angeles Times*, November 23, 2002

The money moved into the family's bank account beginning in early 2000, just a few months after hijackers Khalid Almidhar and Nawaf Alhazmi arrived in Los Angeles from an Al Qaeda planning summit in Kuala Lumpur, Malaysia, according to the sources. Within days of the terrorists' arrival in the United States, Al Bayoumi befriended the two men who would eventually hijack American Flight 77, throwing them a welcoming party in San Diego and guaranteeing their lease on an apartment next door to his own. Al Bayoumi also paid $1,500 to cover the first two months of rent for Al Midhar and Alhazmi, although officials said it is possible that the hijackers later repaid the money.

—Michael Isikoff, *Newsweek,* November 22, 2002

Prince Bandar and Princess Haifa professed their ignorance of the whole affair.

Mark Stein speculates about the recent visit Prince Bandar and Princess Haifa paid to George and Laura at the Crawford ranch, where they were received with the accolades usually reserved for heads of state. Bush must have known about the money transfers and Bandar must have known Bush knew, but apparently a good time was had by all.

Meanwhile, Majeda Ibrahin, the woman the princess was sending all that money to, turns out to be married to Osama Basnan, another buddy of the al-Qa'eda duo, and one who subsequently celebrated 11 September as a 'wonderful, glorious day'. But here's an odd little thing: Mr. Basnan is known to have been in Texas in April when Crown Prince Abdullah and his entourage flew in to the state to see Bush at the ranch. Just another coincidence? Well, sorta: he's supposed to have had a meeting in Houston with some big-time Saudi prince who deals with 'intelligence matters.' This seems an unusual degree of access for some schlub from San Diego who's in the US illegally, as it transpires. He is variously described as a Saudi government agent and al-Qa'eda sympathizer, as if these positions are mutually exclusive. The Saudi embassy say they've only received queries about this matter from the media, not from the FBI. Odd that. The federal government claims it needs vast new powers to track every single credit card transaction and every single email of every single American, yet a prima facie link between the terrorists and Prince Bandar's wife isn't worth going over to the embassy to have a little chat about.

—Mark Steyn, "Bush and the Saudi Princess"
The Spectator, November. 30, 2002

Apparently it is not only the Saudis' oil riches that insulates them from criticism, but also their calculated distribution of largesse. The Saudis have contributed to every presidential library in recent decades. Not surprisingly, former ambassadors to Saudi Arabia from the United States end up being apologists for the corrupt, despotic Saudi regime. The Saudis have arranged that American ambassadors to their country *not* speak Arabic. The American embassy in Saudi Arabia gets all its information about the reactionary regime from the rulers.

Some of the Washington politicians who found the Saudi connection lucrative include Spiro Agnew, Frank Carlucci, Jimmy Carter, Clark Clifford, John Connally, James Baker, George H. W. Bush, William Simon and Caspar Weinberger.

—Daniel Golden, James Bandler and Marcus Walker, *Wall Street Journal*,
September 27, 2001 Posted at *globalresearch.ca* 5 October 2001

Profits before Patriotism

The Bush dynasty has always been comfortable putting profits before patriotism. Prescott Bush, Bush Senior's father, extended credit to Adolph Hitler and supplied him with raw materials during Word War II. The U. S. seized his assets under the Trading with the Enemy Act, but grandfather Bush found other ways to replenish the family coffers.

Bush Senior struck it rich in oil and in the defense industry. Mahfouz (yes, that Mahfouz), Prince Bandar and Prince Sultan (Bandar's father) were also heavily invested in the defense industry through their holdings in the Carlyle Group, where Bush Senior served on the board of directors. Founded in 1987 as a private investment group with strong connections to the Republican Party establishment, Carlyle increased its original investment of $130 million to $900 million when it went public in 2001.

In recent years, Carlyle has been successful both at raising and making money. It has raised $14 billion in the last five years or so, and its annual rate of return has been 36 percent. Its 550 investors consist of institutions and wealthy individuals from around the world including, until shortly after September 2001, members of the bin Laden family of Saudi Arabia. The family — which has publicly disavowed links with Osama bin Laden — had been an investor since 1995.

—James Hatfield, "Why would Osama bin Laden want to kill Dubya, his
former business partner?"
Online Journal, July 13, 2001

As the eleventh largest US defence contractor, Carlyle is involved in nearly every aspect of military production, including making the big guns used on US naval destroyers, the Bradley Fighting Vehicle used by US forces during the Gulf War and parts used in most commercial and military aircraft. United Defense has joint ventures in Saudi Arabia and Turkey, two of the United States' closest military allies in the Middle East.

—Steve Lohr, "Gerstner to Be Chairman of Carlyle Group," *New York Times*, November 22, 2002

It's passing strange that even as the hijacked planes smashed into the World Trade Center, the Carlyle Group was holding its annual investor conference. Shafig Bin Laden, brother of Osama Bin Laden, attended.

Bush Junior once served as an executive with Caterair, one of hundreds of companies Carlyle has bought and sold over the past 15 years, but he removed the record of this period from his resume.

In 1986, Bush Junior, to date a flop as a businessman, joined Harken Energy Corporation as a director and was awarded 212,000 shares of stock and other plums.

In 1987, Khalid bin Mahfouz arranged for BCCI investor Abdullah Bakhsh to purchase 17% of Harken. A Harken official acknowledged that Bush's White House connections had everything to do with the appointment. Somehow, the inexperienced, obscure firm was awarded a prime drilling contract by Bahrain, and Harken's stock price soared.

> In June 1990, Bush Junior sold his Harken stock for a juicy $848,000, enabling him to pay off the loan he had assumed on buying shares in the Texas Rangers. Never mind that the Harken stock promptly tanked when Saddam Hussein invaded Kuwait, for Abdullah Bakhsh, a major Harken shareholder and an investor in BCCI, who had purchased 17% of Harken Energy in 1987, got his money's worth. By 1990, Bakhsh's representative on Harken's board, Talet Othman, began attending Middle East policy discussions with President Bush Senior. Now that Bush Junior occupies the White House, Bush Senior receives frequent CIA briefings (his prerogative as a former president). "In July 2001, Bush personally contacted Saudi Crown Prince Abdullah to 'clarify' his son's Middle East policies. Also during the summer of 2001, Bush forwarded his son a North Korea policy plan penned by 'Asia expert' and former ambassador to Korea, Donald Gregg. Gregg is a 31-year CIA veteran and the elder Bush's former national security adviser whose expertise involved participation in the Vietnam-era Phoenix Program (death squads), Air America heroin smuggling, 'pacification' efforts in El Salvador and Guatemala, the 'October Surprise,' and the Iran-Contra operation (for which Gregg received a Bush pardon in 1992)."
>
> —Tim Shorrock uncovers the Bush connection to US defense giant the
> Carlyle Group, *New Internationalist 347*, July 2002

Bush Junior has received more than advice from his father. He has taken on the team of hustlers and criminals that worked with George Herbert Walker Bush when he was Vice President and President of the United States of America.

Just as his father did, he invokes executive privilege to hide all evidence of collusion with the petroleum pashas who have enriched the Bushes and intimidated the rest of us.

Sandy Tolan, an I.F. Stone Fellow at the Graduate School of Journalism at UC Berkeley, asserts that what the Bush administration really wants in Iraq is a remapping of the Mideast. "The plan is, in its way, as ambitious as the 1916 Sykes-Picot agreement between the empires of Britain and France, which carved up the region at the fall of the Ottoman Empire. The neo-imperial vision, which can be ascertained from the writings of key administration figures and their co-visionaries in influential conservative think tanks, includes not only regime change in Iraq but control of Iraqi oil, a possible end to the Organization of the Petroleum Exporting Countries and newly compliant governments in Syria and Iran -- either by force or internal rebellion."

The Bushes are carriers of the deny-destroy-and-be-damned virus. Prescott Bush never apologized for trading with the Nazis. George Bush Senior professed to know nothing of the drug and arms dealing that funded the bloody, illegal Iran-Contra operations, although it was common knowledge that he directed them. He and his sons enriched themselves through shady real estate deals and financial manipulations that brought down entire banking and savings and loan institutions. They are all consummate inside traders, looting and leaving ruin in their wake.

President-Select George Bush is no exception. He has no scruples about exploiting his office for personal and family gain. The Texas governor who could joke about frying prisoners in the electric chair will not, as president, agonize over the decision to send young men and women into battle--or over denying them medical care when they are injured.

There is irrefutable evidence that highly-placed Saudis aided and supported the terrorists who murdered over 3000 American citizens on September 11, 2001. Yet George Bush persists in protecting and colluding with those who sponsor terrorists. Is this not an act of treason?

George Bush should be impeached.

Chapter Seven

How Both Bushes Attacked Iraq

By Michelle Mairesse

In 1990, Hussein was preoccupied with Kuwait (one of the Persian Gulf states the British had carved out in the 1920s), which severely limited Iraq's access to the Gulf. Not only did that tiny country demand repayment of war loans, but it had also been slant drilling and siphoning oil from Iraqi territory.

Saddam Hussein had reason to believe that the U.S.A. still backed him. After all, the C.I.A. had helped install him as dictator of Iraq in 1979, and the U.S.A. had supplied him with arms, including chemical and biological weapons, during the war with Iran (19801988).

On airing his concerns to U. S. Ambassador April Glaspie in July, Hussein was encouraged by her response. She told Hussein that Washington had "no opinion on Arab-Arab conflicts, like your border disagreement with Kuwait," a statement, she said later, she regretted.

In September 1990, Glaspie told the *New York Times*, "We didn't think he'd take all of Kuwait."

The Invasion of Kuwait

As early as April of 1990, both Kuwaiti and American intelligence services were aware of Iraqi invasion plans, and American policy-makers were informed several days beforehand, but there were no public pronouncements or warnings to Hussein.

When Iraqi tanks rolled into Kuwait on August 2, 1990, President George Bush Senior compared the invasion to Nazi Germany's occupation of the Rhineland.

Nevertheless, the day before the invasion, the Bush administration approved the sale of $395,000,000 worth of advanced data transmission devices to Iraq, just one item in the 1.5 billion dollars of advanced technology that both the Reagan and Bush administrations sold to Hussein from 1985 to 1990.

Exploiting the Crisis

The first President Bush, aided by Dick Cheney, Paul Wolfowitz, and Colin Powell, now jumped at the opportunity to justify a more militaristic foreign policy.

Bush proposed "a new world order--free from the threat of terror." The United States would lead a coalition against the aggressor.

Arab leaders suggested a compromise: allow Iraq to annex a small segment of Kuwait after withdrawal. The administration refused that offer and all others, not because the plans were unreasonable, but because the Bush administration had decided on a war designed to enhance American power in the oil-rich Mideast.

Fake Satellite Photos

In early January, Hussein's troops began to withdraw from Kuwait, but the Pentagon claimed to have satellite photographs showing an enormous buildup of Iraqi forces and weapons, 250,000 Iraqi troops and 1500 tanks massing in the desert for their impending attack on Saudi Arabia. This announcement stunned the anti-war protesters, and world opinion gradually shifted, although no one saw the alleged photos, which were, of course, classified.

Jean Heller, an ace journalist from the St. Petersburg Times in Florida, persuaded her editors to buy two photos from the Russian commercial satellite, the Soyuz Karta, taken September 11 and September 13. The photos proved that the entire Iraqi air force was parked in Riyadh and that Iraqi troops were nowhere to be found massing in the desert. The editors asked two former Defense Intelligence Agency analysts to examine the photos. They, too, were surprised that the pictures showed American jets arrayed on the Saudi Arabian border but no troops at all on the Kuwaiti border.

Peter Zimmerman, a satellite expert at George Washington University, said,

> We could see clearly the main road leading right through Kuwait, south to Saudi Arabia, but it was covered with sand banks from the wind and it was clear that no army had moved over it. We could see empty barracks where you would have expected these thousands of troops to be billeted, but they were deserted as well.

Then a strange thing happened. Major news organizations, including *Newsweek,* the *Chicago Tribune,* and ABC, perused the photos but decided not to publish a story that would contradict the government's information. The Iraqi military buildup, which did not exist, was Bush's justification for dispatching troops, yet the American media refused to expose the government's lie. The only honest American journalists were in St. Petersburg, Florida.

After the war, the House Armed Services Committee concluded that at the beginning of the ground war in February, the Iraqi troops numbered 183,000, not the 250,000 "discovered" by the Pentagon satellite.

The alleged Pentagon satellite photos are still classified.

Fake Dead Babies

The propagandists for the Gulf War had to reach back to World War I for the ultimate staged outrage--our evil enemy attacks innocent babies.

Here is how it unfolded. Kuwaiti citizen Nijirah al-Sabah, wiped her eyes and described a horrifying scene she saw when she was a volunteer in the Al Adnan hospital in Kuwait City. She had witnessed Iraqi soldiers looting incubators to take back to Baghdad, throwing Kuwaiti babies on "the cold floor to die."

This story, told and retold, incensed the public and congress as nothing else had done. The Senate resolution to go to war passed by five votes. Six senators said the baby incubator story had overcome their reluctance to send troops.

Months later, Nayirah was exposed as the daughter of the Kuwaiti ambassador to Washington. She had no connection to the Al Adnan hospital, as nurses there would testify. She and several other "witnesses" had been coached by the Hill and Knowlton public relations firm, which had a contract worth over $10,000,000 with the Kuwaiti government.

Brent Scowcroft, Bush's national security adviser, later said in an interview with the *Guardian* that the administration had not known at the time that the story was false. He admitted that "it was useful in mobilizing public opinion."

Fake Statistics

After the war, Bush's Secretary of Defense Dick Cheney said that the government did not know and probably would never know how many Iraqi casualties resulted from the Gulf War.

Beth Osborne Daponte, a Commerce Department demographer, prepared a report estimating that 13,000 civilians were killed by allied forces, 70,000 civilians died from infrastructure damage, and 40,000 troops were killed in battle. Her supervisors dismissed her, confiscated her report, and issued a new one with much lower estimates of Iraqi mortality rates.

Later, after Beth Osborne won her appeal and had been reinstated in her job, U.S. officials provided higher estimates: 100,000 Iraqi soldiers killed, 300,000 wounded, and 2,500 to 3,000 Iraqi civilians killed by bombing. International organizations estimated that the war created 5,000,000 refugees and that sanctions had killed more than 500,000 Iraqi children.

A Grateful Nation

Returning Gulf War veterans experienced the same government obstinacy that Vietnam veterans had run into when they reported illnesses caused by chemical warfare agents. After both wars, the U. S. government insisted that the veterans' symptoms were psychological and had no known physical cause. After both wars, even sympathetic Veterans Administration physicians were ordered to treat such claims as stress related. As recently as January 23, 2003, the Veterans Affairs Department announced that Vietnam veterans suffering from chronic lymphocytic leukemia probably contracted the disease after exposure to Agent Orange (a defoliant the American army used extensively in the Vietnam War) and were entitled to benefits.

Of an estimated 540,000 Gulf War veterans, two out of five are on disability. Not all disability claims are honored. Veterans suffering from what is known as Gulf War Syndrome are encountering the same official blindness to the after-effects of chemical warfare agents. Despite international opposition to weaponized depleted uranium, the Pentagon is still denying its toxic effects and still employs the radioactive substance in shells and armor. Despite mounting evidence of the health hazards created by the forced inoculations of troops, the Pentagon blandly persists in requiring them.

During a press interview in October 2000, the retired commander of French forces in the Gulf War said his French troops took anti-nerve-gas tablets" (pyridostigmine bromide) for four days only. The British and American troops took them for months at a time. General Roquejoffre had never allowed his troops to be inoculated with the untried, controversial American "cocktail" vaccination. British and American troops had all been inoculated. British and American troops who had served in the same areas as the French came down with Gulf War Syndrome, but not a single French soldier suffered from the disease. The Pentagon continues to blow smoke about this issue and still forces troops to be vaccinated.

Question: How many retired military officers own stock in the pharmaceutical companies who make components of the "cocktail"? The anthrax vaccine alone goes for $18 a pop.

Like Father, Like Son

John MacArthur, author of *Second Front: Censorship and Propaganda in the Gulf War,* reminds us that both Bush administrations shared many of the same top officials. "These are all the same people who were running it more than ten years ago," he says. "They'll make up just about anything--to get their way."

It's the same old crew, all right, the wonderful folks who brought us the too-soon-forgotten Iran-Contra scandal.

Obviously, Big Oil is over-represented in Bush Junior's administration. The Bushistas, including Vice President Dick Cheney (Halliburton Oil), Commerce Secretary Don Evans (Colorado Oil), National Security Advisor Condoleeza Rice (Chevron), Secretary of Commerce and State Department official Richard Haas, have served as executives and consultants for international oil firms. They have traded valuable stock in companies that extract, refine, and market petroleum. They have profited from companies that build pipelines, obtain drilling concessions, and provision the industry. Enron used to be busy in all those capacities.

Robert Zoellick, U.S. Trade Representative, served on Enron's advisory council; I. Lewis Libby, Cheney's Chief of Staff, was a major Enron stockholder; Secretary of the Army Thomas White was an Enron executive for a decade and cashed in millions of dollars in stocks and options before the crash. Karl Rove, Bush Junior's Gray Eminence, owned about $250,000 worth of Enron stock at the time he conferred with Ken Lay in the White House about Enron's difficulties with federal regulators.

It's the same old crew, all right, refusing to negotiate, comparing Hussein to Hitler, accusing him of "gassing his own people" although the preponderance of evidence shows that the Iranians gassed the Kurds during the Iran-Iraq War, while the U.S. was supporting the Iraqis.

Charley Reese reminds us how easily this administration resorts to obfuscation or lies.

> Bush has repeatedly cited the 1988 gassing of Kurds in Halabja as evidence of Iraqi cruelty. Recently, Stephen C. Pelletiere, a former CIA analyst, has reminded us of a Defense Intelligence Study that concluded that (1) the Kurds were casualties in a battle for the city between Iraqi and Iranian forces and not the object of the attack; and (2) that it was the Iranian gas that killed the Kurds.

> I remember reading a story in The Washington Post about this report. Now, one of two things is inescapable: Either the U.S. government was lying when it issued the report, or the president and his people are lying today when they blame it on Iraq. It has to be one or the other.

No one should be surprised that the majority of hawks, the men who want to go to war rather than resort to diplomacy, have never seen military service. They managed to avoid the draft during the Vietnam conflict. Vice President Dick Cheney boasts, "I was smart enough to get five deferments." Bush Junior served in the National Guard, went AWOL for most of his enlistment. and somehow avoided imprisonment. Abrams, Card, Thompson, Wolfowitz, Ashcroft, Rove, Perle, etc.--none of them served, and all of them are eager to draw blood in Iraq.

The notable exception is Colin Powell, the only Bushista to have credibility in the realm of tactics, strategy, and diplomacy. Unfortunately, he is in the same position he occupied during Bush Senior's regime when he repeatedly covered up the Iran-Contra crimes. Against what we hope must be his better judgment, he exercises the same function for Bush Junior.

How sad, then, we were to see Powell standing before the United Nations Security Council with a pathetic show-and-tell presentation. The incriminating aerial photographs of Hussein's hidden weapons facilities could have been a Hollywood set or a Bakersfield truck stop as far as the audience was concerned. The photos required, Powell hastened to explain, expert interpretation. Sigh. Maybe the Pentagon should buy its photos from Soyuz Karta, the commercial Russian satellite.

Powell made points when he read earnestly from the thick British intelligence dossier, only to be ridiculed days later when the "intelligence dossier" proved to have been cobbled together from decade-old public sources, such as *Jane's Intelligence Review* and an unattributed article from the *Middle East Review of International Affairs* written by a lecturer at the U.S. Naval Postgraduate School.

While Powell was brandishing his vial of simulated anthrax, he failed to mention the significant facts about the anthrax letters. F.B.I. investigators have concluded that the powdered anthrax mailings were a weaponized form of an American strain produced at an American facility. Furthermore, weapons inspectors declare that Iraq has never possessed a dry preparation of anthrax.

No, General Powell. You had your chance and you blew it. Instead of holding up the vial of white powder and announcing that Hussein could do a whole bunch of damage with a teaspoonful of this anthrax stuff, you should have thrown your head back, swallowed it, and declaimed, "It is a far, far better thing I do than I have ever done before."

It looks like we'll be hearing about dead babies pretty soon.

Chapter Eight

The California Recall Plot

By Michelle Mairesse

It was an extraordinary moment. Congressional Representative Darrell Issa stood before a press microphone array and wept. He had just spent two million of his estimated $300 million fortune gathering signatures and running campaign ads urging citizens to recall California Governor Gray Davis and replace the governor with Issa himself.

Issa had reason to hope. Ben Ginsberg, the attorney who headed the Bush team in the Florida courts in the 2000 presidential election, had been Issa's advisor during these months of importing, organizing, and deploying petition circulators from out of state. Then a thunderclap came out of the blue and Issa's dream collapsed: The night before Issa cried on camera, a movie star announced on Jay Leno's Tonight Show that he, Arnold Schwarzenegger, was preparing to be California's next governor.

Issa's resume neglected to mention that, like several of Bush's cabinet members, he had been charged with four felonies and convicted of one, but he thought his neoconservative outlook and his rags-to-riches immigrant's story would compensate for any past mistakes. He was wrong. Although the Republican wheeler-dealers kindly allowed him to pick up the recall tab, they never considered backing his run for the statehouse. Arnold was their boy from the beginning-- and had been for years.

Think back to the manufactured electrical power crisis of 2001. While Gray Davis was unsuccessfully trying to get through to Vice President Dick Cheney, Enron official Ken Lay, Texas energy traders, and Bush and Cheney cronies were conferring with Vice President Cheney in Washington and scheming to create power shortages in the golden state.

They gamed the system so successfully in California that they soon were raking in fortunes and flicking the lights on and off all over the state. After the third rolling blackout had occurred in California, Lay called a secret meeting of high Republican honchos at the Beverly Hills Hotel. He invited such notable Republicans as then-mayor of Los Angeles Richard Riordan, convicted junk-bond scammer Michael Milken, and steroid-enhanced movie star Arnold Schwarzenegger.

At that time, Lay was collecting allies for his plan to bring even more deregulation to California while he and his "competitors" were busy creating a rigged market that was to cost California more than $7 billion. Mighty Enron, favored and well-connected as it was, overreached and crashed, but not before it had thrown myriad businesses into receivership, annihilated billions of dollars of its own assets and workers' pensions, and wrecked public utilities in several third world countries. Although Lay and other Enron executives were convicted of fraud in July 2006, a federal judge ruled that Lay's death on July 6 prevented him from appealing, thereby invalidating Lays' conviction.

Not everyone was unhappy about the rolling blackouts. California Republicans gleefully announced their strategy on the Internet, with such conservatively compassionate messages as: "Use blackouts to break Davis, and use Davis to break the Democrats." The strategy seemed to be working. The Federal Energy Regulatory Commission declined to intervene, although ratepayers in San Diego County eventually saw their energy bills increase by 300%. In pursuit of petty, partisan politics, the Bush administration allowed corporate outlaws to inflict grievous harm on the citizens and businesses of California. With electricity selling for $1500 per megawatt hour, Silicon Valley workshops, hospitals, and schools went dark; the poor dispensed with gas and electricity, and small businesses closed their doors. Belatedly, the FERC capped prices at $273 per megawatt hour. In a desperate attempt to spike energy prices, Gray Davis bought futures in the hope that California could buy natural gas for less than the market price. When natural gas prices fell through the floor, California actually had to pay *more* than market price for gas.

Again, the Bush administration could have prevented this move, but chose to play politics with the welfare of California citizens. Energy Secretary Spencer Abraham knew that Saudi Arabia had contracted with the seven major Anglo-American oil companies and Enron, which specialized in liquid natural gas, to distribute liquid natural gas worldwide.

Abraham knew that gas prices would drop. If he been a real public servant instead of a political time-server, he would have consulted with Davis and warned him against purchasing the gas futures.

Gray Davis was not responsible for deregulating energy in California. Davis did what he legally could do to get the energy leeches off California's back, but the Bush administration colluded with the leeches. The person responsible for the deliberately manufactured crisis, the person who promoted and signed the energy deregulation bill that Davis inherited, was California governor Pete Wilson.

Schwarzenegger's campaign manager is, of course, Pete Wilson.

On April 12, 2003 while Issa was circulating recall petitions, Schwarzenegger conferred at the White House with Karl Rove, the man who has been called "Bush's brain." He appears to be Arnold's brain as well, for Schwarzenegger has surrounded himself with political consultants who are as ethically-challenged as any of Bush's appointees.

Take Schwarzenegger's media director, Don Sipple, for example. He accepted $120,000 from California Insurance Commissioner Chuck Quackenbush to produce an underground political campaign ad for the commissioner. Sipple's payment came from a $13 million fund intended for earthquake victims, who never saw a cent of it. Quackenbush encouraged insurance companies to donate money to foundations in lieu of paying larger fines for mishandling Northridge earthquake claims. For this and other scams, Quackenbush faced impeachment and was forced to resign in disgrace. In 2000, the Assembly Insurance Committee censured Sipple, Jeff Randle, Marty Wilson, and Joe Shumate for participating in Quackenbush's fun and games and racking up six figure payments diverted from the general fund. It is mind-boggling to learn that these men served as consultants to Schwarzenegger, who vows "to clean up Sacramento."

Last November, the citizens of California elected Gray Davis to serve as their governor for another four years. An elected official can be removed for malfeasance, but Davis is no malefactor. His budget figures were no worse than those of the Republican governor of New York, not to mention the Republican president of the United States.

Funding George "leave no millionaire behind" Bush's tax-cuts for the rich was costly for all the states, including California, but California is far from collapse. An August 17 *Los Angeles Times* editorial maintains that the state of the state is not nearly as grim as the doomsayers claim. California has no more unemployed workers than has the rest of the country, and unemployment is greatest in Silicon Valley, where the high-tech bubble burst and created much of the budget deficit. The number of businesses actually increased during the energy crisis in 2000, the latest year for which statistics are available. Another Schwarzenegger advisor, Democratic billionaire Warren Buffett, in a pronouncement that was not much bruited abroad, said, "California has a vibrant economy."

According to Paul Krugman, news reports continue to talk about a $38 billion deficit, although next year's (2004) projected gap is only $8 billion.

For what crime, then, have the Republicans conspired to flout the will of the California electorate? It's simple. Davis is a Democrat. He was on their hit list. He fit their pattern: After removing 90,000 qualified voters from the rolls and falsifying returns in Florida, the Republicans stole an election they could not win from Al Gore.

Six states, after installing voting machines manufactured by right-wing Republican companies, noticed voting irregularities in the 2002 congressional elections, some resulting in surprising Republican victories. The companies would not permit their machines to be examined.

Every ten years, all the states redraw electoral districts based on the federal census. Texas reapportioned its electoral districts three years ago, giving Democrats 17 seats and Republicans 15 seats in the U. S. Congress. After the jiggered Republican victory in the 2002 elections, House Majority Leader Tom DeLay tried to install a new districting map, based on fuzzy Republican math or dowsing or divine inspiration, which would give the Republicans 22 seats and the Democrats 10. Understandably, the Democrats left town to avoid being steamrollered.

The California recall election allowed Schwarzenegger to complete Governor Davis's term and cost the taxpayers an estimated $67 million. Now Schwarzenegger was favorably positioned as a candidate, an incumbent with outstanding name recognition.

Despite an undistinguished record and a program roundly rejected by voters, Arnold had a makeover and won the election that had so carefully been scripted for him.

The California recall vote fit very nicely into the Republican plan for winning elections: If you can't win or steal an election, recount, reverse, or recall.

Don't make the mistake of thinking that the Bush Cabal is stupid. Unscrupulous, yes. Even crazy. But not stupid.

Chapter Nine

Terri Schiavo and the "Culture of Life"

By Michelle Mairesse

Nothing in Theresa Marie Schindler's early life foreshadowed the sinister celebrity of her last years. A shy brunette who wore glasses and had a permanent weight problem, she grew up with her younger brother and sister in a comfortable suburban community near Philadelphia. When she attended an all-girls Catholic high school, she was 5 feet 5 inches tall and weighed 250 pounds. She shared the musical and cinematic preferences of her girlfriends--except for clothes-shopping. Nothing she wore could disguise her obesity. From an early age, she liked and empathized with animals. Her collection of stuffed animals, over a hundred of them, reflected her ambition to work in a zoo one day.

Under the direction of a pediatrician, she slimmed down considerably when she attended Bucks County Community College. There she met and dated Michael Schiavo. Michael, according to Terri's sister, was the first boy to pay attention to Terri. In November 1984, their long engagement culminated in a huge nuptial celebration attended by 250 wedding guests.

For a few months, money was so tight for the newlyweds that they roomed in the Schindler family's basement. In 1988, they moved to Florida, where Terri's parents, Robert and Mary Schindler, had retired. Terri and Michael quickly found employment and rented a small apartment. In sunny Florida, Terri was experimenting with a new version of herself. She had become a svelte blonde weighing 110 pounds. Clothes-shopping was fun. She drove a new Toyota. Her job as an insurance clerk gave her free time to sunbathe on the beach and visit clubs with friends.

Mary Schindler worried that her daughter was not eating properly, but Terri reassured her. An obstetrician had found no obstacles to conception, so she was undergoing fertility therapy. She and Michael hoped that she would eventually become pregnant. She did not confide to her mother or anyone else how her obsession with weight control had led her to follow meals with bouts of induced vomiting.

At 5:30 in the morning of February 5, 1990, Michael, who worked nights as a restaurant manager, was startled awake by the sound of a loud thump in the hall. He found his wife lying face-down on the floor and making a gurgling noise. He quickly rushed her to the hospital.

For weeks, Michael haunted the intensive care unit hoping for signs of recovery. Attending doctors believed that his wife's heart, deprived of oxygen, had stopped beating for five minutes owing to a potassium imbalance resulting from Terri's eating disorder. The oxygen deficiency had devastated her cerebral cortex, they said, leaving it filled with scar tissue and spinal fluid. They diagnosed her condition as a persistent vegetative state.

Neurologists make definite distinctions between coma and persistent vegetative state. Coma patients have closed eyes and are unresponsive to stimuli. Persistent vegetative state patients have a normal sleep-wake cycle and open their eyes. However, persistent vegetative state patients exhibit no awareness of self or environment; they exhibit no evidence of sustained, reproducible, purposeful, or voluntary behavioral responses to visual, auditory, tactile, or noxious stimuli and no evidence of language comprehension or expression. A persistent vegetative state generally results from traumatic brain injuries or metabolic imbalances.

In a March 2005 television interview with Dan Abrams, Dr. Ronald Cranford, assistant chief of neurology at Hennepin County Medical Center in Minneapolis and faculty member at the University of Minnesota's Center for Bioethics, described how he diagnosed Terri Schiavo after examining her in 2002 and testifying to her condition in court. Of the eight neurologists who examined her in 2002, seven of them said Terri Schiavo was in a vegetative state. Cranford said that her CT scan showed severe atrophy of the brain, her EEG was flat, and she had undoubtedly been in a permanent vegetative state since 1990. He believes that the parents are indulging in wishful thinking when they attribute responses to her.

No credible neurologist has come along who's examined her who's said she's not in a vegetative state. It's just what they want to see. And you can see how scary the tapes are that show her apparently interacting with her eyes open. But her eyes are open, but she's not even looking at her mother when you look at those tapes.

The dissenting neurologist was one Dr. William Hammesfahr, who devised a discredited treatment for stroke victims. He was disqualified by the Florida Medical Board and never published in any legitimate peer-reviewed journal. Nevertheless, television host Sean Hannity falsely introduced him as a Nobel nominee and never questioned Doctor Hammesfahr's contention that with the right treatment Terri would be going out, seeing movies, and enjoying life.

While showing Dan Abrams the most recent CT scan done on Terri, one dating from 2002, Dr. Cranford commented that the scan showed severe atrophy.

> Where those black areas are, that should be white. That should be cerebral cortex, and so really there is no cerebral cortex left. It's just a shrinkage of the cerebral cortex. It's a thin band of white on the outside and any neurologist or any radiologist looking at those CT scans will tell you that her atrophy could not be more severe than it is. So even if she were mentally conscious, which she's not, she's irreversible. She's been like this for 15 years, Dan, and that CT scan shows the most extreme severe atrophy of the higher centers of the brain.

Later in the interview, Dr. Cranford commented that edited tapes and still photos falsely make it appear that the patient is interacting. "That's what the vegetative state is. It looks like they're interacting, but they're really not. And there's nothing I can do to change that."

The talk shows continued to feature Dr. Hammesfahr and his ilk anyway. Dr. Theresa Buck, the staff physician at Terri's hospice, was unable to convince her mother and her mother-in-law that Terri was in a vegetative state. The physician's relatives believed what they heard on television--that Terri Schiavo was talking and making requests.

Early on, both families continued to hope that Terri would revive. Michael sold hot dogs on the beach to raise money for the various therapies he ordered for Terri. He even flew her to California for an implant of platinum electrodes. Nothing availed, but he continued to oversee her care, dressing her in new clothes, perfuming her, bringing flowers to her room. Finally, to better supervise the care of his wife, he enrolled in school and became a registered nurse. The hospice nurses resented his constant demands, although they admitted that Michael was the kind of man they wanted in their corner when they were ill.

In 1992, the Schiavos were awarded over a million dollars in two medical malpractice suits. $750,000 went into a trust fund for Terri's care, and $300,000 went to Michael. In February 1993, Michael and his father-in-law were permanently estranged when Robert Schindler demanded a share of the money, according to Michael. Untrue, say the Schindlers.

Whatever happened, the Schindlers launched an all-out campaign to have Michael removed as Terri's guardian, charging neglect, abuse, and adultery. (Michael was now living with his girlfriend.) A judge dismissed their action.

The Schindlers enlisted the support of the ultra-conservative Philanthropy Roundtable, a collection of foundations with assets of two billion dollars to lavish on their pet causes: abolishing social security, outlawing birth control and abortion clinics, making prayer mandatory in public schools, and prohibiting stem cell research. Some of these foundations have contributed hundreds of thousands of dollars to the Schindlers' cause. The Schindlers themselves solicit donations for the Schindler-Schiavo Foundation on their website. They recently agreed to give the names of all their contributors to a conservative direct-marketing firm in exchange for the firm's services in soliciting more donations.

In 1998, Michael petitioned a Florida state court to permit removal of Terri's feeding tube. The Schindlers opposed him in court. The court-appointed guardian for Terri was perturbed by the Schindlers' vehemence; they said they would never remove the feeding tube under any circumstances, even if their daughter had specifically requested them to do so. The judge ruled for Michael, and the tube was removed in 2001. The Schindlers appealed the decision, and the tube was reconnected.

In November 2002, the court found that Mrs. Schiavo would not recover and ordered her feeding tube removed again. Almost a year later, the tube was removed, prompting Governor Jeb Bush and the Florida Legislature to pass a new law, Terri's Law, specifically demanding that the tube be reconnected.

In September 2004, the Florida Supreme Court ruled Terri's Law unconstitutional. At this time, House Majority Leader Tom Delay was fending off widespread criticism of his possibly criminal and definitely unethical conduct. Never one to miss an opportunity, he expressed his outrage over the Florida court's decision and vowed to leap into the breach on Terri's behalf.

Tom Delay and Senate Majority Leader Bill Frist summoned Congress back from recess to pass emergency legislation requiring federal courts to hear the Schiavo case. With only faint protests from House Democrats and none from Senate Democrats, Congress, after midnight, approved the law.

For the first time since he took office, President George Bush interrupted a leisurely Crawford vacation. He headed to the capital on Air force One and signed the bill in the wee hours of the morning.

Considering that approximately forty judges in six courts had reviewed the case, federal jurists were unimpressed with the congressional fiat. One Republican appointee on the U.S. Court of Appeals wrote that the intervention of Congress violated the Constitution. By March 30, the Florida Supreme Court and a United States District Court had denied the Schindlers' appeals. For the sixth time, the United States Supreme Court refused to hear another appeal.

Meanwhile, the Schindlers and their supporters gathered outside the hospice where Terri lay dying. They carried protest signs, shouted and mugged for the cameras, heckled the workers entering the hospice, and provided bits of fairground entertainment for the cameras and bystanders.

A Christian husband-and-wife juggling team said God had sent them to perform for Terri. Antiabortion crusader Scott Heldreth and his son also claimed to be present on God's orders. It just goes to show that the deity works in mysterious ways, because Heldreth is a registered sex offender. The animal rights people showed up. Perhaps it was one of theirs who paraded a hat-wearing chicken around the arena. Randall Terry, another antiabortion crusader with an arrest record, assumed a prominent role in the circus, helpfully staging such maudlin events as "innocent" children being arrested by the police.

Terri died on the morning of March 31. Outside, a trumpet player was on hand to sound a requiem. Forty-one-year-old Theresa Marie Schiavo had died peacefully, with a stuffed tabby cat tucked under one arm, surrounded by flowers, and embraced by her husband. When he announced his intention to bury her in the family plot in Pennsylvania, the Schindlers announced that they would be holding their own service in Florida. In lieu of flowers, the Schindlers preferred that donations be made to their foundation.

Despite the hysteria, despite the false witnesses, and despite the inaccurate reports issuing from politicians, pulpits, press, cable television, and radio, the public refused to be stampeded. They believed in the separation of powers and the integrity of our court system. Most of all, they believed that politicians and religious fanatics had no business interfering with an anguished family's private decisions.

On the day Congress intervened, an ABC poll showed that citizens opposed congressional and presidential involvement by 70% and approved by only 27%. In seven days, Bush's approval rating dropped from 52% to 45%. A Gallup poll spokesman said the numbers probably reflected the public's response to the Schiavo controversy.

Dizzy with defeat, the old pols lined up to bluster. House Judiciary Committee Chairman

F. James Sensenbrenner Jr. declared that the federal courts had not given the case the new, full, and fresh review that the law required. Tom Delay threatened, "This loss happened because our legal system did not protect the people who need protection most, and that will change. The time will come for the men responsible for this to answer for their behavior, but not today."

The hypocrisy of the political right has never been greater. The Schiavo case was not unique. Families and doctors make the decision to remove life-support on a daily basis. Within a fortnight, Tom Delay made the decision to withdraw life-support from his father, who had suffered brain damage in an accident. Terri Schiavo's father made the same decision for his own mother after one week. Even the three Franciscan Brothers of Peace, who accompanied the Schindlers everywhere, had withdrawn life-support from their Order's brain-damaged founder in 2003.

It was unseemly for notably randy congressmen and talk-show hosts to deplore Michael Shiavo's adultery. It was vicious for fanatics to hurl death threats at Michael Shiavo, his family, and County Judge George Greer. It was vile for conservative fundraisers to use Terri Schiavo's image in their promotions.

Finally, it was and is outrageous for radical conservatives to preach to us about the culture of life while their actions promote the culture of living-death. When, after being raped, a pitiful, retarded girl asked for an abortion, Governor Jeb Bush appointed a guardian--for the fetus. As Governor of Texas George Bush chalked up a record number of executions, making jokes about his refusal to extend reprieves. As president, he has brought back thousands of dead soldiers' bodies--all under cover of darkness, no photos allowed.

Your living-death conservative, like his peers in North Korea and Saudi Arabia, approves the death penalty for criminals. He allows corporations to determine how much poison water we drink and how much toxic air we breathe. He rejects any scientific conclusions that interfere with his agenda. He finds the sight of an exposed feminine breast more offensive than the sight of beggars and homeless people. He justifies torture.

He prefers deadly lies to liberating truths. Because he blights the ground he walks on, we must strip him and his kind of any power over us and reclaim the true culture of life!

Chapter Ten

Enronization: Global Epidemic

By Michelle Mairesse

By November 2001, Chairman Ken Lay of Enron Corporation, a man who had hobnobbed with presidents and potentates, wasn't getting his telephone calls returned. His attempts to reach the ears of those who had enjoyed his patronage were unavailing, and by December 2, 2001 it was all over. Enron filed for chapter 11 bankruptcy protection. In the meantime, Enron's head honchos had surreptitiously sold their stock, raked in huge bonuses, and were now unconvincingly declaring that they were shocked, shocked by these sudden developments. Left holding the bag were thousands of employees, shareholders, creditors, and states and municipalities that signed contracts with Enron. Losses are estimated at $50 billion and counting.

Ratepayers in Connecticut are outraged at the mess Enron left behind when it signed up the state's trash disposal agency. Not only did the state take a $220 million hit, but it then tried to recap its losses by gouging ratepayers. The state attorney general believes that the Connecticut Resources Recovery Authority negotiated an illegal loan contract with Enron and hid the documentation. An investigation is in progress.

Only a short time ago, the billionaire boys who ran Enron were still riding high. They always got their phone calls returned.

From August 2000 to June 2001, while California's energy consumers were screaming about gas and electric bills that kept doubling and redoubling, Enron executives communicated with federal energy regulators in twenty-five meetings and telephone calls, doubtless counseling the feds to let the "free" market work its magic. In the Golden State, the only cities not begging the federal government for price caps were those, like Los Angeles, with publicly-owned utilities. The new Federal Energy Regulatory Commission chief, nominated by Enron and installed by President Bush II in August 2000, did nothing for six months, made minor adjustments in April, and finally imposed price caps in mid-June 2001, at which time the "crisis" disappeared.

Investigators discovered that an unprecedented one-third of the state's generators had been closed "for maintenance" during the "crisis" thereby creating an artificial shortage. After the FERC belatedly imposed price caps, the shortage vanished.

But deregulating utilities had been only the second step in Enron's grand strategy. At the center of Enron's grand strategy was what American journalist Greg Palast referred to as "briberization." Enron ran a candy store for government officials, media figures, and influence peddlers. Political contributions, grants, consulting fees, favors, and salaried positions gushed out of the cornucopia in Houston.

Not surprisingly, the Bush II administration is loaded with former Enron officials and consultants, and Enron chairman Ken Lay has had close ties with the Bush family.

Lay was perhaps the most important figure in Bush's political career, having earlier supported the re-election campaign of his father, then hiring a number of former Bush Sr. officials. Over the years, Lay and Enron contributed $2 million to the younger Bush. He helped Bush win passage of energy deregulation and other initiatives in Texas. He also lent the use of his corporate jet for the Bush presidential campaign. Enron gave $300,000 to the Republican National Convention host committee and another $300,000 to the inaugural committee. Joan Claybrook, *Public Citizen News*, January/February 2002

Other good friends of Enron included lobbyist Wendy Gramm, serving simultaneously on the Chicago Board of Trade and Enron's board and audit committee, assisted by her husband, Senator Phil Gramm, who held out his bucket and received $97,350 in political contributions from the cornucopia.

Enron's Ken Lay and Vice President Dick Cheney go way back. When Cheney was CEO of Halliburton, his Houston-based Brown & Root subsidiary built Enron's new baseball park in Houston. Secretary of the Army Thomas E. White was vice chairman of Enron Energy Services, U.S. Trade Representative Robert Zoellick served on Enron's Advisory Board, and White House Chief of Staff Karl Rove and the Vice President's Chief of Staff Lewis Libby both owned sizable amounts of Enron stock.

Enron lavished donations on conservative think tanks and foundations. It contributed to the American Enterprise Institute, which gave grants or salaries to such future Bush II administration staffers and supporters as Lawrence Lindsey, once a paid Enron consultant ($50,000) and future Secretary of the Treasury Paul O'Neill, who was an American Enterprise trustee for seven years, and future Vice President Dick Cheney's wife, Lynne, a senior fellow there. Enron's largesse flowed to the Institute for Policy Innovation (founded by Dick Armey), Citizens for a Sound Economy, which got a $20,000 contribution, and a Republican fund-raising machine benefiting Congressman Tom De Lay, which Enron gifted with $50,000. All of the Enron-financed institutions fervently supported deregulation, laissez-faire capitalism, globalization, and banking secrecy. Enron contributed to the political campaigns of thirty-three members of Congress who urged both the Clinton and the Bush administrations to ignore international demands for offshore banking regulations.

> Not content simply to deregulate energy markets, Enron deregulated futures markets, making itself exempt from government oversight and from fraud laws." The maneuver "was tantamount to the company giving itself permission to launder massive amounts of money. Which it did.
>
> —Larry Chin, *Online Journal*, February 1, 2002. Transcript from *http:// globalresearch.ca/articles/CHI202C.html.*

During the Clinton administration the Enron brigade successfully thwarted Clinton's attempts to regulate offshore tax havens. Treasury Secretary Paul O'Neill, speaking for the new Bush II administration, endorsed total banking secrecy everywhere in the world. After the attack on the World Trade Center, he modified the policy, but curiously, even though the Cayman Islands offered to open its banking records, he did not immediately accept the offer.

Security Exchange records show that by January 2001, Enron had incorporated subsidiaries in a number of offshore banks: 692 accounts in the Cayman Islands, 110 accounts in Turks and Caicos Islands, 43 accounts in Mauritius, nine accounts in Bermuda, five accounts in Barbados, four accounts in Puerto Rico, two apiece in Hong Kong, and one each in Aruba, the British Virgin Islands, Guam, Guernsey, and Singapore.

Using its offshore subsidiaries, Enron borrowed its own stock, traded with itself and reported the trades as income, hid debt and losses, paid extortionate sums to its executives, and moved its paper profits to avoid taxation for four of the previous five years. The subsidiaries offered cover for an orgy of speculation in derivatives, another facet of the Enron grand strategy. *Public Citizen* comments that having access to this number of unregulated accounts provided Enron "with potentially thousands of phantom accounts to hide money from U.S. tax officials, California energy crisis investigators or creditors during Enron's bankruptcy filing."

Enron's nimble accountant-auditor-consultant, Arthur Andersen, shredded reams of documents after the bankruptcy meltdown, but some paperwork survived, including a memo indicating Enron's intention to grease palms at the International Accounting Standards Board with a $500,000 donation. Enron was never a company that thought small. Buying influence was the cost of doing business, but unfortunately, they were better at the former than the latter. After softening foreign officials with its briberization ploy, Enron positioned itself among the movers and shakers of globalization, the last phase of its grand strategy.

In the hyperactive atmosphere of the nineties, Enron was driving in stakes all over the map. After the Gulf War resulted in the doubling of Kuwaiti oil production, three former Bush I administration officials employed by Enron talked Kuwaiti officials into awarding the giant firm a contract to rebuild the bombed-out Shuaiba power plant, even though Enron charged a higher price for power than other bidders did.

Frank Wisner, U. S. Ambassador to the Philippines in 1991, helped Enron win the contract to manage the two power plants in Subic Bay. Under Enron's management, energy prices jumped 20%, and the entire National Power Corporation Board resigned in disgust.

Wisner, now an Enron consultant, used his influence in 1992 to help Enron secure a lucrative contract for the Dabhol power plant in India. Sandip Roy's devastating report on the project appeared on the *Pacific News Service* Website, February 8, 2000. Here is an excerpt:

> From the get-go, the Dabhol project was mired in controversy. Enron worked hand in hand with corrupt Indian politicians and bureaucrats in rushing the project through. Charges filed by an Indian public interest group allege Enron and the Indian company Reliance bribed the Indian petroleum minister in

1992-93 to secure the contract to produce and sell oil and gas from the nearby Panna and Mukta fields to supply the plant.

A Human Rights Watch report recounted incidents of farmers' land stolen, water sources damaged, officials bribed and opponents of the project arrested on trumped-up charges. In 1997, the state police attacked a fishing village where many residents opposed the plant. The pregnant wife of one protest leader was dragged naked from her home and beaten with batons.

The state forces accused of abuses provided security to the Dabhol Power Corporation (DPC), a joint venture of Enron, the Bechtel Corp. and General Electric, overseen by Enron.

The U.S. State Department issued the DPC a human rights clean bill of health. Charged with the assessment was U.S. Ambassador Frank Wisner, who had also helped Enron get a contract to manage a power plant in Subic Bay in the Philippines in 1993. Shortly after leaving his post in India in 1997, Wisner took up an appointment to the board of directors of Enron Oil and Gas, a subsidiary of Enron.

Thanks in part to Wisner's positive rights review, Washington extended some $300 million in loan guarantees to Enron for its investment in Dabhol --even though the World Bank had refused to finance the project, calling it unviable.

A recent Indian investigative committee report exposed an 'utter failure of governance'--bribery, lack of competitive bidding, secrecy, etc. --by both the Indian federal government and two successive state governments as they rushed the Enron project through.

By June 2001, the Maharashtra state government had already broken off its agreement with DPC because its power cost too much. That was the plant's one and only customer.

By December, news of Enron's collapse was in newspapers across the world. But the company still filed a $200 million claim with the U.S. government's Overseas Private Investment Corporation, a U.S. taxpayer-funded insurance fund for American companies abroad, in an attempt to recoup losses from the DPC. Indian newspapers reported that Vice President Dick Cheney, Treasury Secretary Paul O'Neill and Commerce Secretary Don Evans tried to twist the Indian government's arm into coughing up the money. Otherwise, U.S. officials warned, other investment projects would be jeopardized. International media reported last month that U.S. government documents showed Cheney tried to help collect the debt.

Today in Dabhol, the power plant is considered polluting and undependable. Spring water has become undrinkable, the mango crop is blighted and the fish catch is dwindling. Often at nightfall, the electricity fails.

According to Reuters, Enron's $2.9 billion gas-fired power plant and adjacent liquefied natural gas facility at Dabhol, about 155 miles south of Bombay, has been idle since June 2001 due to a tariff dispute with the government.

After Enron-favored candidate Bush Senior lost his re-election bid in 1992, the pragmatic corporation poured money into the treasury of the Democratic National Committee. In 1994, Clinton's Secretary of Commerce Ron Brown helped Enron secure a construction contract with Paiton Power Plant through a sleazy deal with Indonesia's rapacious dictator, Suharto.

In 1995, Clinton's National Security Advisor, Anthony Lake, helped Enron secure a contract to build a gas pipeline from Mozambique to South Africa, and to develop a gas field in southern Mozambique. During the 1998 World Economic Summit in Davos, Enron received Clinton administration help in the marketing of Russian gas in Europe. Ken Lay and Boris Brevnov of Unified Electricity Systems of Russia signed a 10-year strategic alliance.

Enron, like many other big corporations, was committed to globalism. Not everyone was happy with this development. Some of the reasons for their discontent are highlighted in an Alec Jones Radio Show interview with investigative reporter Greg Palast, an American with a true global perspective. (March 4, 2002).

Palast said that an interview with former World Bank official Joseph Stiglitz and a gift of documents from other sources at the World Bank and the International Monetary Fund detailed the sordid secret practices of international banking.

Palast: "So what we found was this. We found inside these documents that basically they required nations to sign secret agreements, in which they agreed to sell off their key assets, in which they agreed to take economic steps which are really devastating to the nations involved and if they didn't agree to these steps, there was an average for each nation that signed one-hundred and eleven items that they are required to sign on to. If they didn't follow those steps they would be cut-off from all international borrowing. You can't borrow any money in the international marketplace. No one can survive without borrowing, whether you are people or corporations or countries . . ."

Palast said the Argentinian plan, signed by Jim Wolfensohn, the president of the World Bank, forced Argentina to sell all publicly owned assets, including the water system.

Palast: "And by the way, it's not just anyone who gets a piece of the action. The water system of Buenos Aires was sold off for a song to a company called Enron. A pipeline was sold off, that runs between Argentina and Chile, was sold off to a company called Enron."

Jones: "And then the globalists blow out the Enron after transferring the assets to another dummy corporation and then they just roll the theft items off."

Jones summarizes after a break in the interview: "They come in, pay off politicians to transfer the water systems, the railways, the telephone companies, the nationalized oil companies, gas stations--they then hand it over to them for nothing. The Globalists pay them off individually, billions a piece in Swiss bank accounts. And the plan is total slavery for the entire population. Of course, Enron, as we told you was a dummy corporation for money laundering, drug money, you name it, from the other reporters we have had on. It's just incredibly massive and hard to believe. But it is actually happening."

Palast expands on the devastation: "They hand it over, generally to the cronies, like Citibank was very big and grabbed half the Argentine banks. You've got British Petroleum grabbing pipelines in Ecuador. I mentioned Enron grabbing water systems all over the place. And the problem is that they are destroying these systems as well. You can't even get drinking water in Buenos Aires. I mean it is not just a question of the theft. You can't turn on the tap. It is more than someone getting rich at the public expense."

Palast describes Enron's dealings in the Texas and California energy markets as a three-card Monty game. "Well, you have to understand that some of the guys who designed the system in California for deregulation then went to work for Enron right after."

Jones: "Go back into privatization. Go through these four points. That's the key. It sends billions to politicians to hand everything over."

Palast says that former World Bank official Joseph Stiglitz calls the process "briberization," where "you sell off the water company and that's worth, over ten years, let's say that that's worth about 5 billion bucks, ten percent of that is 500 million, you can figure out how it works. I actually spoke to a Senator from Argentina two weeks ago. I got him on camera. He said that after he got a call from George W. Bush in 1988 saying give the gas pipeline in Argentina to Enron, that's our current president. He said that what he found was really creepy was that Enron was going to pay one-fifth of the world's price for their gas and he said how can you make such an offer? And he was told, not by George W. but by a partner in the deal, well if we only pay one-fifth that leaves quite a little bit for you to go in your Swiss bank account. And that's how it's done."

Palast describes the influence of Enron campaign donations: "In fact, we saw some interesting documents, a month before Bush took office, Bill Clinton, I think to get even with Bush's big donor, cut Enron out of the California power market. He put a cap on the prices they could charge. They couldn't charge more than one-hundred times the normal price for electricity. That upset Enron. So Ken Lay personally wrote a note to Dick Cheney saying get rid of Clinton's cap on prices. Within 48 hours of George W. Bush taking office, his energy department reversed the clamps on Enron. OK, how much is that worth for those guys? You know that has got to be worth, that paid off in a week all the donations."

Returning to the globalization theme, Jones asks what happens after the foreign banks have collected 21% to 70% interest and destroyed the economy of the debtor nations.

Palast: "Like I said, you open up the borders for trade, that's the new opium wars. And once you have destroyed an economy that can't produce anything, one of the terrible things is that they are forcing nations to pay horrendous amounts for things like drugs--legal drugs." After that, the ruined country can only survive by trafficking in illegal drugs.

Jones: "And so, drive the whole world down, blow out their economies and then buy the rest of it up for pennies on the dollar. What's Part 4 of the IMF/World Bank Plan?"

Palast: "Well, in Part 4, you end up again with the taking apart of the government. And by the way, the real Part 4 is the coup d'etat. That's what they are not telling you. And I'm just finding that out in Venezuela. I just got a call from the President of Venezuela."

Jones: "And they install their own corporate government."

Palast: "What they said was here you've got an elected president of the government and the IMF has announced, listen to this, that they would support a transition government if the president were removed. They are not saying that they are going to get involved in politics--they would just support a transition government. What that effectively is is saying we will pay for the coup d'etat, if the military overthrows the current president, because the current president of Venezuela has said no to the IMF. He told those guys to go packing. They brought their teams in and said you have to do this and that. And he said, I don't have to do nothing. He said what I'm going to do is, I'm going to double the taxes on oil corporations because we have a whole lot of oil in Venezuela. And I'm going to double the taxes on oil corporations and then I will have all the money I need for social programs and the government--and we will be a very rich nation. Well, as soon as they did that, they started fomenting trouble with the military and I'm telling you watch this space: the President of Venezuela will be out of office in three months or shot dead. They are not going to allow him to raise taxes on the oil companies." [The CIA-IMF sponsored coup happened, just as Palast predicted, but the popular President Chavez survived and resumed his elected status as Venezuela's president.]

Jones observes that the Bush administration set up a shadow government without advising Congress. "This looks like a coup d'etat here. I'm going to come right out with it. We had better spread the word on this now or these greedy creatures are going to go all the way."

Palast concludes that only the mainstream press in Britain will carry his stories. "And I'm just very sorry that we have to have an alternative press, an alternative radio network and everything else to get out the information that makes any sense. I mean this information should be available to every American. I mean, after all, it's our government."

The URL of this interview is: *http://globalresearch.ca/articles/PAL203A.html*

On March 22, 2002 The Institute for Policy Studies released an exhaustive study exposing public financing of Enron's overseas expansion. "It should be a national disgrace that the U.S. government was subsidizing Enron's far-flung and often harmful global operations," said John Cavanagh, Director of IPS.

The report details how, over the past decade, twenty-one agencies representing the U.S. government, multilateral development banks, and other national governments helped supply $7.2 billion in public financing approved for thirty-eight projects in twenty-nine countries. The study also reveals that the company was infamous for predatory policies in the developing world. Bolstered by taxpayer financing from agencies like the Overseas Private Investment Corporation and the World Bank, Enron began privatizing national energy sectors during the Reagan Administration, promising to supply reliable energy at a low price. Once Eron bribed officials and took charge, there followed price hikes, blackouts, and street riots in which people died. Enron's accounting firm, Arthur Andersen, was a big player in the piratization-privatization game. It assessed utilities at bargain basement prices so that Enron could acquire the properties on the cheap. For example, in the Dominican Republic, Enron paid almost $1 billion less than the public utility's actual value.

—http://www.seen.org

Marc Edelman, a professor of anthropology at Hunter College and the CUNY Graduate Center, and author of *Peasants Against Globalization*, describes the Central American famine resulting from these policies.

> Many are abandoning farms that failed because of globalized trade and the dumping of U.S. grain. Others are fleeing liberalized interest rates so high that they have no hope of ever starting a small business. Still others are trying to escape life in the free trade zones, where factory owners enjoy huge public subsidies and workers face immense obstacles in organizing for a living wage.

> Central American land could produce decent living standards for small farmers if they could obtain small-scale irrigation systems, better access to land, secure title to property, low-cost credit and shelter from unfair competition and the ravages of global market forces.

—Marc Edelman, The *Los Angeles Times,* March 22, 2002.

So there it is--deregulation, briberization, hidden speculation, and globalization, a recipe for disaster. At each step of the process, shock waves travel around the world. As long as America permits legally sanctioned financial rape and pillage, Enronization will continue to reward the greedy and pauperize ordinary citizens.

In his testimony before the Senate Banking Committee March 21, 2000 SEC Chairman Harvey Pitt advised the committee against banning accounting firms from providing consulting services to companies whose books they audit, admitting, though, that auditing and consulting for the same corporate clients "can, and in a number of situations clearly does, create conflicts." So, what's your problem, Harvey?

Let's hope that when President Bush visits El Salvador he won't convince his audience that the Central American Free Trade Agreement will make them rich and prosperous. Only one word is the key to their devastated economies: Enronization.

Barry Crimmins, in *Dollars and Sense*, March/April 2002 has a unique view of the fiasco:

- Enron has had to keep shredding files; otherwise they could have fallen into Arthur Andersen's hands.

- Imagine how much sooner Enron would have gone broke had the corporation paid ANY TAXES in the last five years.

- Clayton Vernon was fired from Enron when he wrote on an Internet bulletin board, "Ken Lay is the sorriest sack of garbage I have ever been associated with, a truly evil and satanic figure." Enron apparently dismissed Vernon for disclosing company secrets.

- Connecticut Senator Joe Lieberman, who received campaign and PAC contributions from Enron, has promised a thorough inquiry that will not become "a witch hunt. Responding to calls for Lieberman to recuse himself over the Take the Money Enron scandal, an indignant Lieberman sputtered, "To say Enron owns me is absurd. Anyone who knows me knows that I am first, last and always a pawn of the insurance industry!"

- "Americans trust the Republicans to do a better job of keeping our communities and our families safe," White House Director of Scoundrelism Karl Rove told the Republican National Committee. He continued, "That is, unless those communities have poor people, Enron employees, or drinking water."

- Once again Ralph Nader's political incompetence is clear. How could he have called himself a politician and not gotten at least a few thousand from Enron?

- What's the difference between Osama bin Laden and Ken Lay? When bin Laden commits major crimes against innocent people, he goes into hiding. When Lay commits major crimes against innocent people, he goes to Aspen.

- The biggest challenge facing the Bush administration during its second year will be to find a way to link Enron's victims to the al Qaeda network.

- Little did we know that when Bush promised to return ethics to Washington, it was because he wanted them rounded up and destroyed. So where do the Houston Astros play next year? Enron Memorial Field?

Chapter Eleven

The Global Water Crisis

By Michelle Mairesse

More than a decade ago, I was a foot soldier in the environmental movement. I held up posters at Coastal Commission meetings, coaxed the Audubon Society to do bird species counts at ponds, read stacks of environmental impact reports, telephoned bureaucrats, researched California state, county, and municipal law codes, attended city council meetings, and bored my friends with indignant accounts of life on the front lines.

A melancholy feature of life on the front is the realization that the war is never won. I might delude myself that yesterday's battle settled the matter: the acre of wetlands essential to twenty-four species of migratory birds won't be paved. But money and politics could regroup, strike a crushing blow, and proceed to drain and pave the acre right under my nose. The winning sortie can come from any direction--a zoning change, a new ordinance, a twisted ruling, a disinformation campaign, a bribe-taker hidden under a shell corporation, a missing document, a suborned inspector, or a shift in the political climate--city, county, state, federal, and, recently, international.

Globalization has brought some new forces into the fray. The multinational corporations and the international financial and trade organizations that aid and abet them want the title to all the earth's resources. In comparison, the robber barons were pussycats. Still, the robber barons cleared the way for the multinationals to conduct the ultimate fire sale.

Think about it. You can buy a building today without owning the underground mineral rights. You can operate a smoke-belching industrial plant and buy the "pollution rights" of another industrialist who isn't using his "quota" of pollution. If you want to build your skyscraper higher than the law allows, you can buy "rights" to extra air space from the owner of a less aspiring building.

What the multinationals have in mind is far more audacious, and they're using tactics that make Enron and World. com look like pikers. If we don't fight back with everything we have, we'll end up as serfs on a dying planet.

Water Wars

Bad news and ominous predictions issue from every quarter. In 1995, World Bank vice president Ismail Serageldin predicted an acute water shortage for the new millennium: "If the wars of this century were fought over oil, the wars of the next century will be fought over water."

While the world's population has tripled, water demand has sextupled.

Both the United Nations and the United States government estimate that by 2015, at least 40 percent of the world's population will lack an adequate water supply. Water shortages will affect the livelihood of one-third of the world's population by 2025, experts predict.

Pollution has so diminished the world's fresh water resources that less than one percent of it can be used for drinking or agriculture, and even as the Green Revolution increased food production it was creating depleted aquifers, saline soil, and chemical pollution.

If American bureaucrats took chemical pollution seriously, we would not be reading stories like this one:

> The Environmental Protection Agency and Department of Agriculture announced an unprecedented plan Friday to entrust testing for water pollution from atrazine, one of the most heavily used weed killers in the country, to the chemical's manufacturer.

> The EPA called the plan for monitoring by Syngenta Crop Protection 'an innovative protective approach.' Syngenta, based in Greensboro, N.C., is a subsidiary of the Swiss agribusiness Syngenta. . . .

> Last year, a UC Berkeley study showed that quantities 30 times lower than allowed in drinking water still caused gross malformations in frogs. Earlier this year, University of Missouri-Columbia epidemi-

ologists found reproductive problems in humans. Their study found male semen counts to be almost 50% lower in Missouri farm country where atrazine was used than in big cities, where it wasn't. 'The results were very surprising to me,' said the study's author, statistician Shanna H. Swan. . . .

The European Union recently announced a ban on use of atrazine. Syngenta plans to replace the chemical in Europe with an alternative, terbuthylazine. However, the company has not sought permission to market the chemical in the U.S., said Syngenta spokeswoman Sherry Ford. 'It did not work as well on U.S. weeds,' she said. (*Los Angeles Times,* November 1, 2003)

The ultimate cost of the Green Revolution has not yet been assessed. The Green Revolution promised to end hunger by introducing high-yield seeds to developing nations, but to replace their drought-resistant native crops with thirsty varieties, farmers had to abandon their traditional irrigation methods for deep wells that sucked up already scarce groundwater.

"Water cannot be looked on as the next gold or oil," said Jean-Michel Cousteau, speaking at the World Water Forum in Kyoto, March 2003.

Now 65 percent of the world's fresh water flows into industrialized agriculture, which requires huge irrigation projects. To solve the irrigation problem, government planners and developers build big dams that create further ecological damage. The Global Water Policy Project, a water conservation advocacy group, estimates that two large dams more than 15 meters high have been constructed every day for the past 50 years. Dams prevent streams and rivers from replenishing groundwater. The Ganges, Nile, Yellow, Indus, and Colorado Rivers often run dry before reaching the ocean. Unreplenished aquifers have been strained to the limit.

The Ogallala Aquifer, underlying land from the Texas Panhandle to South Dakota, has probably lost over half its bounty. More than 200,000 wells draw 13 million gallons from the aquifer a minute, faster than Nature can replenish it. Nevertheless, corporate raider T. Boone Pickens compelled a Texas state water district to allow him to pump and sell up to 65 billion gallons of water a year from the Ogallala Aquifer.

Governments all over the world are squabbling over water. Syrians, Jordanians, and Palestinians condemn Israeli manipulation of water resources. Syria and Iraq object to Turkey's plans to dam the Euphrates River. Turkey, in turn, is opposed to Kurdish independence because the Kurds control the snow-covered mountains that augment their water supply. Egypt resents Ethiopia's plans to take more Nile water, and Bangladesh, downstream from India, is drying up because India has dammed and rerouted so much of its water.

China's dam construction has displaced whole populations and created severe ecological imbalances. The former Soviet Union's vast irrigation plan to support water intensive crops in Central Asia has turned the Aral Sea, one of the largest inland bodies of water, into a shrunken, salty puddle.

Twenty-five percent of the world's fresh water goes to non-agricultural industrial projects, everything from automobile production to silicon chip manufacturing, which laps up immense quantities of pure water.

Manufacturing plants that were once welcomed in third-world countries have had unexpected impacts on communities and their water deposits. Plachimada, a once prosperous farming village in Kerala, India, is demanding that the largest Coca-Cola plant in India shut down.

Since 1998, the company has drawn up to one million liters of water daily from an underground aquifer that used to feed the village wells, sustain its coconut groves, and drench its crops. Now that the wells have dried up, the company sends water tankers through the village each morning with subsistence allotments of water for the residents. Coca-Cola sells the residual manufacturing sludge as fertilizer, gives it away, or dumps it in dry riverbeds. Exeter University analyzed samples of the sludge and reported finding high levels of lead and cadmium.

Commodification

The ruins of aqueducts throughout Europe attest to the Roman Empire's belief that water was a right of the people. Until recently, public drinking fountains were found in public squares.

The notion that water could be considered a commodity sold for private gain arose in France in the nineteenth century during the reign of Napoleon III. Suez Lyonnaise has been expanding its global reach ever since, recently grabbing the American United Water Resources. The German-based RWE Aktiengesellschaft purchased the British OMI-Thames, as well as the largest private water company in the United States, American Water Works.

These and other multinational water corporations lobbied the World Water Forum meeting in 2001 to change the definition of water from being a "human right" to a "human need."

Maude Barlow, chair of Canada's largest public advocacy group protests, "These companies completely reject the idea that water is a common property belonging to all living creatures. Their only goal is to commodify the earth's most precious resource." According to the World Trade Organization, "human needs can be supplied by private entrepreneurs for a profit, unlike a human right which accrues equally to everyone." National and international trade associations like the WTO and NAFTA define water as a "commodity" and have agreements requiring governments to permit water exports under specified conditions.

Frank Rijsberman, chairman of a consortium of water scarcity researchers, says that "policy decisions taken in the World Trade Organization are possibly the single most dominant factor shaping the global demand for food and consequently the amount of water required to grow that food."

In short, follow the money.

Privatization

Commodification and privatization go hand in hand. Even though the evidence for water scarcity is overwhelming, governments and global bureaucracies, influenced by lobbyists, and, in many documented cases, outright bribery, are disposed to call water a commodity, to transfer what remains to private corporations, and to let the market determine who gets water and the price they pay for it.

The mythological "market" doesn't apply to water traders. As Jim Hightower points out:

> Wielding monopoly power, they slash staff, lower wages, compromise service, cut corners on quality, skimp on long-term investment, raise rates – and call this 'efficiency.' Any savings derived from these tactics are routed into extravagant executive-pay packages, luxurious corporate headquarters, bureaucracy for the parent conglomerate, lavish advertising and lobbying budgets, and profits. All of this is done behind closed doors, for these private empires are not subject to the open-access and disclosure rules of public agencies. Then, when the peasants rebel, the faraway CEO dispatches an army of PR flacks and lawyers, overwhelming the financial resources available to local citizens and governments.

Fortune magazine predicts that water stocks offer consistent returns well into the twenty-first century. And why not? Hightower explains:

> Many of these companies get profit guarantees written into their contracts. For example, if residents use less water than predicted, companies can raise rates so profits don't fall below a predetermined number. Once in control of a water system, they can also take any surplus and sell it off to the highest bidder, usually a neighboring city that's experiencing an unexpected shortfall. In some parts of the world, reports the trade journal *Global Water Intelligence*, water commands the same price as oil.

Although many local governments claim to lack money for improvements to their fresh water and waste water systems, they end up privatizing public assets and subsidizing private profits.

Environmentalists claim that profits come from increased sales, hence the water privateers have no incentive to conserve.

Corporations like the giant Vivendi demur, arguing that their investments in new technology and infrastructure can improve service and conserve water. Theoretically perhaps they can, but in the real world it hasn't happened.

Multinational tentacles reach into sectors and utilities other than water management. In 2000, for example, Vivendi transferred the entire debt of its communications division onto its environmental division--water, energy, waste, and transport operations. While the communications division is now debt free, subscribers to the "environmental" division have a surcharge of 4% added to their bills.

A study compiled by David Hall, director of the Public Services International Research Unit at the University of Greenwich, concludes that privatization of water in Argentina, Brazil, Germany, Nairobi, and the Philippines resulted in enormous price increases that incited public outrage.

Georgia Out of Its Mind

Georgia's House Bill 237, which *Atlanta Constitution* columnist Jay Bookman has called a "wholesale theft of public property," would privatize water "into a commodity that will be bought and sold like bushels of wheat and pounds of coffee."

Under HB 237, water permits would be transformed into property deeds to water, stream, lake, river, aquifer water, that has always belonged to the people of Georgia. Farmers could sell their irrigation permits. Declining wood products companies could auction off the permits that have allowed them to withdraw millions of gallons a day. You would think that the legislators had learned their lesson in January 2003, when Atlanta took back control of its municipal water system from UWR, a subsidiary of Suez Lyonnaise. UWR had promised to make a demonstration project of the public-private partnership.

The company racked up big profits from privatizing Atlanta's water system under its twenty-million dollar yearly contract, yet it still managed to lower bills for customers. What went wrong?

UWR went on a cost-cutting binge, reducing staff from 731 to 327 employees. Fire hydrants didn't function. Service for repairs or installation was reluctant and slow. Worst of all, brown water flowed from the taps. In the year 2000 alone, the health department issued five boil-all-water alerts.

Where oh where were the Georgia legislators hiding their heads when they framed HB 237?

Bechtel versus Bolivia

The World Bank denied a $25 million loan guarantee to Cochabamba, Bolivia unless the local government sold its water system to the private sector. Two years prior to the water deal, World Bank officials threatened to withhold $600 million in international debt relief if Bolivia, the poorest country in South America, did not privatize Cochabamba's public water system.

Immediately after Bechtel bought the municipal water supply in Cochabamba, the American firm raised prices two hundred percent and cut off water access to the poor. When the company refused to lower its rates, there followed a general strike, a transportation stand-still, and demonstrations resulting in mass arrests, hundred of injuries, and at least one death. After only four months, Bechtel fled to the United States and filed a twenty-five million dollar suit against Bolivia that is to be tried behind closed doors in a secret trade court at World Bank headquarters in Washington, D.C.

Ghana Gets Gouged

Here we go again. World Bank and IMF officials laid down disastrous terms to the Ghanaian government in exchange for $400 million in loans to rebuild its publicly owned water systems. The Ghanaian government agreed to sell water at full market rates and to cease subsidizing poor communities at the expense of wealthy industrial customers. Rates increased two hundred percent and seventy-eight percent of poor Ghanaians had to slake their thirst with contaminated water wherever they could find it. Raging epidemics of malaria, cholera, and guinea worm are filling the hospitals.

Down and Dirty Down Under

In the last decade of the twentieth century, Australia began privatizing its water supplies in a big way, awarding over fifty contracts to private enterprise. By 2001, foreign multinationals provided a quarter of Australia's drinking water.

Adelaide was the only Australian city that handed over the entire management and operation of its drinking and waste water systems to a consortium called United Water International and led by Thames Water and Vivendi. Less than a year and a half later, citizens began to complain that the terrible stench pervading the city made them ill with headaches, nausea, sinusitis, and asthma. For three months, the stink's origin remained a mystery until an investigator located it at one of Adelaide's four wastewater treatment plants eleven miles north of the city. Chemical treatment of the plants system eliminated the smell. It was the old story: to cut costs, UWI had neglected maintenance of the treatment plant's large lagoon system. As for the many benefits UWI had promised, they are not forthcoming.

Adelaide is stuck with the contract until 2011. A government study concluded that with the continued salinity of its water source, the Murray River, Adelaide will no longer have potable water by 2020. The convoluted, secret bidding process that secured UWI's contract has been the cynosure of two government investigations and a parliamentary committee inquiry.

Canada Gets Conned

Hamilton, the first privatized large water utility in Canada, was planned as a demonstration project. The city council set up a new entity with Philip Services, a local corporation. Philip Utilities Management Corporation (PUMC) was awarded an unbid, ten-year one hundred-fifteen dollar contract to operate, manage, and maintain fourteen municipal water treatment facilities, three wastewater treatment plants, and one hundred twenty-nine pumping stations. PUMC retained seventy percent controlling interest and the city would be responsible for water rates and investment in the system. PUMC promised to create an export-oriented water company with its head office in Hamilton. Seven months after start-up, PUMC slashed staff by fifty percent.

After a massive raw sewage spill into Hamilton homes in 1996, the corporation held out against lawsuits for damages for more than three years. As sewage spills continued on a regular basis (sewage floated in the harbor and bubbled up from manhole covers in a neighboring town) the operation accumulated sizable environmental fines that were passed along to the frequently changing ownership. By September 2001, when the German RWE corporation took over, Hamilton had suffered multiple indignities and rate increases from five water companies in eight years.

Community sentiment appears to favor public ownership when RWE's contract comes up for renewal in 2004.

Everybody Lives Downstream

Despite the spirit of the age—untrammeled greed, casual cruelty, unabashed corruption, and fatal short-sightedness—we still find people who want to redeem the time, to make a difference. Fortunately for humankind, these people have encouraged conservation of natural resources for the last fifty years.

The Tree People, a California ecological group, for example, have shifted their focus from planting trees to renewing the watershed that nurtures the trees. In Pacoima and Westchester school grounds, they have mounted demonstration projects using landscaping and underground cisterns to retain rainwater. If parks and schools spent a little more on cooling trees and underground watering systems, they would save money on water and energy while preventing pollution and erosion from pavement runoff.

The many proponents of organic farming want us to stop growing water-intensive crops in the desert with scarce irrigation water and government subsidies, as the industrial agriculturists are doing all over the world. Drought-resistant plants grown on pesticide-free small plots prevent pollution and conserve water.

We have learned from the water privateers how important definitions are. Water defined as a right rather than a commodity can be protected from predators. Dianne Wassenich is taking the definition a step farther. The western states have traditionally granted water rights on the basis of "beneficial needs." Beneficial needs have included mining, building, and agriculture, but not conservation.

Wassenich has applied for a permit to allow the water flowing through her property to continue in its course to the Gulf of Mexico and she has set up a one-person foundation that is part of an emerging movement to redefine beneficial use.

One seasoned warrior in the water wars is Rajendra Singh, who makes rivers flow in the desert. Using traditional methods, his organization has rejuvenated land in India's driest area.

In 1985, Rajendra Singh quit his government job and the comforts of the Rajasthani city of Jaipur for rural development work in the Indian outback. Medicine and literacy were all very well, villagers said, but what they needed first was water. So he learned traditional water-management skills, dug ponds with his hands, braved cudgels and hundreds of legal writs and finally, after many battles, was honored with national and international awards.

An interview with Singh was first published in *New Scientist* print edition. Excerpts from the web transcript follow:

Question: How did you learn to build *johad*s?

> The farmers taught me. How you harvest water depends on your objective, the geography, topography, catchment area, pond area and soil type. Between 100,000 and 500,000 rupees ($2000 to $10,000), depending on the size. The first one was built with my efforts. Today, the local contribution is up to 90 per cent. Rajasthan has had drought for the past five consecutive years. But there is no migration from

the region around the Ruparel and Arvari rivers. The water that had flowed away in flash floods is now accumulating underground. Farmers' crops are growing and there is fodder for their cattle.

Question: So why the opposition?

In the beginning the power brokers and moneylenders--those who mistakenly think that economic empowerment of the poor means loss of their riches--were against me. And the government engineers felt illiterate villagers had no right to enter their domain of construction. When we built our first *johad*, the state irrigation department issued warrants for its removal under the Irrigation and Drainage Act of 1954. I told them we cannot stop rain falling on our land. Last year the people of Lava ka Baas village built a pond to collect run-off water. The area became green and farmers started growing vegetables. But the act forbids stopping the flow of water. The state irrigation department sent earth-movers to demolish the water-harvesting structure. How can the government come between nature and people like that?

Question: So the government claims ownership of water?

No king in history has claimed to rule over water. They only had rights in water management. Government alone cannot own water. Civil society has a right in water management but even it does not own water. Nature owns water. Before they lost their rights over common land and forests, these communities had a rich tradition of building *johads* and other rainwater harvesting structures. With government centralisation, the *johads* were neglected and allowed to die.

You know, Jaisalmer in the west of Rajasthan--the last town before the border with Pakistan--is in one of the driest areas in the world. Yet 100 years ago it was India's major trading centre. It had twice the population it has today, and 15 times more camels. It survived on a traditional water-harvesting system. But now society has become indifferent as it thinks that water is the responsibility of the government that collects taxes. Only when a community realises that it owns water will it treat it with care and stop misusing it.

Communities should manage their water resources and the government should help them. In a democracy, it is the duty of the government to make sure every person has drinking water. If the government is unable to provide it, it should take help from communities. They can work together. The government should have declared water a common natural resource.

Question: Is there a role for the private sector?

Government has failed in water management. So it is handing over to the private sector. Fine. But what private sector? Communities or multinational corporations? If multinationals gain control of water, they will squash the rights of the poor. The National Water Policy implies water privatization. That would spell doom for society.

Question: If the solution is so simple, then why has the government gone for huge dams and irrigation projects?

Maybe because big projects mean more money and more scope for corruption.

Question: Are you against such schemes? You also support the protests against the dams on the Narmada river in Gujarat and neighbouring states.

It is not a question of big or small structures. Small projects are not automatically sustainable either. Sustainability comes with a sense of community ownership and participation. Big dams displace a lot of people and raise issues of equity. You have to think hard, and go for such projects only if there is no other option.

It is the modern engineers who destroyed the traditional water-harvesting systems. The new technocrats and scientists have not concerned themselves with nature and ecology. They are intellectual giants, experts in calculations and research. But more problems arise when you seek solutions without understanding the underlying circumstances. Consider massive, centralised schemes like the Indira Gandhi Canal. Is this wise in a desert state like Rajasthan? There are problems with increasing soil alkalinity and rises in malaria due to water logging and waterborne diseases like diarrhea. No local would have advised such a canal here.

Question: Why this clash between traditional and modern systems?

Traditional knowledge is dismissed as unscientific. But what's really unscientific is not trying to understand local agro-ecology-climate dynamics, local culture and needs, and soil characteristics. Our scientists think problems should be solved by any means necessary. But they looked only at the benefits of their schemes, not the harm. You should not dismiss everything emanating from illiterate villagers as unscientific.

May the wisdom of Rajendra Singh prevail. Think globally and act locally.

Chapter Twelve

Keys to 9/11

By Michelle Mairesse

Our Web journal, the *New Enlightenment*, first published this article in 2002. The questions it raised then are still unanswered.

The largest crash in stock market history occurred on Tuesday October 29, 1929, the day that ushered in the Great Depression and was ever after known as Black Tuesday. The Hoover administration had ignored all the mounting evidence for a financial debacle and did little to intervene after Black Tuesday. Hoover stubbornly insisted that an untrammeled market would correct itself and refused to acknowledge the Hunger Marchers and Bonus Marchers who besieged the capital. Hoover deservedly lost the 1932 presidential election to Franklin D. Roosevelt.

Largely owing to the safeguards Roosevelt put in place, the second big stock market crash (which occurred recently and was met with the same fatuous, Hooverian, laissez-faire philosophy) did not devastate the nation in the same way. Unhappily for us, the most secretive, repressive administration in our history is determining our destiny after the second Black Tuesday, September 11, 2001, and we are in for even darker days ahead.

The Outrage

The horrifying image of the blasted, crumbling World Trade Center twin towers erupting in black clouds of smoke and debris flickered on our television screens again and again during the anniversary observance of September 11, 2001, Black Tuesday.

A parade of politicians, pundits, and publicists lied to us again, declared the attack unprecedented and unexpected, and urged us to surrender our liberties in exchange for a specious promise of protection. Once more the pitiful bleating of intelligence officials was heard in the land. We were asked to believe that twenty-six intelligence services with a budget of more than thirty billion dollars didn't have a clue.

Truth to tell, they had myriad clues. Let's begin with the date, September 11. Exactly five years earlier, September 11, 1996, Ramzi Yousef, Wali Khan Shah, and Abdul Hakim Murad were convicted as conspirators in the first attack on the World Trade Center. The three conspirators had been at large since March 1993 and would probably still be at large had not a quick-thinking Filipina policewoman investigated a suspicious flash fire.

Operation Bojinka

In January 1995, a patrolman told Manila Senior Inspector Aida Fariscal not to worry about the smoke plume rising from a sixth-floor apartment down the street from the station because some Pakistanis had accidentally started a blaze with firecrackers. Fariscal decided to walk down the street and have a look anyway. These days nothing was routine. A typhoon had just left a trail of wreckage in its wake, and Manila was still preparing for the upcoming visit of the pope.

The apartment was littered with chemicals, cotton, and electrical wiring. After refusing a $2000 bribe, Fariscal and a patrolman took a man of many aliases (later identified as Abdul Hakim Murad) into custody. Murad's two companions escaped.

When she returned with the bomb squad, Fariscal knew that from the generals and officials arriving on the scene, this was no ordinary bust. The entire apartment was a manufacturing site for explosive devices. The bomb squad discovered two complete remote controlled pipe-bombs, an extensive array of explosive chemicals funnels, timers, hotplates, reference manuals, as well as a number of varied passports hidden in a wall divider, the pope's schedule and maps of his procession through the city, and a laptop computer belonging to one of Murad's escaped companions, whose identity emerged from many layers of aliases as Ramzi Yousef.

Murad confessed to Philippine police that he and his companions were ready to carry out an ambitious terror attack. Murad, a pilot who had received some of his pilot training in the United States, was primed to crash a plane into C.I.A. headquarters in Langley, Virginia. A second pilot would crash his plane into the Pentagon, and another would crash his plane into some major federal building. These suicide bombings would be coordinated with other crashes. Murad described an elaborate scheme to hide bombs on eleven American airliners (United, Delta, and Northwest), bombs timed to explode simultaneously over the Pacific Ocean. Investigators found detailed plans, including maps and flight schedules, for this fiendish design on Yousef's laptop computer, part of an operation codenamed Bojinka (Serbo-Croatian for big bang).

Philippine police in Manila arrested Murad's partners in crime, Ramzi Yousef and Wali Khan Shah, Islamic militants linked to Osama bin Laden's Al Qaeda network. As fugitives from justice, the trio was extradited to the United States, where they were convicted and imprisoned.

Ramzi Yousef, the mastermind of the 1993 World Trade Center bombing, was unrepentant. His only regret was that he did not bring down the twin towers in 1993 because he lacked funds to buy enough explosives. Intelligence officials in the Philippines say that a round-faced Indonesian cleric known as Hambali was Yousef's main moneyman. He funded and coordinated Yousef's cell through a Malaysian trading company. Both Hambali and Wali Khan Shah were on the board of directors. (In 1994, Wali Khan Shah directed hijackers of a Philippine Airlines plane who killed a Japanese businessman. According to Murad, this was a practice run for Project Bojinka.) Here was a strong clue linking Hambali, Al Qaeda, and the terrorists, but no one followed it. A second source of funding came from a local charitable foundation headed by Mohammad Jamal Khalifa, brother-in-law to bin Laden. No one followed that clue, either.

Hambali's Al Qaeda network, say Philippine officials, built a formidable logistics operation, providing money, housing, and fake documents to terrorists involved in attacks on the 1993 World Trade Center, the October 2000 bombing of the U.S.S. Cole in Yemen, and the September 11 attacks. They say Hambali and his subordinates met with at least two of the September 11 suicide hijackers in Malaysia in January 2000.

Hambali's organization provided money and documents identifying Zacarias Moussaoui (currently on trial for conspiracy in the 9/11 attack) as a consultant for a Malaysian company, Infocus Tech, to expedite his entrance into the United States. Yazid Sufaat signed a letter as Managing Director of the Malaysian company, declaring that Moussaoui was a marketing consultant for Infocus Tech and would receive a $2,500 monthly allowance. (Infocus Tech, a real company, denies that Moussaoui was ever an employee.) Significantly, Sufaat also owned the Kuala Lumpur condominium where crucial terrorist meetings took place. One gathering was attended by a man later identified as a leading suspect in the October 2000 bombing of the U.S.S. Cole in Yemen. Moussaoui stayed at the same condo eight months later.

The Sleuths

Zacarias Moussaoui, who was arraigned on six counts of conspiracy to commit murder and terrorism, declared in court that the U.S. government chose not to arrest hijacker Hani Hanjour last summer because that would have tipped off the attackers to surveillance by the F.B.I. "They arrested me and not Hanjour who was a few weeks before me at Pan Am Flight School (and has been reported was a danger) because they knew that I was not with the 19 hijackers and therefore they will not be alerted . . . by my arrest." Moussaoui's story received corroboration May 24, 2002, when ABC News reported that paid F.B.I. informant Auki Collins claimed he had monitored the Arab and Islamic communities in Phoenix, including Hani Hanjour while he attended flight school in Phoenix. The F.B.I. admitted that Collins had worked for them, but denied he had told them anything about Hanjour.

Moussaoui claimed he had been under observation before 9/11 and that the hijackers' movements *had been facilitated by the U.S. government.* Assistant U.S. Attorney Robert Spencer denied Moussaoui's allegation in court, maintaining that Moussaoui had not been under physical or electronic surveillance, that he knows of no such surveillance by any foreign government, and also that the U.S. government did not facilitate the movement of any of the 19 hijackers or have any of them under surveillance while they were in the United States. Spencer's sweeping denials don't stand up under scrutiny.

Steve Fainaru's and James V. Grimaldi's *Washington Post* article of September 23, 2001 concludes: "Since 1996, the F.B.I. had been developing evidence that international terrorists were using US flight schools to learn to fly jumbo jets. A foiled plot in Manila to blow up U.S. airliners [Bojinka] and later court testimony by an associate of bin Laden had touched off F.B.I. inquiries at several schools, officials say." So it appears that at least the flight schools were under surveillance.

Three days after the 9/11 attack, the F.B.I. released a list of 19 suspected hijackers, complete with birth dates, photographs, and aliases. The gullible American press never questioned the authenticity of the list, but professionals in Europe did. Andreas von Buelow, a former German cabinet member, expressed his dissatisfaction with the official account in a full-page interview in the January 13, 2002 edition of the *Berlin Tagesspiegel*. "For 60 decisive minutes, the military and intelligence agencies let the fighter planes stay on the ground; 48 hours later, however, the F.B.I. presented a list of suicide attackers. Within ten days, it emerged that seven of them were still alive."

Von Buelow wondered why the F.B.I chief took no position regarding contradictions, where the list came from, and why he did not give ongoing reports on the investigation.

F.B.I. director Robert Mueller said the agency was "fairly confident" that the hijackers' names were not aliases, but before the end of September at least four of the men should have been removed from the list. All four had reported their passports stolen, and none of the four were in the United States at the time of the hijacking.

Relatives declared that two other young men were alive and working with relief agencies in Chechnya. Social Security officials reported that six of the nineteen F.B.I. suspects had used stolen Social Security numbers. Yet, since September 27, the F.B.I. has not revised the list.

At least five of the F.B.I. suspects were actually in other countries at the time of the attack:

- Ahmed Alnami, manager at Saudi Airlines

- Saeed Alghamdi, taking flying lessons in Tunisia

- Salem Alhazmi, working at a petrochemical plant in Saudi Arabia

- Waleed Alsheri, a pilot with Saudi Airlines and studying in Morocco

- Abdulaziz Alomari, who protested from Saudi Arabia that his passport had been stolen when he studied electrical engineering at the University of Denver in 1995.

Clearly, some or all the hijackers used stolen identities. Why hasn't the F.B.I. clarified the mix-up? Who is responsible for releasing the original list and photos of the hijackers?

U. S. military officials gave the F.B.I. information that during the nineties, five of the hijackers were trained at secure U.S. military installations. Saeed Alghamdi, Ahmad Alnami, and Ahmed Alghamdi all listed their address at the Pensacola Naval Station. A high-ranking Pentagon official said another of the hijackers may have been trained in strategy and tactics at the Air War College in Montgomery, Alabama. The fifth man may have received language instruction at Lackland Air Force Base in San Antonio, Texas. Both were former Saudi Air Force pilots who had come to the United States, according to the Pentagon source. Why were they there?

Ziad Samir Jarrah, identified on the F.B.I.'s list as a hijacker aboard the airliner that crashed in western Pennsylvania, was on an American watch list of terrorists in January 30, 2001. Officials from the United Arab Emirates detained and questioned Jarrah that day and noted that he had visited Afghanistan and Pakistan (a red flag to border watches). He was returning to Florida, where he had taken flight training for more than six months. Jarrah then re-entered the U.S. without hindrance. (Jarrah's Lebanese family claims, however, that their son was visiting his hospitalized father on that date.) Someone closely resembling Jarrah and calling himself Jarrah leased an apartment in Brooklyn in 1995 while the Lebanese Jarrah was studying in Beirut. Were there two Jarrahs? Was one or neither of them aboard that airliner?

The agencies keep changing their stories. On August 21, 2001, the F.B.I. listed Kahlil Almidhar and Nawaf Alhamzi as suspects for border-watch. Shortly afterward, the bureau learned the two were already in the country and began an unsuccessful search.

The C.I.A. initially said they were unaware of Alhazmi's presence in this country until immigration officials notified them in August 2001. The C.I.A. later admitted that months earlier Malaysian intelligence reported a meeting in a Kuala Lumpur condo between Khalid Almidhar, Salem Alhamzi, and other suspects.

Those in attendance were videotaped by Malaysia's Special Branch at the request of the United States and were later identified as including not only hijackers Alhazmi and Almidhar, but also a one-legged al Qaeda fighter named Tawfiq bin Attash, alias Khalad. (The F.B.I. had identified Khalad as a leading suspect in the U.S.S. Cole bombing in October 2000.)

Newsweek reported that the Malaysian agency continued to watch the condo, though the C.I.A. seemed to lose interest. "'We couldn't fathom it, really,' Rais Yatim, Malaysia's Legal Affairs minister, told *Newsweek*. 'There was no show of concern.'" Too bad, because Zacarias Moussaoui stopped by on his way to the United States later that year.

Moussaoui entered the United States in February 2000 and enrolled in the same Oklahoma flight school Murad had attended. After flunking out in Oklahoma, he resumed lessons on flight simulators in Eagan, Minnesota, where his eccentric behavior aroused suspicions. The F.B.I. detained him on immigration charges on August 17. Among his possessions, they discovered a laptop computer.

Eager to examine the computer, Minneapolis F.B.I. agents repeatedly requested a special warrant to examine Moussaoui's computer, and bureau attorneys in Washington repeatedly denied their requests, claiming there was insufficient evidence. The special court that reviews warrants covered by the Foreign Intelligence Surveillance Act has approved more than 12,000 Justice Department applications for covert search warrants and wiretaps and rejected only one since the act was passed in 1978.

After the 9/11 attacks, F.B.I. agent Coleen Rowley, general counsel in the Minneapolis field office, wrote a scorching 13-page open letter to F.B.I. Director Robert S. Mueller III and the Senate Intelligence Committee. She asserted that the French government had shared ample intelligence on Moussaoui, including information on his links to Osama bin Laden, information that supported requests for a special surveillance warrant to search Moussaoui's laptop computer in the weeks before the terrorist attacks. (The French, who had put Moussaoui on a watch list in 1999 because they suspected him of terrorist activities, insisted that they had shared their thick dossier with American intelligence agencies.) Rowley said some field agents were so frustrated that they joked about spies and moles for bin Laden working at Washington headquarters.

Rowley complained that agents' reports from Arizona and Minneapolis landed on the desk of David Frasca, head of the Radical Fundamentalists Unit, who had actually telephoned Rowley as she and other agents watched the 9/11 attacks on television. He instructed her not to proceed with the Moussaoui investigation, with the cryptic explanation that Minneapolis *might screw up something else going on elsewhere in the country*. Makes you wonder, doesn't it?

Even Senate Investigating Committee members wondered why Yemen-born Ramzid Binalshibh was refused a visa four times when his roommate Moussaoui breezed right through. Binalshibh wired some nice chunks of money to Moussaoui without raising any red flags, though. Perhaps he should have applied as a Saudi resident because Saudis always got service with a smile.

J. Michael Springmann, formerly chief of the visa section at the U.S. Embassy in Jeddah, Saudi Arabia, claims that he rejected hundreds of suspicious visa applications, but the C.I.A. officer overruled him and ordered the visas to be issued. Springmann protested to the State Department, the Office of Diplomatic Security, the F.B.I., the Justice Department and congressional committees, but was told to shut up. Springmann observed that 15 of the 19 people who allegedly flew airplanes into buildings in the United States got their visas from the same CIA-dominated consulate in Jeddah. As a special favor to residents of Saudi Arabia (including non-Saudi citizens), applicants for non-immigrant visas could apply at private travel agencies anywhere in Saudi Arabia and receive their U.S. visa through the mail. During the month *following the 9/11 attack*, 102 applicants received their visas by mail, two more were interviewed, and none were rejected.

No doubt about it--the Saudis always got special treatment. In a November 6, 2001 BBC broadcast Greg Palast revealed just how special that treatment was. After Pakistan expelled the World Association of Muslim Youth (WAMY) and India claimed that the organization was linked to terrorist bombings in Kashmir and the Philippines military accused WAMY of funding Muslim insurgency, the F.B.I. got orders to leave them alone.

The bin Laden family members got extra special treatment. Palast says that days after the hijackers took off from Boston aiming for the Twin Towers, " a special charter flight out of the same airport whisked 11 members of Osama Bin Laden's family off to Saudi Arabia. That did not concern the White House. Their official line is that the Bin Ladens are above suspicion -apart from Osama, the black sheep, who they say hijacked the family name. That's fortunate for the Bush family and the Saudi royal household, whose links with the Bin Ladens could otherwise prove embarrassing. But Newsnight has obtained evidence that the F.B.I. was on the trail of other members of the Bin Laden family for links to terrorist organisations before and after September 11th."

The owner of a motel outside Oklahoma City had a strange story to tell Jim Crogan (*Los Angeles Weekly*, July 26, 2002). About six weeks before 9/11, three men tried unsuccessfully to rent a room at the weekly rate. He later saw photos of the men and recognized them as suspected conspirators and terrorists.

The motel owner said that Moussaoui and a man who appeared to be Marwan al-Shehhi --who helped crash a jetliner into the south tower of the World Trade Center--were friendly and said a few things, but Atta was clearly the leader.

"'He did most of the talking and seemed very serious,' said the owner, adding, 'I was standing face to face, about two feet away from Atta, and talked to the three of them for about 10 minutes.'"

After the owner reported the incident to the F.B.I., he heard from the bureau several weeks later. "'The agent told me they had passed on a copy of my statement to Moussaoui's defense team, and I might be getting a call from them. But I was under no obligation to talk to them. However, I don't know if that was the truth. Since then, I have never heard from anyone connected to Moussaoui's case.'"

Cogan says that the convicted Oklahoma City bombers, Timothy McVeigh and Terry Nichols, were said to have stayed at the some motel, "interacting with a group of Iraqis during the weeks before the bombing."

Television reporter Jayna Davis also interviewed motel staff and former guests, collecting signed affidavits about their contacts with McVeigh and the Iraqis. The bureau twice refused to accept her materials.

Cogan notes that the absence of this information from the public record "raises new questions about the FBI investigation of Moussaoui and even the 1995 destruction of the Federal Building in Oklahoma City."

The purported ringleader of the hijackers, Mohammed Atta, has been the focus of Daniel Hopsicker's investigations since the twin towers fell. Hopsicker says that Atta and at least four other hijackers trained at South Florida flight schools that locals believed were C.I.A. proprietaries. Atta was the beneficiary of a U.S.-German scholars exchange program who never lacked for cash and spent some of it partying in a very un-Islamic fashion.

Witnesses told Hopsicker that records from the flight school Atta attended "were deemed sensitive enough to have merited being escorted back to Washington by Florida Governor Jeb Bush aboard a C130 cargo plane, which left Sarasota less than 24 hours after the September attack."

Who knew?

Unexplained Anomalies

1. On September 10, 2001, there were 4,526 put options bought on United Airlines and only 748 call options. For American Airlines, the number of puts is 60 times the daily average. Who were these traders?

2. The chief of the Pakistani Intelligence Service wired $100,000 to Mohammed Atta before the attacks. On September 11, he met with the heads of the House and Senate Intelligence Committees in Washington, D.C. Why did he send the money and why was he meeting with congresspersons on September 11?

3. Why were Standard Operating Procedures, designed to prevent, intercept, or terminate an attack, utterly ignored or suspended on 9/11?

4. Why did George W. Bush continue to chat with Florida elementary school children after he learned of the attack?

5. Why did Pentagon officials cancel their airline flights on 9/11?

One Possible Conclusion

Mary Schiavo, former Inspector General for the U.S. Department of Transportation under both Bush I and Clinton, and a lawyer for thirty-two families from all 9/11 hijacked planes, stated that every single aviation disaster in history, except for 9/11, had been followed by not only a criminal investigation but a national transportation safety investigation.

What are they hiding? Why is no one held accountable? Despite massive evidence of incompetence and dishonesty, no heads have rolled. Each time a falsehood is exposed, a new and stranger story replaces it. The trail gets muddier and muddier.

Let's follow tradition in this matter. We must convene an independent investigative commission like those convened after Pearl Harbor and the Kennedy assassination, but with a difference. In addition to the learned professionals who sit on the committee, let us, the American people, be represented by some members of the families whose loved ones perished on Black Tuesday.

Chapter Thirteen

America Has Partially Awakened

By Norman D. Livergood

Hurray for the American people! We've delivered a clear repudiation of cabal policies: the war in Iraq, attacks on constitutional rights, the debased economy, rampant corruption, and the Bush junta in general. But we must not settle for false promises, assuming that the 2006 election results will produce some kind of magic.

And we must not be deluded into believing that members of the Democratic Party are intrinsically more on the side of working-class American citizens than Republicans.

The New American Revolution

We must fully awaken to the real meaning and import of the 2006 election: we, the American people, kicked some of the rascals out. Many fuzzy-thinking people are going to try to get us to misinterpret our citizens' rebellion against forces we recognize as destructive of the country and the people. For example, as the election evening wore on and the political implications of the massive anti-Bush, anti-corruption, antiwar vote became unmistakable, both Democratic pundits and cynical media spinmeisters tried to misconstrue the election results in completely reactionary and bland terms--pretending that a political revolution had not taken place. One self-appointed expert bemoaned that America had already had its revolution and didn't want another.

If we look carefully at the 2006 election, we see that it reflects the broad, deep popular opposition not only to Bush, but also to the reactionary media, to the Iraq war, to beltway corruption, and to members of Congress in general. American citizens didn't choose Democrats because we see them as more competent and more ethical than Republicans--we simply chose the lesser of two evils because we had only two alternatives (unfortunately).

We, the American electorate, repudiated all members of Congress--Republican and Democrat--who backed the administration's war drive, promoted Bush's lies about weapons of mass destruction and Iraq-Al Qaeda ties, stood idly by and allowed the Bush junta to destroy quintessential constitutional rights such as habeas corpus, and continue to support the massive slaughter of American soldiers in the perverse cabal plan to privatize Iraq's oil resources and re-structure the geopolitical map in the Middle East.

The American People Express Their Revulsion

What Americans conveyed through the 2006 election was: *We're mad as hell and we're not going to take it anymore.* At least 29 Republican incumbents went down to defeat in the House of Representatives and the Democrats gained a large number of state legislatures and governorships. This was no mild expression of easygoing discontent; it was a vehement outburst of revulsion at how the cabal--through its Bush junta--has been destroying our nation and our fundamental principles.

American citizens expressed themselves in such extreme terms that it horrified the political and media establishment. The politicians and the media sycophants simply refuse to recognize that the American public is expressing its disgust in this intemperate manner because it is furious with the status quo. During his Wednesday White House press conference to announce Rumsfeld's resignation, Bush said, "I recognize that many Americans voted last night to register their displeasure with the lack of progress being made there [in Iraq]." But he quickly added: "Yet I also believe most Americans and leaders here in Washington from both political parties understand we cannot accept defeat."

No, Mr. Bush, the American public is not merely amiably discontent with what your propaganda calls "lack of progress in Iraq," we're up in arms at your temerity in imposing a dictatorship on this country and turning it into a totalitarian state. What the 2006 election says to you is that we're not going to be taken in by your indoctrination and propaganda any more and we will no longer tolerate your lies, equivocations, and pretenses; we're going to clean out the entire Potomac swamp.

The Present State of the American People

The political and media pundit-pretenders still haven't understood that the 2006 election showed that the American people have started thinking for themselves; they're no longer willing to be the pawns of the spinmeisters and propagandists. The political and media charlatans still want to pretend that they control American voters. So we get the outlandish explanations by people like Rahm Emanual and Howard Dean saying they produced the 2006 election results by "expanding the conservative center" and "asking more people to vote." And in elections where Republicans won, Karl Rove and his Nazis are saying that they controlled the results by "getting out the base."

Hello imposters? The American people voted in the 2006 election the way they did because they're beginning to make their own judgments and act accordingly. They rejected the propaganda on the right *and* the left. And they showed that they're no longer going to tolerate lies and false accusations in election campaigns and campaign ads. The Republicans, it is now evident, can no longer assume that merely getting conservative voters to the polls will automatically result in a win for the GOP.

We mustn't mistake our being irate and appalled at Bush and his Democratic and Republican collaborators, however, as evidence of our having come fully awake; we've just partially awakened from a suicidal sleepwalking state. We must come fully awake and work assiduously to overcome remaining elements of somnolence.

Many Americans had allowed themselves to be entranced and possessed by cabal lies. Those persons willingly succumbed to Bush junta propaganda, accepting the Republican false reality as true. Whether it was swallowing the Big Lie of the weapons of mass destruction and the necessity of a unilateral invasion of the sovereign state of Iraq or the necessity of giving up our constitutional liberties for the sake of the war on terrorism, a large number of Americans have mindlessly acquiesced to Bush junta falsehoods. Here are other cabal delusions from which the American people must free themselves:

1. Now that we've expressed our outrage at the Bush junta, they'll completely change their policies and tactics.

In a White House ceremony accepting Rumsfeld's resignation and introducing his replacement, former CIA director Robert Gates, Bush left no doubt that the fundamental policy of the administration remains unchanged.

In nominating Gates, Bush praised the career CIA official as someone who 'understands the challenges we face in Afghanistan' because of the role he played as Reagan's deputy director of the CIA when he 'helped lead America's efforts to drive Soviet forces from Afghanistan.'

In other words, he is one of the American intelligence officials who established intimate ties with Osama bin Laden during the CIA-backed war that shattered Afghan society. As such, he played a role in fostering the very Islamist terrorists who ultimately carried out 9/11.

Nothing could express more starkly the cynicism of America's ruling elite than Bush's touting such a record as a qualification for leading the 'war on terror.'

Gates's ties to terrorism do not end with bin Laden. In the mid-1980s he was tied to the network of White House operatives and CIA agents who organized the 'Iran-contra' operation, in which covert arms sales to Iran were used to provide illegal funding for the US-backed 'contra' terror war against Nicaragua. He has likewise been linked to covert efforts in the 1980s to supply weapons to the Iraqi regime of Saddam Hussein during its war against Iran.

That such a figure is being introduced as the champion of a 'fresh perspective' on Iraq is the clearest warning that even more horrific crimes are being prepared.

—World Socialist Web Site: "Rumsfeld's firing: First casualty of post-election crisis in US ," 11/9/06

2. A second delusion from which we must free ourselves is that by voting in a new Congress all our problems have been solved.

> To the extent the Democrats gained the majority in the House, it was on the backs of some very right wing Democrats who won the election against right wing Republican incumbents. And so, there was no mandate for any progressive agenda.

> —Ralph Nader, Interview with Amy Goodman, 10/8/06

"Under conditions in which the population is so alienated from official politics that only 40 percent of those eligible even cast ballots, the sweeping defeat of the Republicans is a pale reflection of the seething discontent that exists throughout America."

> —World Socialist Web Site: "Rumsfeld's firing: First casualty of post-election crisis in US ," 11/9/06

The American People's Revolutionary Agenda

The message we sent in the 2006 election demanding change will not be acted upon unless we come fully awake and *make sure* that policies and procedures are enacted that will:

- Stop the Bush junta from bankrupting our country through its military spending and corruption (e.g. Halliburton no-bid contracts)

- Halt the destruction of our constitutional rights by repealing the Patriot Act and recent legislation that legalizes torture and destroys *habeas corpus*

- Pass legislation that will end illegal immigration, penalizing any employer who hires undocumented workers

- End the Bush junta's plan to loot Social Security

- Bring the Iraq war to an end as soon as possible

- Put an end to the tax giveaways to the top 1% of obscenely wealthy Americans and raise the minimum wage nationwide

- End the corporate control of government through the buying of politicians

- Bring Bush and other junta members to accountability for their war crimes

- Make sure that all Americans have health insurance

- Terminate corporate outsourcing of American jobs

- Enact legislation that will require paper ballots and a paper trail in all elections

We *cannot remain asleep* to the likelihood that the Democratic Party will make only cosmetic changes and basically continue the cabal policies. The Democratic Party in the 2006 election is the beneficiary of overwhelming anti-Bush, antiwar sentiment that that party did nothing significantly to encourage.

In fact the majority of Democrats, fearing political reprisal, have maintained that the Iraq war was legitimate. This stands in stark opposition to the American people's anti-Iraq-war feelings. American citizens made it clear in the 2006 election that we have a strong antiwar sentiment which is contradictory to the Democratic Party leaders' pro-Bush stand on Iraq.

The Cowardice, Backpedaling, and False Bipartisanship Has Begun

The American people spoke in extremes in the 2006 election because we want to see radical, fundamental changes in the ways of governing. This was a call for sweeping rectification of the outrages the Bush junta has perpetrated. We painted in bold, defiant strokes to register our total rejection of malefactors such as Dubya, Cheney, Rumsfeld, Rove, et al.

We don't want the newly elected Democrats playing footsy with these monsters as though they were reasonable persons deserving of solicitude. We haven't forgotten that they've debased our country into a police state, destroyed all checks and balances in a befouled Congress, and passed legislation and used Presidential violations of laws to destroy constitutional liberties and sanction crimes such as false imprisonment and torture.

Failing to acknowledge the deception which the appointment of Robert Graves as Secretary of Defense represents, the empty-headed Democratic party leaders began a chorus of praise for Bush's action, following in the wake of a series of statements by Democratic leaders pledging collaboration with the Bush White House. Incoming Democratic House Speaker Nancy Pelosi vowed that the Democrats would pursue "partnership with the president and the Republicans in Congress, and not partisanship."

The Bush junta made it clear that it would pretend to work in a bipartisan manner with the Democrats--while all the while pushing through more of their police-state measures before the 2006-2007 congressional term expired.

The clearest indication that we'll have to complete our citizen revolution ourselves is the Democratic leadership's preemptive promises to Bush and Schwarzenegger and other criminals that they will not be impeached or indicted. Our revolutionary agenda is something we the people will have to carry out almost entirely on our own.

In her 2006 election victory speech, New York Senator Hillary Clinton, considered to be the front-runner to win the Democratic nomination for president in 2008, declared that American politics had to return to the "vital center," and pledged her commitment to work with the Republicans in prosecuting the war on terror.

Looking Forward to the 2008 Election

Hillary Clinton represents the kind of "bait and switch" scams that the Democratic Party is already pulling in regard to 2007 and 2008. Both she and her husband are agents of the criminal cabal which seized control of America in the early decades of the twentieth century. This cabal "smoke and mirrors" tactic of controlling both Democratic and Republican politicians has been one of their hallmarks.

To recognize that Bill Clinton was a cabal agent, you have only to look at illustrative operations during his presidential tenure:

- He complied with the cabal's insistence that he instigate the war in Kosovo--so the former Soviet Union satellite countries could be pulled into the cabal-dominated NATO and a strategic U.S. military base could be located in that region

- He saw to it that NAFTA (North American Free Trade Agreement) passed, which has resulted in American jobs being outsourced to lower-wage countries and has decimated the American economy

We must make certain that we're not taken in by such counterfeit Democratic candidates as Hillary Clinton in the 2008 presidential election. We already suffered from the cabal ringer John Kerry going back on his promise to contest the stolen 2004 election, standing in solidarity with his Skull-and-Bones brother George W. Bush.

Our Unfinished Work

The day after the 2006 election, Al Franken (a self-styled progressive) told his Air America audience that the outcome proved that the Republicans never steal elections--never have and never will. He then pretended humility--and contradicted himself--in saying that he never spoke about election fraud because he didn't want to discourage people from voting.

As Democrats began to appear as newly-minted pundits on television news programs, we did not hear any of them mention such quintessential elements as getting rid of the Patriot Act and restoring constitutional liberties such as *habeas corpus*.

Activists in the new Citizen Revolution must not be fooled by such dimwits as these into forgetting what we've suffered over the past six years under the Bush junta. Bush II was brought into the presidency in 2000 through a coup d'etat set up by Jeb Bush, Jim Baker, and the Supreme Court. That changed the entire structure of our government. The

2002 and 2004 presidential elections were stolen by the Republicans, through the connivance of Karl Rove and his Nazis. The fact that the Democrats became vigilant and created election oversight operations in the 2006 election, doesn't prove that the Republicans will not try--and perhaps succeed--in rigging the 2008 election. Even in the 2006 mid-term election, it appears that at least four percent of the votes were "misplaced."

The 2006 election is the first of many victories for the American people. In our ongoing battle to overthrow the criminal cabal that's seized control of American political and financial systems, we're fortunate to be joined by a growing number of courageous women and men.

We have an excellent chance of success in this crusade if we prepare assiduously and act fearlessly. In setting the foundation for this absolutely indispensable citizen revolution, we need to assimilate the information contained in this book.

> The people is the grand canyon of humanity
> and many many miles across.
> The people is Pandora's box, humpty dumpty,
> a clock of doom and an avalanche when it
> turns loose.
> The people rest on land and weather, on time
> and the changing winds.
> The people have come far and can look back
> and say, "We will go farther yet."
> The people is a plucked goose and a shorn
> sheep of legalized fraud
> And the people is one of those mountain slopes
> holding a volcano of retribution,
> Slow in all things, slow in its gathered wrath,
> slow in its onward heave,
> Slow in its asking: "Where are we now? what time
> is it?"
>
> —— Carl Sandburg

Chapter Fourteen

Realizing A New America

By Norman D. Livergood

Many Americans partially awakened in the 2006 mid-term elections to vote against lies, corruption, and a murderous war. And not a minute too soon, because while Americans were sleeping the criminal cabal's Bush junta puppets were destroying our constitutional liberties, looting our tax dollars and our Social Security fund to finance a senseless, murderous war, and wrecking our country and the world in every way possible.

However, many Americans are still fast asleep, allowing themselves to be deluded by Republican propaganda. Most California voters, for example, are still under the reactionary Republican spell, doing the unthinkable of electing cabal henchmen such as Governator Schwartzenegger and Representatives Brian Bilbray and Darrell Issa.

So we mustn't mistake our partial stirring for being fully awake. Our outcry at the Republicans and their Democratic collaborators during the 2006 mid-term election was basically a momentary uprising at being startled into awareness by their *outrages.*

Those Americans who came partially awake put the Democrats in control of both houses of Congress--ridding themselves of the intolerable situation where there were no countervailing powers in our federal government. But we haven't solved our larger, more pervasive, ongoing problems.

As the momentum from the 2006 mid-term election winds down, the Republicans began to lull Americans to sleep again by pretending to make substantive changes, when they really just continued business as usual. They appointed the equally criminal Robert Gates to replace Rumsfeld—who was unanimously approved by Republicans and traitor-Democrats on the Senate confirmation committee. They've made it clear that they would try to follow through on their efforts to legalize domestic spying and they put their worst goons such as Trent Lott in charge of blocking any Democratic legislation that might work against their looting of the country.

Educating Ourselves During this Dangerous Time

We must recognize the absolute necessity of changing ourselves and our country in a permanent manner:

1. We need to educate ourselves so we understand:

   - How we allowed ourselves to be lulled asleep by a tyrannous gang of crooks

   - How we can prevent it happening again

2. We must *realize* a new American commonwealth of, by, and for all the people.

America is such a rich and dynamic country that it's easy for its inhabitants to merely enjoy its fruits and feel no obligation to understand and preserve its precious heritage. However, the Bush junta and its Republican and Democratic collaborators became so outrageous in their corruption and oppression, that they momentarily aroused many Americans from their slumber of ignorance. Now we must make sure that the cabal doesn't lull Americans back into somnolence. Our first task is to gain an understanding of what kind of people we've allowed ourselves to become and how we've permitted our nation's principles to be degraded and destroyed.

We're going to have to do the hard work of waking up to what elements in our makeup allowed us to be duped by reactionary ideologies, lies, and divisiveness. It will be necessary for us to create *a means of educating ourselves,* to gain an understanding of ourselves and our world.

A Pedagogy of the Oppressed

In creating this new pedagogy, we can learn a great deal from someone who worked with people like ourselves to develop techniques of self-education in activist groups. Paulo Freire developed what he called a "pedagogy of the oppressed" by working in literacy campaigns throughout northeast Brazil in the early 1960s. The techniques he and his coparticipants developed were so revolutionary that when a military coup seized power in Brazil in 1964, Freire was immediately jailed. Released seventy days later, Freire was told to leave the country. He did so, and began working with similar groups in other parts of the world to continue developing a people-centered "pedagogy of the oppressed."

You may find yourself reacting to the word "oppressed." It may seem to you that a "pedagogy of the oppressed" would have no relevance to you and other Americans because you don't consider us to be oppressed. What do you consider it to be when Americans are needlessly dying in a totally fraudulent war, when working people are losing their jobs to corporate outsourcing, when a despotic administration spies on citizens and tortures war prisoners, when no-bid contracts to Bush junta cronies are putting America into appalling debt?

The Answer is Oppression!

We're being economically, politically, and socially oppressed--and it has degraded many Americans into mindless humanoids. These people are so brainwashed by Republican propaganda that they can't see that Americans are being duped into dying for cabal war profits? The fact of the almost three thousand dead American soldiers stares you in the face every time you turn on your TV or read your newspaper.

To see just how far the oppressive brainwashing has debased many Americans' minds, consider this analogy. We're appalled when we see the carnage caused by Muslim extremist suicide bombers. How could they sacrifice their lives for their ideology and their religion? we ask. If we look closely at the essence of Muslim suicide bombers, it's this:

- They've allowed themselves to be totally possessed by a political/religious ideology.

- Their ideology and their political/religious leaders tell them that giving their lives for their cause is courageous and patriotic.

If we look honestly and discerningly at what's happening in America it's almost identical:

- Americans are being duped into thinking that the Iraq war is legitimate (even after the WMD lies have been exposed).

- American soldiers are going into a battle situation which is *suicidal* because of lack of planning and necessary protective devices.

- American soldiers are being told by their political/religious leaders (the Bush junta pseudo-religious neo-conservatives) that giving their lives for their cause is courageous and patriotic.

Discovering Ourselves

Realizations such as the above allow us to come awake to the fact that reactionary forces have brainwashed many of us into a mindless state. So it's essential that we educate ourselves as to the condition of our minds and the full reality of what's happened and is happening in America and the world.

We must comprehend the bewitched mind-state that many of us are still in. A useful way to become aware of our benumbed mental condition is to look full in the face at some of the obvious absurdities and lies which the neo-con political/religious charlatans pass off as the veriest truth:

- Lie: Iraq is a war to bring democracy to a struggling people. Truth: Iraq is a war to allow the cabal to seize Iraqi oil and re-configure the Middle-East.

- Lie: We're fighting against terrorism.
  Truth: There is NO connection between Iraq and the 9/11 catastrophe.

- Lie: If you're not for our troops you're for the terrorists. Truth: We're in sympathy with our troops in a genuine way, not the jingoistic way --in synch with our troops so much that we detest seeing them senselessly slaughtered by the Bush junta.

- Lie: We must remain in Iraq until we achieve victory. Truth: There is no way of being victorious in the civil war conditions which the Bush junta has deliberately imposed on Iraq.

A Pedagogy for Literary and Intellectual Illiterates

Freire worked to help third-world people overcome illiteracy. We don't like to think of ourselves as illiterate in any sense, but let's look at the facts:

- Some thirty million adults in the U.S. do not have the skills to perform even the most basic tasks such as adding numbers on a bank slip, identifying a place on a map, or reading directions for taking a medication. Eleven million Americans are totally illiterate in English.

- Only twenty-nine percent of Americans have basic reading and computing skills. One out of every twenty Americans lacks the ability to understand what is going on in the world or to develop an informed opinion for voting.

Today, Freire's insights can be applied to two different kinds of illiteracy in America and other countries of the world:

1. *Literary illiteracy:* Those who cannot grasp the sense of letters or symbols

2. *Intellectual illiteracy:* Those who can "read" (in the grammar school sense) but who cannot *read* in the sense of understanding the meaning of the words they scan

- There are Americans today, for example, who "read" about such things as worker layoffs and American corporations relocating their manufacturing plants in China or Indonesia, but who do not *understand* the meaning of what they "read."

- Another kind of modern-day "illiteracy" occurs as people "read" or "hear" the "news" in newspapers or on TV, and allow themselves to be taken in by the propaganda that such "news" involves. We might call this brainwashing illiteracy.

Now more than ever we need to begin developing a critical consciousness in all of us who are oppressed by the criminal cabal. We're up against a number of obstacles:

- The lack of awareness that *we are the oppressed*, that we are members of an oppressed class

- The lack of solidarity among oppressed people

- The loss of the tradition of fellow feeling and human rights

- The indifference of oppressed people to their situation

Living in an age of repression, we become accustomed to it. So what if our schools no longer teach people how to read or think, no longer help students gain an understanding of why human liberty is so precious and precarious. Our movies, TV shows, and books present images of "cool," illiterate, violence-prone savages dressed in the latest styles and exhibiting the popular ego-centered attitudes. Unable to understand the creativity of a well written novel or screenplay, no longer capable of appreciating the depths of classical music, people today move in a gray world of ego-gratification and violence. Soon the false values become identified as the true, and we have movies such as *Pulp Fiction*, *The Godfather*, and *As Good As It Gets* touted as masterpieces.

In *Critical Path,* R. Buckminster Fuller explains our predicament. "The world's power structures have always 'divided to conquer' and have always 'kept divided to keep conquered.' As a consequence the power structure has so divided humanity--not only into special function categories but into religious and language and color categories--that individual humans are now helplessly inarticulate in the face of the present crisis. They consider their political representation to be completely corrupted, therefore, they feel almost utterly helpless."

—R. Buckminster Fuller, *Critical Path*

We only become aware of the oppressive nature of contemporary society when we become the victim of unemployment or a mugging or some other mishap. Trained to be oblivious to the plight of others, we fail to see the hundreds of thousands who suffer from homelessness, lack of medical care, and wage slavery.

Since people are encouraged to pursue their own interests, there is no feeling of solidarity and hence no possibility of concerted effort to overcome the oppressive conditions. It seems perfectly normal that a two-class society is rapidly developing, with new billionaires being created every year while millions of workers are laid off, denied welfare, and their tax money stolen by wealthy looters. Meanwhile the American working class is subjected to such scams as the Iraq war swindle, the Patriot Act fraud, and the no-taxes-for-the-rich con job.

We must begin to awaken ourselves to what's happening in the world and take action to overcome the oppressive conditions. And here Freire's books are exceptionally helpful. As oppressed people we must become aware of what has happened to us and develop our own sense of what it means to be truly human.

How can the oppressed, as divided, unauthentic beings, participate in developing the pedagogy of their liberation? Only as they discover themselves to be 'hosts' of the oppressor can they contribute to the midwifery of their liberating pedagogy. As long as they live in the duality in which to be is to be like and to be like is to be like the oppressor, this contribution is impossible. The pedagogy of the oppressed is an instrument for their critical discovery that both they and their oppressors are manifestations of dehumanization.

As we begin to struggle against oppressive conditions, we must retain an optimistic attitude, with assurance that the struggle for freedom will ultimately succeed. In order for the oppressed to be able to wage the struggle for their liberation, they must perceive the reality of oppression not as a closed world from which there is no exit, but as a limiting situation which they can transform.

Realizing a New America

Let's remind ourselves of why we're examining and re-educating our personal mental and moral states and working toward a new American culture. We recognize that the partial awakening of many Americans which resulted in positive results in the 2006 midterm elections was a momentary outburst of popular outrage. Putting the Democrats in control of the House and Senate, we recognize, doesn't solve our fundamental problem of the manipulation of American political and economic systems by corporations for their own profit and power.

So we need to begin a long-range program of re-educating ourselves so the destructive forces are unable to program and brainwash Americans back into an acquiescent stupor. The Bush junta must face a fully-awakened citizenry intent on terminating their corruption and tyranny. We recognize that there are basic flaws in our political and economic structures to allow the cabal to seize power and obliterate American principles and values. So we have to make basic changes not only in ourselves but also in the basic design of our government and our economy.

It's clear that we must begin to evaluate just what in our heritage we can use in building a new America. Our past and recent experience has made it evident that we *must* transform our psychological, political, and economic foundations so our nation becomes a true commonwealth, operating to the benefit of all citizens.

This will require our adopting more appropriate values to undergird this new culture. We'll need to examine our current TV-radio-movie mindless gratification culture and substitute positive role models and humanizing and unifying ideals.

We cannot continue in our present mode of cultural irresponsibility, celebrating criminals, illiterates, and inane "celebrities," and expect to have an enlightened citizenry. The current Keith Olbermann show is an allegory for the schizoid cultural state America is in. On the one hand the Olbermann show highlights infantalizing "Oddball" bizarrities, which

Keith himself admitted on the day after Thanksgiving episode: "We're part of the problem, not part of the solution." However, Olbermann also periodically presents an outstanding commentary which gets at the heart of the present totalitarian oppression, helping to inform Americans about what's really going on in the world.

In realizing a new America, we must understand what values, structures, and principles we need as foundational elements. We will need to revivify the values of genuine intelligence, authentic fellow-feeling, true person-enhancing art, service to others, and genuine (not inflated) self-esteem.

As we go forward in this long-term operation of self-and cultural-transformation, we can be assured that our opponents have adopted values and a definition of power which are ultimately self-defeating: money, control of political and economic systems, ignorance, and egomania.

By adopting the elemental, deathless values of truth, justice, freedom, understanding, unity, and fellowship, we can be certain that our struggle will ultimately succeed.

Prayers of Steel

Lay me on an anvil, O God.

Beat me and hammer me into a crowbar.

Let me pry loose old walls.

Let me lift and loosen old foundations.

Lay me on an anvil, O God.

Beat me and hammer me into a steel spike.

Drive me into the girders that hold a skyscraper together.

Take red-hot rivets and fasten me into the central girders.

Let me be the great nail holding a skyscraper

through blue nights into white stars.

—Carl Sandburg

Chapter Fifteen

Oliver Stone's Radical Films

By Michelle Mairesse

It goes without saying that those who strive to maintain the status quo are the most immoral of all. To them the great sin is to question the prevailing order. Yet every great thinker, every great artist, every great religious teacher did just that.

—Henry Miller, "The Immorality of Morality"

Oliver Stone has no reverence for the status quo. He asks embarrassing questions about the prevailing order. He despises official lies. He is a serious patriot. These qualities alone are enough to irritate the complacent cynics who report and comment on national events, so Stone is accustomed to caustic attacks on his work and character. But in December 1991, he was taken aback by the critical fusillade aimed at *JFK* when he opened his complex, technically dazzling, consummately directed film in the nation's capital. Instead of welcoming Stone's investigation of a national scandal, a majority of the media savaged the film wherever it was exhibited in the United States.

The press accused Stone of misrepresenting the historical record. Stone patiently explained that *JFK* was not a documentary, but a drama, a drama employing dramatic devices, including composite characters. (If the press considered the Warren Report history, then they had missed the point of *JFK*.)

Instancing the twenty-six volumes comprising the Warren Report, and confusing its sheer bulk with substance, the press charged Stone with sensationalism and superficiality. On the contrary, Stone's film is packed with more relevant information than is contained in all twenty-six volumes of the Warren Report, for as Mark North points out in *Act of Treason: The Role of J. Edgar Hoover in the Assassination of President Kennedy*, the director of the FBI withheld vital evidence (including Oswald's status as an FBI informant) and blitzed the commission with reams of irrelevant information. Oliver Stone had doubtless researched the characters, events, and background of the assassination more intensively than had any member of the commission or, for that matter, any member of the press. He purchased Jim Marrs's outstanding *Crossfire: The Plot That Killed Kennedy* as well as Jim Garrison's *On the Trail of the Assassins*. He hired a researcher who turned up significant new evidence. Zachary Sklar, who edited Garrison's book, co-authored the screenplay with Stone. "Mr. X," who the press presumed was a figment of Stone's imagination, was largely based on retired U.S. air force Colonel L. Fletcher Prouty, who served as the chief of special operations for the Joint Chiefs of Staff and acted as an advisor on the film. His articles about the assassination were included in his book *JFK: The CIA, Vietnam And The Plot To Assassinate John F. Kennedy*.

The press complained that JFK was really the story of Jim Garrison, and an idealized Jim Garrison at that. In James Riordan's *A Biography of Oliver Stone: the controversies, excesses, and exploits of a radical filmmaker*, Stone agrees that he omitted Garrison's failings. "The film was already going to run over three hours because I was not just dealing with Jim Garrison. It was like four movies. I was doing the Lee Harvey Oswald history, I was doing Dealey Plaza. Garrison was never there, but I was showing it again and again. And I was doing this Mr. 'X' story in Washington."

The film does precisely that--and a good deal more. It captures the ambiance of the decade. In clubs, in offices, in restaurants, in homes, the omnipresent television set intrudes with its catalogue of insouciance, mendacity, and brutality. The film's participants see, as do we, live events and news bulletins--President Eisenhower delivering his farewell address warning us of the military-industrial complex; the CIA's secret war on Castro; the Bay of Pigs debacle; the Soviet missile crisis; Kennedy's determination to limit the Vietnamese conflict; Walter Cronkite announcing that of the three shots fired at the president, one bullet entered at the base of the president's throat, and, with a weak voice, that President Kennedy died at 1 p.m. Central Standard Time. We view, on television screens, the president's funeral; Lyndon Johnson being sworn in; Ruby blasting away on camera, mortally wounding Lee Harvey Oswald; the formation of the

Warren Commission; a Vietnamese war zone; troops firing on anti-war demonstrators; Garrison accused of bribing and drugging witnesses and of concealed mob ties; news of the Martin Luther King assassination; Attorney General Robert Kennedy assassinated on camera.

That's the way it was. Somehow Stone manages to weave all of these bizarre happenings into a gripping, beautifully acted, finely-wrought narrative that depicts the assassination and the cover-up in astonishing detail:

An anonymous woman is heaved from a speeding car onto a bleak stretch of highway. Torn and bleeding, she lies here sobbing. President Kennedy banquets. The anonymous woman is in a hospital bed babbling about Jack Ruby and an underworld plot to kill Kennedy in Dallas. The Kennedys emerge from Air force One in Dallas. At the parade in Dealey Plaza, a bystander appears to have an epileptic seizure. Blackout. A flight of pigeons lifts off the roof of the Texas Schoolbook Depository building. Walter Cronkite announces the president's death on television. New Orleans District Attorney Jim Garrison and his staff are stunned by the announcement. The anonymous woman was Rose Cheramie. Her story, confirmed by a Louisiana State Police lieutenant and doctors who declared she was not psychotic, appears in the House Select Committee's report but not in the Warren Report. Her prediction occurred two days before the assassination. On the day of the assassination, the Louisiana police officer contacted Dallas police captain Will Fritz, who was in charge of the assassination investigation. Fritz wasn't interested.

November 22, 1963. It was a warm, sunny day, fine parade weather. Despite the rumblings of the rich troglodytes who considered Dallas their private fief, ordinary citizens lining the motorcade route smiled, cheered, and waved at President Kennedy and his wife as they wended slowly through Dealey Plaza in their open limousine. Immediately after the presidential car made a sharp slow turn from Houston to Elm Street, shots rang out, and horrified onlookers saw the president's exploded head spew out brain tissues and blood. Stone withholds the Zapruder film until Garrison displays it to the jury. Until Garrison subpoenaed the film, the general public had not been allowed to view it.

Bystanders describe their stunned reactions. They have heard a volley of shots, more than three. Some of the shots came from the grassy knoll near the railroad tracks.

Bulletin: Dallas police officer J. D. Tippit is shot and Oswald is arrested in the Texas Theater as a suspect in the Tippit killing. Immediately, FBI director J. Edgar Hoover telephoned Attorney General Robert Kennedy with a biography of Oswald before the Dallas police had even connected him to the president's assassination. The Dallas police interrogated Lee Harvey Oswald without benefit of counsel. Claiming they had made no transcript of the interrogation, the police confidently informed the press that Oswald had murdered President Kennedy. Two days later, Jack Ruby a gambler, nightclub owner, and Mafia bagman with ties to the Dallas police, the FBI, and the CIA gunned down Oswald in front of television cameras and sixty Dallas policemen.

For reasons never adequately explained, the Secret Service and the Dallas police had neglected the most rudimentary security precautions. The Secret Service and the Dallas police utterly failed to explain the egregious security lapses that exposed both the president and his suspected assassin to ambush, but those who were most derelict in their duties received promotions. The vice president (violating another routine security measure) had traveled with the presidential party to Dallas. Vice President Lyndon Johnson, who would legally assume the presidency in the event of the president's death, insisted on taking the oath of office in Texas before flying back to Washington.

Garrison was troubled. Oswald had some strange associates in New Orleans who might be able to throw some light on the investigation. On a tip, the district attorney interviewed David Ferrie, and when Ferrie gave a lame explanation for his whereabouts on the day of the assassination and denied knowing Oswald, Garrison turned him over to the FBI for questioning. The FBI cleared and released him immediately. Oswald was a member of David Ferrie's Louisiana Civil Air Patrol Unit in the mid-fifties. Six witnesses, considered credible by the House Select Committee, testified to seeing Ferrie and Oswald together less than three months before President Kennedy was assassinated. Egregious errors and distortions were discovered in the autopsy report. British acoustics experts determined that indeed *four shots had been fired*. The evidence of malfeasance is overwhelming.

Hoping to squelch the rumors of conspiracy bruited at home and abroad, President Johnson authorized a special commission to investigate the Kennedy assassination. The Warren Commission spent ten months sifting through information and interviewing witnesses funneled exclusively through the FBI and the CIA. We know today that the FBI lied to the commission, intimidated witnesses, and altered transcripts of their testimony. The bureau lost and destroyed files, seized photographs of the motorcade and Dealey Plaza that were never seen again, suppressed and tampered with evidence, and had input and output from FBI Director J. Edgar Hoover's cronies on the Warren Commission (and later on the House Select Committee). We know now that the FBI and the CIA withheld significant information about Clay Shaw and Lee Harvey Oswald that is surfacing in files released under the Freedom of Information Act. We know today that the CIA, pleading national security, failed to release significant information about the principals in the investigation. We know today that there was a cover-up at the highest levels of government.

At the time, critics of the Warren Report saw an investigative pattern emerge: the commissioners preferred witnesses who confirmed the theory that Oswald was a lone assassin. They did not interview many dissenters. They did not call on independent experts to evaluate conflicting evidence. The Warren Commission was intent on establishing Oswald's guilt. If more than three bullets had been fired, Oswald could not have acted alone. Therefore, the commission brushed aside the mountain of evidence that more than three bullets were fired and accepted the FBI's contrived explanation that a single bullet had inflicted seven wounds on Governor Connally and the president.

Serious researchers expressed their dismay at the commission's findings. On their own, they had uncovered substantial evidence that supported a conspiracy theory, but the bureaucracy was keeping a tight grip on documents. Government agencies, pleading national security, blocked freelance investigators at every turn. Other organizations kept mum. Clearly, Oswald's association with the intelligence community began when he served in the Marine Corps, yet the documentation was withheld for decades. The "official" history of the Kennedy assassination contained in the Warren Commission report looked more and more like an official lie.

New Orleans district attorney Jim Garrison wanted to change all that. On March 1, 1967 Garrison filed stunning charges against prominent businessman Clay Shaw, to wit: conspiring to assassinate President Kennedy. Although he had quietly begun to investigate some of Oswald's associates in New Orleans--Ferrie, Banister, Shaw, and anti-Castro Cuban exiles--the news of his investigation leaked, and the press hampered and harassed Garrison, while government agencies continued to stonewall. He went to trial with a case that the press, the FBI, and the CIA had literally sabotaged from within. All of his major witnesses died before trial, some under mysterious circumstances.

Two years later, the case went to court. Although Garrison was ill during much of the trial, and the assistant district attorney delivered the summation, Stone wrote the climactic scene with Kevin Costner (as Garrison) addressing the jury. Looking directly into the camera, the district attorney tells the jury and the audience that history is in our hands. On February 28, 1969, the jury found Shaw not guilty.

The jury *did* believe that there had been a conspiracy to kill the president, and assassination researchers redoubled their demands for information and documents.

And Garrison was absolutely right about Clay Shaw. He lied about his identity, beginning with the CIA affiliation he denied under oath. An agency document released in 1977 shows that Shaw was a CIA informant. Three former intelligence agents have fingered Shaw as an agent who worked with Guy Bannister and David Ferrie. In 1979 former director Richard Helms testified that Shaw had worked for the Domestic Contact Division of the CIA. In 1993 a declassified CIA document refers to Shaw's covert clearance for a top CIA project. As for Oswald's acting alone, Stone's film allows us to view Dealey Plaza from the sixth-floor through the tree-obstructed window where Oswald allegedly took aim. Oswald's service records reveal that he was a poor shot, yet he would have had to fire three rounds from a cheap, mail-order 6.5 Italian carbine in under six seconds. Not one of the sharpshooters who attempted that feat succeeded. Although the "magic bullet" which supposedly inflicted seven wounds on the president and Governor Connally came from the Italian carbine, tests proved that it was not the bullet that wounded Connally. No one could explain why the bullet was in pristine condition after traveling through flesh and bone, or how it came to rest on a stretcher at Parkland Hospital.

Sadly, the official lie lives on. As late as 1993, Gerald Posner, in *Case Closed: Lee Harvey Oswald and the Assassination of JFK*, maintains that Oswald was a lone assassin and that Jim Garrison's case was totally fabricated. In *Hasty Judgment: A Reply to Gerald Posner*, Michael T. Griffith dismantles Posner's book.

Serious researchers have amassed extensive evidence concerning the assassination of John F. Kennedy, enough to vindicate Garrison, enough to expose the conspiracy to cover up the conspiracy.

But it's all too easy to get caught up in the details of the assassination. A few Americans transcend the national appetite for mere scandal. They have made a solemn commitment to restoring democratic freedoms and to shining floodlights into the dark corners of our hidden government. Prouty did that. Marrs did that. Garrison did that. Not only did Oliver Stone do that, but he gave us a masterpiece into the bargain.

Critics who complain of school children's learning inaccurate history from Oliver Stone's *JFK* may as well admit that an accurate history has not yet been written.

History may be servitude, History may be freedom. See, now they vanish, The faces and places, with the self which, as it could, loved them, to become renewed, transfigured, in another pattern.

—T. S. Eliot, "Little Gidding"

Each of Oliver Stone's cinematic creations embodies at least one of the dramatic themes that have obsessed the writer-director throughout his career. Even the exciting visual effects--the moody lighting; wild camera angles; mixed film stock; color, black-and-white, and sepia blends; videos; computer graphics and morphing; animation and cartoons; grainy old newsreels, flashing, flickering, and lingering on the screen--illuminate the mystery and paradox of character confronting destiny, of will imposed on fate. *Salvador* (1985), his first major film, marks off the territory Stone will explore over and over again: an unlikely hero is transformed in his struggle to comprehend and expose illusion, institutional deception, the consensual lie, the official lie.

Based on journalist Richard Boyle's autobiographical manuscript, the film begins with the breakup of Boyle's marriage and his capricious decision to drive from California to war-torn El Salvador searching for action and cheap highs. Accompanied by a stoned disc jockey who provides comic relief, the jaded, unemployed newsman cons his way into the battle zones and back into the good graces of an old girlfriend. At first, Boyle is detached as he scratches for a story, but his indignation mounts as he follows a blood-soaked trail of smoking villages and mass graves, for he knows that his own government supplies the military junta's bullets, bombs, tanks, and aircraft. A press photographer who helps Boyle document American covert support is killed in a bombing raid, while the docile press corps continues to accept the U.S. embassy version of the conflict, even when American nuns are ambushed and murdered. Boyle breaks the story and focuses the world's attention on the ruinous regime.

James Woods's flawless performance depicts Boyle as a shifty rogue who gradually revives conscience and commitment as he argues policy with American authorities, sabotages government raids, marries his Salvadoran girlfriend, and makes a hairbreadth escape from El Salvador primed to reveal the truth about the CIA in Central America. Although immigration authorities apprehend his bride, Boyle has redeemed himself. He has the will to fight for both Maria and his convictions.

In *Platoon* (1986), once again Stone shows us an American trying to make sense of a senseless war. Chris Taylor is an innocent, middle-class youth who waives his draft exemption and, in a burst of patriotic fervor, volunteers for service as an infantryman in Vietnam. The director-screenwriter, himself a wounded and decorated veteran of that war, recreates the grunt's lot in every war--weariness, ache, grime, and gut-wrenching fear relieved only by brief instinctive surges of survivalist adrenaline. Attacks can come at any time from any quarter--from a magnesium-lit jungle clearing to a dirt-floored lean-to packed with peasants--and Chris experiences each encounter with the Vietcong as tumult and confusion.

Chris's feelings towards the Vietnamese villagers range from rage to pity, for each one of them is a potential assassin or potential victim. Within the platoon itself there is tension between the two veteran leaders, the cold killer Barnes and the compassionate Elias. When Barnes betrays and abandons Elias to die, Chris feels that the virtue has departed from the platoon, and he avenges the good soldier's death. As he grows battle-hardened and almost inured to the war's futility, the young infantryman finds reserves of strength and courage he didn't know he possessed. Now when his breast swells, it is not with reflex patriotism but with outrage that the poorest and least privileged men of his generation are being fed to Moloch, for he has discovered a bond with his comrades in arms and a new sensitivity to injustice. Chris Taylor restructures his soul while searching for truth in the valley of the shadow of death. *Platoon* is a great war film, devoid of callousness, sentimentality, or false theatrics. Like *All Quiet on the Western Front*, which exposed the murderous futility of World War I, Stone's *Platoon* will endure as a classic of filmmaking.

In *Wall Street* (1987), Stone instructs his audience in the workings of American high finance without slowing the action--no mean feat, considering his complex subject. Charlie Sheen plays the innocent hero whose goals and outlook mirror America in the eighties. An airline mechanic's son who cold-calls from a brokerage firm's phone bank, Bud Fox admires the legendary trader and corporate marauder Gordon Gekko, the embodiment of Reagan Revolution greed. Bud ingratiates himself with Gekko, (played with reptilian magnetism by Michael Douglas) who uses the insider tip Bud heard from his father to make a big score.

The in-your-face camera work charges everything in Gekko's orbit with danger, but Bud sees only the glittering trophies. He discards his father's old-fashioned values so he can swim with the barracudas. Bud's intrigues for and with Gekko soon win plaudits and prizes. He gets the long-legged girl, the big-windowed apartment, the power office in the firm, and more money than his father will earn in a lifetime of honest toil. Yet Stone's takes of the narcissistic girl, the impersonal apartment, the affected dinners, and the politics of the brokerage house depict how joyless Bud's victory is.

Unlike Gekko, Bud has not developed a taste for raw meat, either as steak *tartare* or life-destroying takeovers. When he learns that Gekko is about to scoop up the airline's assets, including his father's pension fund, Bud foils Gekko's raid and reaps a whirlwind of vengeance, paying with everything but his soul for his compact with Gordon Gekko. At film's end, Bud is about to stand trial. He knows he will be convicted and imprisoned, but he has the satisfaction of exposing Gekko's criminal empire.

Everyone who hated this film was deeply invested in the official fable of eternally benevolent *laissez faire* capitalism, even though Stone, with an uncanny sense of timing, premiered *Wall Street* shortly after several Gekko-like figures were being dragged away in handcuffs. The same media pundits who sat through the infamous savings and loan debacle without uttering a peep declared that Stone had hit an anomaly, not a vein. What Stone had really hit was a nerve.

In *Talk Radio* (1988) Stone introduces a hero who does not redeem himself, a hero whose hubris destroys him. Barry Champlain broadcasts his gab fest from a Houston radio station, where most of the film's action occurs. Sepia flashbacks take us out of the studio and into Champlain's bleak private life. His waspish disposition has alienated everyone--wife, colleagues, and the unseen call-in audience that fills the airwaves with ranting, blustering, and whining. Champlain, wittier, more articulate, more perceptive than anyone in his audience, goads them, insults them, and enrages them. He tells the self-pitiers that their suffering is not noble, but rather unattractive. He tells the fanatics that they are fools and liars. He tells the egomaniacs that they are sniveling nonentities. He reminds them all that his show is the biggest thing in their insignificant lives.

The corollary, of course, is that his callers, pathetic, vacuous, vicious though they be, are the biggest thing in his life, and he despises himself for catering to them. Champlain dumps a load of sarcasm and invective on the hotheads who threaten him with bombs and bullets, finally inciting one to murder him in the station parking lot. Stone sustains our interest in this uncomplicated plot by focusing on the complicated psyche of Champlain, who begins as an innocent clown and ends as a misanthrope without a scintilla of compassion for himself or anyone else.

The comedy of humiliation is an ancient genre. Greek and Roman comedies abound in reprobates who get their comeuppance. But how severely should coxcombs and louts be punished or humiliated? Champlain amuses us but makes us uneasy, too. After the talk show host is gunned down, we must conclude that Champlain's show is entertainment only if we think Russian roulette is entertainment.

Talk Radio is first class entertainment, a textbook demonstration of what a master can do with a tiny cast, a tiny set, a tiny budget, a significant theme, and an unfettered imagination.

In *Born on the Fourth of July* (1989) Stone again exposes the liars in high places who orchestrated the Vietnam War. Based on veteran Ron Kovic's poignant autobiography, the film lays bare the official lies that duped idealistic young Americans into enlisting, the official lies that interpreted the conflict to those at home, and the official lies about America's appreciation and concern for veterans.

Tom Cruise vividly depicts every stage of Kovic's journey. The popular athlete has never questioned the values inculcated at home, in church, or in school. When Marine Corps recruiters come to Kovic's high school, he volunteers, eager to show his mettle fighting America's enemies abroad. In Vietnam, he quickly learns that the enemy is hard to identify, hard to find. The neat distinctions of American football matches do not obtain here. We are still recoiling from the shocks inflicted on guileless recruits being reprogrammed for their new profession when we, the audience, are suddenly plunged into a chaotic fire-fight. We lose our bearings and understand how easy it is for Kovic to lose his bearings and accidentally shoot a comrade. But Kovic does not forgive himself, and he is slow to blame anyone else for his second tour of hell, even after a bullet shatters his spinal cord and leaves him paralyzed from the waist down.

Stateside, he tastes bitterness for the first time when he enters the next circle of hell, the under-funded, over-crowded Veterans Hospital. Back in his home town, Kovic enjoys the applause when he is wheeled onto the VIP's platform during an Independence Day celebration, but jeering anti-war demonstrators darken his moment in the sun. We watch Kovic's disillusionment gnaw him day by day.

Kovic's visit to the family of the Marine he accidentally shot is futile because they will not absolve him of blame. They would have been happier believing that the dead marine made the supreme sacrifice for his country, not that he was a victim of friendly fire. Americans, Kovic realizes, prefer to slap another coat of whitewash over the sepulcher of Vietnam than to admit it contains a hecatomb of rotting corpses. Only in the company of other veterans can he communicate his feelings, but increasingly he clashes with friends and family, who subscribe to the entire menu of official lies. Kovic's growing frustration and rage erupt in family quarrels and barroom brawls. His parents find his opinions and conduct so shocking that they ask him to leave the household.

Kovic descends into an even lower ring of hell in Mexico, consorting with whores, drunks, and drug-addicts in an enclave of disabled American veterans. In one horrifying scene, Kovic and another veteran, alone in the desert, fight each other until they are both unhorsed (thrown from their wheelchairs) and lie helpless on the ground. Clearly, Kovic will not find solace for his troubled spirit here.

So he returns to the United States and bravely admits that he sacrificed his body for an illusion, a chimera. When Kovic lends his powerful voice and his clear vision to the antiwar movement, we see him undergoing a spiritual transformation. He has joined that elite portion of humankind that will always prefer painful truth to soothing lies. Because Oliver Stone belongs to that elite corps of light-bringers, he created this finely-wrought, moving film--and another masterpiece.

Chapter Sixteen

Lewis Mumford's Green City

By Michelle Mairesse

Civilization is hooped together, brought

Under a rule, under the semblance of peace

By manifold illusion

—William Butler Yeats

The Greeks believed the civilizations that preceded theirs were characterized by the metals used for ornaments, implements, and weapons: the earliest was the Age of Gold, its successor the Age of Bronze, and the last was the Age of Iron.

During the nineteenth century, European production of iron and steel increased *four hundred-fold*, and may be said to have inaugurated the Age of Steel. Public transportation systems proliferated, along with mechanized factories. England, richer and more intensely industrialized than the continent, saw mass migrations from country districts to factory towns. Deprived of the traditional communal lands that yielded fuel, game, and pasturage, poor agricultural families, children included, labored in mines and factories up to eighteen hours a day at bare subsistence wages. Hunger and misery were so widespread that the government grudgingly and gradually enacted a series of reforms to avert a revolution.

In America, too, industrialized cities attracted displaced and unemployed workers. In 1790, there were fewer than a million residents in American cities. By 1860, there were eleven million. The poor were crowded into dark, airless tenements and damp basements, where they suffered from poor sanitation, epidemics, and fires, but the plight of the "huddled masses yearning to breathe free" was no concern of the real estate speculators and factory owners yearning to be rich.

In New England, led by Emerson, a group of intellectuals persistently denounced the new commercial ethic. They warned their fellow citizens against money-lust and its consequences.

Henry David Thoreau didn't mince words. In an essay titled "Life without Principle," he said, "This world is a place of business. What an infinite bustle! I am awaked almost every night by the panting of the locomotive. It interrupts my dreams. There is no Sabbath. It would be glorious to see mankind at leisure for once. It is nothing but work, work, work. I cannot easily buy a blank-book to write thoughts in; they are commonly ruled for dollars and cents. An Irishman, seeing me make a minute in the fields, took it for granted that I was calculating my wages. If a man was tossed out of a window when an infant, and so made a cripple for life, or scared out of his wits by the Indians, it is regretted chiefly because he was thus incapacitated for--business! I think that there is nothing, not even crime, more opposed to poetry, to philosophy, ay, to life itself, than this incessant business."

Thoreau took to the woods to escape incessant business, but his famous retreat to Walden Pond was less wild and solitary than he intimated. He brought manufactured implements for building and planting, friends from Concord helped him roof his cabin, and he supplemented the diet he describes in *Walden*--plants he gathered or cultivated himself--with the suppers he ate during his frequent visits to his sister's house in town.

A lifetime fugitive from regimentation and acquisitiveness, Thoreau sporadically reentered the money economy as a handyman, surveyor, writer, and lecturer. He could not be accused of truckling to his audience. He began a lecture on "Walking" with this declaration: "I wish to speak a word for Nature, for absolute freedom and wildness, as contrasted with a freedom and culture merely civil--to regard man as an inhabitant, or a part and parcel of Nature, rather than a member of society. I wish to make an extreme statement. If so I may make an emphatic one, for there are enough champions of civilization: the minister and the school committee, and every one of you will take care of that."

Despite his expressed contempt for civilization and civilized conventions, Thoreau was enough a member of his society to find Walt Whitman's erotic references offensive rather than "part and parcel of Nature." He recognized Whitman's originality, but his ascetic soul was as much repelled by the poet's sensuality as by his fellow citizens' luxurious living.

It is this streak of asceticism in the neo-Thoreauvians that our contemporary consumer society rejects. Asceticism posits limits, and the consumer society, by definition, repudiates limits: as long as there is as drop of oil or a speck of gold to be wrung out of Nature, it belongs to the takers for marketing.

Lewis Mumford (1895-1990), like Thoreau, deplored the effects of the new cities on "a world of professional illusionists and their credulous victims." Unlike Thoreau, he did not believe in arrant individualism. He decried the new economy's creation of alienated individuals. " Freed from his sense of dependence on corporation and neighborhood, the 'emancipated individual' was dissociated and delocalized: an atom of power, ruthlessly seeking whatever power can command. With the quest for financial and political power, the notion of limits disappeared--limits on numbers, limits on wealth, limits on population growth, limits on urban expansion: on the contrary, quantitative expansion became predominant. The merchant cannot be too rich; the state cannot possess too much territory; the city cannot become too big. Success in life was identified with expansion. This superstition still retains its hold in the notion of an indefinitely expanding economy."

He argued that humans, who belong both to the natural world and the artificial world of their own making, are capable of designing wholesome living environments, that cities are as much natural structures as anthills or beaver colonies. In *The Story of Utopias* (1922) he admonishes planners of ideal communities to be practical, to study the intricate human, natural, and commercial networks both of the site of settlement and the entire region. Influenced by the Scotch botanist Patrick Geddes, who urged planners to adopt a wider scheme of ecological reference, Mumford helped found the Regional Planning Association of America, which promoted detailed regional surveys, decentralization, green urban spaces, and lower density in dwellings and commercial buildings.

Like Thoreau, Mumford was a great walker and observer. Traipsing through the mean streets and great avenues of New York, he saw the juggernaut of laissez faire capitalism destroy neighborhoods, pack tenants into small spaces, pollute the air and water, and create a mass of rootless workers. There seemed to be no limits to exploitation and destruction. "Instead of being penalized for his anti-social exploitation of land, the slum landlord, on capitalist principles, was handsomely rewarded: for the values of his decayed properties, so far from being written off because of their age and disrepair, became embedded in the structure of land values taxes. If a new use were proposed for the land, it could only be done profitably by maintaining a slum level of congestion, or by admitting even higher densities."

As an alternative to urban growth and suburbanization, he envisioned new towns surrounded by greenbelts as satellites to older metropolises, with the greenbelts serving as open space and as boundaries to the urban area. Boundaries limit both the physical size of cities and population density, and ensure a human scale. The new towns would maintain a balance of town and country as well as an equilibrium between home, industry, and market.

In *The City in History* (1961), Mumford traces the malaise of modern cities to the new mechanistic, scientific outlook in the service of mercantilism. "The generating agents of the new city were the mine, the factory, and the railroad. But their success in displacing every traditional concept of the city was due to the fact that the solidarity of the upper classes was visibly breaking up: the Court was becoming supernumerary, and even capitalist speculation turned from trade to industrial exploitation to achieve the greatest possibilities of financial aggrandizement. In every quarter, the older principles of aristocratic education and rural culture were replaced by a single-minded devotion to industrial power and pecuniary success, sometimes disguised as democracy."

Mumford insisted on putting human values ahead of avarice, on re-examining the premises of city planners. "That a city could not control its growth without controlling the development of its land, and that it could not even provide space for its own public buildings, in the right situation, unless it could at least acquire and hold land long before the actual need for it arose, had not even entered the new urban mind. The very notion of public control was from the outset taboo. Where profits were concerned, private interest was held superior, on classic capitalist theory, to public interest. True, the powers of the state or the municipality were never entirely rejected by capitalist enterprise. Capitalism greedily demanded large subventions and subsidies, vast outright gifts, like those that originally promoted the western railroads and that now, just as improvidently subsidize private air and motor transportation.

> Thus the city, from the beginning of the nineteenth century on, was treated not as a public institution,
> but a private commercial venture to be carved up in any fashion that might increase the turnover and

further the rise in land values. The analysis of this condition by Henry George, and its bold rectification by Ebenezer Howard in his proposal for the new Garden City, which would corporately hold all its land, marks a turning point in the conception of both municipal economics and municipal government.

Mumford asked the municipal movers and shakers to regard the assets already in place before they unleashed their bulldozers. "In the interest of expansion, capitalism was prepared to destroy the most satisfactory social equilibrium. Just as the new ideas of business resulted--gradually after the sixteenth century, rapidly after the eighteenth--in the suppression and destruction of the guilds, so these new ideas brought about the demolition of old buildings and the effacement of playing fields, market gardens, orchards, and villages that stood in the way of the growing city. No matter how venerable these old uses might be, or how salutary for the existence of the city itself, they would be sacrificed to fast-moving traffic or to financial gain."

In a series of books that appeared between the two world wars, Mumford examined the impact of technology on every aspect of civilization. The unifying theme of these books was the importance of organic planning, of open spaces for interaction, of greenbelts, of taking into account the wisdom, skills, traditions, institutions, and history of the local community, of the renewal of life.

In 1944, when much of Europe lay in ruins after World War II, a war in which Mumford's own son perished, he called for a re-evaluation of Western civilization in *The Condition of Man*. "Western man has exhausted the dream of mechanical power which so long dominated his imagination. If he is to preserve the instruments he has so cunningly created, if he is to continue to refine and perfect the whole apparatus of life, he can no longer let himself remain spellbound in that dream: he must attach himself to more humane purposes than those he has given to the machine. We can no longer live, with the illusions of success, in a world given over to devitalized mechanisms, desocialized organisms, and depersonalized societies: a world that had lost its sense of the ultimate dignity of the person almost as completely as the Roman Empire did at the height of its military greatness and technical facility. All that the Nazis have done has been to bring to a more rapid climax a process that was more slowly, more insidiously, undermining our whole civilization."

When *The Condition of Man* was reprinted eighteen years later, it had lost none of its force. In the preface to the 1962 edition he says that he had pointed out that "the now obsolete economy of expansion might be maintained by continued preparations for war, which would absorb by sheer waste the surplus that orthodox capitalism had never learned to liquidate without bringing on an economic depression; and that stabilization by 'financial insurance and corporate monopolies' might frustrate a more viable social form for achieving a dynamic equilibrium. Both these possibilities have come to pass."

Like Henry Adams, Mumford repudiated machine-life and machine-thought. In an essay on Adams, he says that the historian, seeking a corrective to the perverse direction of civilization, realized that we did not need more information, statistical data, or exact knowledge. "Adams saw that we needed more feeling, feeling and gentling such as infants first get at their mothers' breasts: such feeling as women symbolically embodied and projected from the Paleolithic Venus of Wilmersdorf to the Venus of Milo; from Egyptian Isis to the Virgin of the Thirteenth Century: feeling that has poured into a thousand benign cultural forms, pictorial, musical, architectural and expressed itself in every sustaining mode of embrace . . . from the kiss of greeting to the hot tears with which we take our leave from the dead." In this, as in so much of his work, Mumford demonstrates that the greatest thinkers are able to think with the heart.

There are whole universes of discourse in Mumford's huge body of work, and anyone who chooses to quote him regrets having to omit hundreds of equally brilliant passages, but here is a timely message for the bureaucrats and politicians who are intent on reforming American education:

> If we are to create balanced human beings, capable of entering into world-wide cooperation with all other men of good will--and that is the supreme task of our generation, and the foundation of all its other potential achievements--we must give as much weight to the arousal of the emotions and to the expression of moral and esthetic values as we now give to science, to invention, to practical organization. One without the other is impotent. And values do not come ready-made: they are achieved by a resolute attempt to square the facts of one's own experience with the historic patterns formed in the past by those who devoted their whole lives to achieving and expressing values.

> If we are to express the love in our own hearts, we must also understand what love meant to Socrates and Saint Francis, to Dante and Shakespeare, to Emily Dickinson and Christina Rosetti, to the explorer

Shackleton and to the intrepid physicians who deliberately exposed themselves to yellow fever. These historic manifestations of love are not recorded in the day's newspaper or the current radio program: they are hidden to people who possess only fashionable minds. Virtue is not a chemical product, as Taine once described it: it is a historic product, like language and literature; and this means that if we cease to care about it, cease to cultivate it, cease to transmit its funded values, a large part of it will become meaningless, like a dead language to which we have lost the key. That, I submit, is what has happened in our own lifetime.

Chapter Seventeen

Harold Bloom's The Western Canon

By Michelle Mairesse

The European Enlightenment was the matrix of the American Revolution and of our national character, but not all European intellectual imports have been as felicitous. In this century, two expiring philosophical ideas from France, existentialism and deconstructionism, got a second wind in America. Now, college students are lapping up deconstructionism as avidly as their credulous parents swallowed existentialism. Combining incompatible Marxian and French republican ideals with the grandiose yet solipsistic ideas of French deconstructionists, multiculturalists on American college campuses are demanding that we jettison the literary canon and substitute for it a more politically correct one.

But today's politically correct celebrities may be tomorrow's artistic nonentities. If you doubt it, compare the banal poster pieces of Third Reich artists with those of any condemned "decadent" painter or writer who fled Germany. Compare the boy-meets-tractor epics mass-produced by politically correct Soviet artists and writers with the astonishing compositions of such persecuted underground Russian poets as Anna Akhmatova or Osip Mandelshtam. Before we substitute politically correct instant masterpieces for the Western Canon, whether in the name of moral rectitude or in the name of political correctness, let's listen to wise counselors like Harold Bloom.

In *The Western Canon: The Books and School of the Ages*, Bloom says, "We are destroying all intellectual and aesthetic standards in the humanities and social sciences, in the name of social justice. Our institutions show bad faith in this: no quotas are imposed on brain surgeons or mathematicians. What has been devaluated is learning as such, as though erudition were irrelevant in the realms of judgment and misjudgment."

He is not concerned with "the current debate between the right-wing defenders of the Canon, who wish to preserve it for its supposed (and nonexistent) moral values, and the academic-journalistic network I have dubbed the School of Resentment, who wish to overthrow the Canon in order to advance their supposed (and nonexistent) programs for social change."

Artists' backgrounds and outlooks neither qualify nor disqualify them for inclusion in the Canon. What does qualify them, then? Aesthetic excellence, says the learned, impassioned defender of the Western Canon. Bloom seeks the sources of this excellence, illuminating his selections with deep and sometimes startling insights.

From internal evidence, he speculates that Genesis, Exodus, and Numbers were written by a woman at King Solomon's court, the author whom nineteenth century scholars dubbed the Yahwist. This author, possibly Bathsheba, mother of Solomon, represents the Hebrew god of her story as all too human--eating, drinking, walking in the shade of the evening, having temper tantrums, mischief-making. What surely must be one of the strangest portraits of a god in history (even when softened by subsequent redactors), a jealous, vindictive, often demented deity, no longer seems strange to devotees of three great world religions. We are made to realize that ambivalence between the divine and the human is one of the author's "grand inventions, another mark of an originality so perpetual that we can scarcely recognize it, because the stories Bathsheba told have absorbed us."

Strangeness, irony. Bloom returns to these qualities again and again.

After declaring ironic storytelling about storytelling to be largely Boccaccio's invention, Bloom shows us how Chaucer, the comic ironist, transformed the design.

> It may be that Chaucer's true literary parent was the Yahwist and his true child, Jane Austen. All three writers make their ironies their principal instruments for discovery or invention, by compelling readers to discover themselves precisely what it is that they have invented.

The position of honor in the Canon belongs to Shakespeare. "If we could conceive of a universal canon, multicultural and multivalent, its one essential book would not be a scripture, whether Bible, Koran, or Eastern text, but rather Shakespeare, who is acted and read everywhere, in every language and circumstance."

Shakespeare casts a very long shadow in Western literature. One way or another, all his successors in the Canon are his progeny. His magnitude and influence are unique. "Without Shakespeare, no canon, because without Shakespeare, no recognizable selves in us, whoever we are. We owe to Shakespeare not only our representation of cognition but much of our capacity for cognition."

Goethe admitted Shakespeare's superiority. Bloom tells us that it was lucky for Goethe that Shakespeare was English, because he could "absorb and imitate Shakespeare without crippling anxieties." (Shakespeare did provoke crippling anxieties in other authors.) Bloom alludes to "the extraordinary strangeness that makes *Faust* the most grotesque masterpiece of Western poetry" and then circles that strange drama repeatedly, casually demonstrating how adept he is at winkling pearls out of unpromising shells, spurring us to reread those classics whose true opulence he has spread out before us.

He reveals the keen intelligence that underlies Emily Dickinson's most audacious metaphors, the split between being and consciousness that is Kafka's theme, the debt of Freud to Shakespeare. He communicates his zest each time he holds up one of his twenty-six candidates for literary canonization. He encourages us to believe that the numinous awaits us, that insights, discoveries, and epiphanies are ours for the asking.

We are not shocked when he asserts that the great writers of the Western Canon are subversive of all values, for Bloom believes in and demonstrates the singular virtue of great literature.

The Canon exists so that we can encounter "authentic aesthetic power" and "aesthetic dignity." "The reception of aesthetic power enables us to learn how to talk to ourselves and how to endure ourselves. The true use of Shakespeare or of Cervantes, of Homer or of Dante, of Chaucer or of Rabelais, is to augment one's own growing inner self. Reading deeply in the Canon will not make one a better or a worse person, a more useful or more harmful citizen. The mind's dialogue with itself is not primarily a social reality. All that the Western Canon can bring one is the proper use of one's own solitude, that solitude whose final form is one's confrontation with one's own mortality."

The rest is silence.

Chapter Eighteen

Notes on Language and Poetry

By Michelle Mairesse

You taught me language, and my profit on it is I know how to curse.

—Shakespeare, *The Tempest*

In Shakespeare's *The Tempest*, the magician Prospero reminds the monster Caliban that he taught Caliban language when the monster had "no language but a cry." Caliban is unappreciative of this boon because he is still a monster, albeit a monster who speaks. Animals can convey information with cries and gestures, but only humans have the vocal and neurological equipment to speak, create meaning, communicate, and understand spoken and written language. The German philosopher Ernst Cassirer believed that humankind's acquisition of an elaborate symbolic system has transformed our lives, so that we live in a "new dimension of reality."

All human societies have languages with complex syntactical structures, and normal children can learn the local version of any language without an accent until they are twelve years old. Feral children who lack the cultural stimulus of language during this crucial twelve-year period never acquire the range and fluency of acculturated children. The poorest, least educated children anywhere in the world who grow up in a community of speakers are the inheritors of incalculable riches, whatever language or dialect they learn to speak. (Linguists bypass the problem of differentiating a language from a dialect by joking that a language is a dialect with a navy.)

During their first twelve years, children learn to attach sounds to the visible and invisible world around them, and the sounds and structure of their primary language creates a kind of template for future language learning. We understand (or misunderstand) our native language directly, but foreign languages have to be translated into our native tongue. One meaning of babble (derived from the Biblical story of the tower of Babel) is "to utter meaningless sounds." Our word barbarian comes from the Greek word for foreigners, which was the Greeks' imitation of the outlandish *bar bar* sounds foreigners made when they spoke. (The barbarians, of course, thought it was the Greeks who were making funny sounds.)

Children and isolated groups who are unacquainted with other languages imagine that their native language provides them with the "real" names of things. The best cure for linguistic provincialism is the study of foreign languages. New concepts and different grammatical forms give us insight into the peculiarities of the mother tongue. The Italian expression "translator-traitor" acknowledges the danger inherent in the confusion of tongues.

The Japanese word *mokusatsu* means both "to ignore" and "to refrain from comment." The Japanese cabinet was preparing to accede to the Allied ultimatum in 1945 but wanted time to deliberate. The press release announcing a policy of *mokusatsu* was not translated as "to refrain from comment" but as "to ignore." Rather than lose face, the cabinet let the misinterpretation stand, and the atomic holocaust followed.

The brilliant amateur linguist Benjamin Lee Whorf discovered that Native American languages reflect different conceptual universes. Of the Hopis he says,

I find it gratuitous to assume that a Hopi who knows only the Hopi language and the cultural ideas of his own society has the same notions, often supposed to be intuitions, of time and space that we have, and that are generally assumed to be universal. In particular, he has no general notion or intuition of TIME as a smooth flowing continuum in which everything in the universe proceeds at an equal rate, out of a future, through a present, into a past; or, in which, to reverse the picture, the observer is being carried in the stream of duration continuously away from a past and into a future.... Just as it is possible to have any number of geometries other than the Euclidean which give an equally perfect account of space configurations, so it is possible to have descriptions of the universe, all equally valid, that do not contain our familiar contrasts of time and space. The relativity viewpoint of modern physics is one such view, conceived in mathematical terms, and the Hopi Weltanschauung is another and quite different one, nonmathematical and linguistic.

—*Language, Thought, and Reality:*
Selected Writings of Benjamin Lee Whorf, Edited by John B. Carroll, The
MIT Press, c. 1956

Where the subject-predicate form of Indo-European languages forces us to say, "The fire flamed up," the Hopis say, "Flame." Hopis have a single word to name everything that flies except birds. We can be more explicit and differentiate between airplanes and bumblebees, simply by naming them.

The Inuit have different words for various forms of snow but no generic term for "snow, generally speaking." All adjectives in Hottentot apply to cows unless something else is specified. Hawaiian has no word for "weather." Quecha has no word for "clean." There are Native American languages and Asian languages that classify things by shape (round, linear, granular), a less arbitrary distinction than some European languages make when they divide the universe into masculine, feminine, and neuter genders.

To the dismay of metaphysicians, all the categories they had believed to be embedded in the universe were merely projected onto the universe by their language systems. A number of twentieth-century philosophers made a career of linguistic analysis in the attempt to expose and eliminate the hidden categories of language. Alfred Korzybski went so far as to write his treatises without using the word "is" so as to avoid implying the category of "existence." (Sometimes, though, he slipped. Anyone who wishes to pursue the subject might want to consult Korzybski's *General Semantics*.)

Korzybski untiringly repeated, "The map is not the territory." A map that perfectly represented a city in its entirety would have to be the size of the city. The map is not the territory, and the word or proposition is not the thing it refers to; the spoken or written word has none of the referent's characteristics.

How many angels can dance on the point of a ball-point pen?

Philosophically, Occidentals have been living off Greek capital for over two thousand years. Greek grammatical classifications, rules for definition, and theory of logic have been basic in Western thinking. Even the term "semiotics," recently revived to describe the philosophical investigation of language, was used by the Stoics.

Paramount among Greek thinkers are Aristotle and Plato. (Alfred North Whitehead said that all of philosophy is a footnote to Plato.) Plato's enduring accounts of the speculations that engaged the best minds of Athens in the fifth century BCE have fascinated readers over the centuries.

Plato immortalized his teacher, Socrates, in the *Apology, Crito*, and *Phaedo*, which depict an extraordinary man who lived by his principles. Even when in 399 the Athenian authorities sentenced him to death for religious heresies and for "corrupting" youths with his teaching, Socrates serenely comforted his students before drinking the poisoned chalice. Socrates thought of philosophy as "the pursuit of meanings." He methodically questioned his students, forcing them to define such terms as *justice, good*, and *piety,* terms they used liberally in discourse without considering what their words meant.

Socrates knew that the great enemy of communication is ambiguity, and abstractions like *justice* are subject to several interpretations. Is *justice* being served when a serial killer is executed by the state? The term *justice* is ambiguous. If you look up "justice" in a dictionary, you will find several definitions. (Dictionaries define words in terms of usage, and usage sometimes changes, which accounts for the frequent revisions and new editions of dictionaries.) One definition for *justice* is "the administration of law." Another is "righteousness." Disputes about the justice of state executions come about because the disputants are using key words in very different ways. Although they may not agree after a discussion, they would certainly understand and communicate their positions better if they defined their terms before arguing.

Speakers sometimes use words for which there are no actual referents. We can discuss griffins, gargoyles, and unicorns without for a moment believing that any of them have ever existed, yet we often think of such theoretical entities as super-egos and neutrinos as if they were pieces of furniture. We call this tendency to turn abstractions into objects *reification.*

The problem of fictions has intrigued many contemporary philosophers. When we make a distinction between something that is real (this computer) and something that is not real (unicorns), to justify our unbelief, we will appeal to the evidence of our senses, authority, or whatever convinces us that unicorns are not real.

A related problem is that of paradoxes. How are we able to make some statements that apparently contradict themselves? Here are some examples:

- The statement after the semicolon is false; the statement before the semicolon is true.

- All generalizations are false, including this one.

- Epimedes the Cretan said, "All Cretans are liars."

- The barber in our neighborhood shaves everyone who doesn't shave himself. Does he shave himself?

The school of Logical Positivists claims that all natural languages lead to paradoxes and verbal quibbles. They invented a calculus to express propositions from natural languages in unambiguous form. A group of words which show relations (*if, and, or, no, all* and *some*) are the constants of their systems. The symbols which represent these terms never represent anything else, just as the arithmetical plus and minus signs refer always to the relations of addition and subtraction. Unfortunately for their theory, symbols cannot stand alone. Just as mathematical formulas must be accompanied by a text in ordinary language so that its symbols can be interpreted, so must the axioms of symbolic logic be translated into ordinary language.

But what about extraordinary language, the rhythmical, metaphorical, singing, swinging language of poets?

A new meaning is the equivalent of a new word.

—Wallace Stevens

Poets make some philosophers uneasy. Plato would have banished them from his ideal republic because they deal with unreality. The poet Wallace Stevens says, "For Plato, the only reality that mattered is exemplified best for us in the principles of mathematics. The aim of our lives should be to draw ourselves away as much as possible from the unsubstantial fluctuating facts of the world about us and establish some communion with the objects which are apprehended by thought and not sense."

But Stevens protests, ". . .poetry has to do with reality in that concrete and individual aspect of it which the mind can never tackle altogether on its own terms, with matter that is foreign and alien in a way in which abstract systems, ideas in which we detect an inherent pattern, a structure that belongs to the ideas themselves, can never be. It is never familiar to us in the way in which Plato wished the conquests of the mind to be familiar. On the contrary its function, the need which it meets and which has to be met in some way in every age that is not to become decadent or barbarous is precisely this contact with reality as it impinges on us from the outside, the sense that we can touch and feel a solid reality which does not wholly dissolve itself into the conceptions of our own minds. It is the individual and particular that does this. And the wonder and mystery of art, as indeed of religion in the last resort, is the revelation of something 'wholly other' by which the inexpressible loneliness of thinking is broken and enriched. To know facts as facts in the ordinary way has, indeed, no particular power or worth. But a quickening of our awareness of the irrevocability by which a thing is what it is, has such power, and it is, I believe, the very soul of art. But no fact is a bare fact, no individual is a universe in itself."

Stevens objects to abstracting the poem's meaning and appraising it by non-aesthetic standards. In *Opus Posthumous* he explains, "The 'something said' is important, but it is important to the poem only in so far as the saying of that particular something in a special way is a revelation of reality. The form derives its significance from the whole. Form has no significance except in relation to the reality that is being revealed."

—Wallace Stevens, *Opus Posthumous*, Alfred A. Knopf,

So we need poetry not only to "purify the language of the tribe," but also to expand the concepts of the tribe.

The poet Charles Simic says it best: "Poetry proves again and again that any single overall theory of anything doesn't work. Poetry is always the cat concert under the window of the room in which the official version of reality is being written."

Chapter Nineteen

Realizing the New Commonwealth

By Norman D. Livergood

In a world brimming over with tyranny and war, it's difficult to see how humans will ever be able to develop a commonwealth (a political unit founded in law by agreement of the people for the common good) in which the interests of all the people are served. Were we living in fourteenth century Europe, oppressed by the Roman Catholic dictatorship as well as whatever political despot we happened to suffer under, we might have felt that it was hopeless that humans would ever realize a society for the common good. But, by the fifteenth century, the West began to be re-invigorated by the creative dynamic of the Perennial Tradition.

By 1463, Marsilio Ficino (1433-99 CE) had completed a translation of the Hermetic writings and in 1469 he completed his translation of Plato's dialogues. Plato's writings provided the fundamental bedrock for the Renaissance and the Enlightenment, resulting in such progressive political documents as the American Declaration of Independence, the Preamble to the U.S. Constitution, and the American Bill of Rights and such liberating movements as the American war for independence. America's struggle for freedom has been long and hard, and has now eventuated in a new form of tyranny under a demonic cabal.

This chapter will examine the foundation principles of a new commonwealth which people must now begin to realize, recognizing that this will involve a difficult and prolonged effort. Work toward a commonwealth is part of our overall effort to realize a new culture. We'll first investigate America's struggle for freedom, discovering the reasons why the American dream of a representative democracy has resulted in a militaristic, imperialistic police state. We'll conclude by considering the Platonic principles which furnish a realistic blueprint for a commonwealth and outline the personal qualities which such a commonwealth requires for its realization.

The American Experience

[The Framers of the Constitution] . . . had no wish to usher in democracy in the United States. They were not making war upon the principle of aristocracy and they had no more intention than had the Tories of destroying the tradition of upper-class leadership in the colonies. Although they hoped to turn the Tories out of office, they did not propose to open these lush pastures to the common herd. They did believe, however, that the common people, if properly bridled and reined, might be made allies in the work of freeing the colonies from British rule and that they--the gentry--might reap the benefits without interference. They expected, in other words, to achieve a "'safe and sane" revolution of gentlemen, by gentlemen, and for gentlemen.

—John C. Milller, *Origins of the American Revolution,* 1943

A small group of wealthy people in America has always ruled the nation for its own benefit, not for the welfare of the people. The huge land holdings of the British loyalists, for example, was one of the obscenities against which poor soldiers fought in the American "War for Independence."

But after the war Lord Fairfax, a friend of George Washington, was allowed to retain his five million acres encompassing twenty-one counties in Virginia. The first American revolution resulted only in a change in rulers: from the British elite to an American plutocracy. Sixty-nine percent of the signers of the Declaration of Independence had held colonial office under England.

But not all of the 56 men who signed the Declaration of Independence were plutocratic chickenhawks. Five signers were captured by the British as traitors and tortured before they died. Twelve had their homes ransacked and burned and two lost their sons who were serving in the Revolutionary Army; another had two sons captured. Nine of the signers fought and died from wounds or hardships in the Revolutionary War. These men signed the Declaration knowing full well that the penalty would be death if they were captured. They had security, but they valued liberty more. They pledged: "For the support of this declaration, with firm reliance on the protection of the divine providence, we mutually pledge to each other, our lives, our fortunes, and our sacred honor."

The national situation in the post-war mid-1780s was incendiary. The merchants and coastal wholesalers had tried to re-establish large-scale trade with Great Britain, but the British merchants stopped giving credit, demanding cash ("specie"). In turn, wholesalers demanded hard money from shopkeepers and the shopkeepers demanded that farmers immediately repay their loans in cash.

American farmers had been used to paying back loans in crops, goods, and labor. Suddenly, farmers were dragged into debtor courts, their land or goods seized when they couldn't pay in cash, or they were imprisoned for unpaid debts.

As an example, in the farming community of Hampshire County Massachusetts:

- 32.4 percent of the county's men over sixteen were hauled into court from 1784 to 1786

- Many were thrown into jail: in one cell, 26 prisoners were held without proper food or ventilation, many got sick and some died

- Not a single retailer went to jail

In Massachusetts, the state government (the instrument of the merchant class) shifted the tax burden away from merchants and onto farmers. State laws demanded that taxes be paid in hard money. The excuse for this attack on the working class was that this promoted commerce.

Nevertheless, there were a number of uprisings by enlightened elements of the middle class and the lower class because they recognized that the nation suffered under an oppressive plutocracy.

According to the view of the merchant class, the state is to be controlled by wealthy elites or "better people" who decide what is best for the "common people." Government's role is to protect the single human capability of *ownership*. All other capabilities--learning, pursuit of happiness, freedom, human concern--are to be subordinated to *property*. The state's only role is to assure that the impersonal *market system* runs smoothly. This requires that the government use violent force when it becomes necessary to protect personal property.

The delegates to the 1787 Constitutional Convention in Philadelphia were selected by state legislatures--*not by popular vote of the people*. The capitalist class was frightened by how much power the working class had been able to muster in the separate colonies and they could see from the Shays rebellion that the people were quite capable of rebelling against the wealthy class when it seized their hard-earned lands, crops, and animals.

Delegates to the Constitutional Convention were instructed that their only job was to amend the Articles of Confederation and that any proposed changes were to be approved by all the states before they were adopted. A conspiratorial junta, led by Hamilton and Madison, had already decided that they would scrap the Articles of Confederation and write an entirely new constitution which would create a centralized government controlled by the wealthy class.

The Convention met entirely in secret, and it would be fifty-three years before American citizens were allowed to see the record of what had transpired in this coup d'etat that enshrined mercantile capitalism as the imposed way of life for Americans. Of the sixty-two delegates appointed to the Convention, fifty-five showed up. At the Convention, no more than eleven states were ever represented at one time. Of the fifty-five members of the Convention, only thirty-nine signed the final draft.

The illegal Constitution these conspirators contrived:

- was in effect an economic document, enshrining property as the primary value

- was anti-majoritarian, making sure that the "common people" could no longer gain political power over the minority capitalist class

- contained no checks against plutocratic (corporate) power

- created the private control of government by the capitalist class, including the creation of domestic and foreign policy

- disallowed city or state assemblies to make decisions which the federal government was to make

- assured that effective political power was unavailable at the local level

Knowing that the popular majority in all the states would oppose this oligarchic document, the framers of the Constitution inserted the provision that it would go into effect *when ratified by only nine states.*

Completing the Second American Revolution

The first post-constitutional major skirmish in the ongoing battle of the "common people" against the wealthy class, was the passage of the Bill of Rights in 1791. These first ten amendments to the Constitution embodied many of the working class's concerns which had been expressed during the ratification process. But it is exceptionally important to recognize that the original Constitution and the Bill of Rights omit any protection for common people against corporations or capitalist employers.

Following the imposition of a plutocratic Constitution on American citizens, there have been continual uprisings by enlightened elements of the working class in America because they have recognized that the nation suffers under an oppressive capitalist class.

The Obscenities of Irresponsible Wealth

Since that time, the rapacious increase in wealth by American plutocrats has been fostered by the U.S. Constitution's plutocratic structure of government. In 1850, 1,000 southern families received about $50 million a year income while all the other 660,000 families combined received about $60 million a year. In 1920s America one-tenth of one percent of the wealthy at the top received as much income as the combined income of 42 percent of the people at the bottom.

In 1995 American corporate CEO salaries increased by 92 percent; corporate profits rose 75 percent, worker layoffs increased 39 percent, consumer prices went up one percent. The highest paid CEO received more than $65 million in 1995. The top one percent in America own approximately 60 percent of all wealth. Approximately 35 percent of American families were living below the poverty line in 1998. For a current exposé of the widespread corruption spawned by a plutocratic society, I would recommend Kevin Phillips's book *Wealth and Democracy.*

Precarious Civil Liberties

No nation in man's history has ever achieved a true commonwealth. American citizens have historically enjoyed a wider range of liberties than most citizens in other countries. But those American liberties have always been at the sufferance of the rulers. When they have felt it necessary they limited or destroyed American liberties without compunction. Americans have suffered under restrictions to civil liberties throughout our history.

- The 1780 Riot Act allowed the Boston authorities to keep people in jail without trial

- The Sedition Act of 1789 made it a crime to say or write anything "false, scandalous and malicious" against the government, Congress, or the President

- The 1917 Espionage Act led to imprisonment of Americans who spoke or wrote against World War I

- President Truman's March 22, 1947 Executive Order 9835 initiated a program to search out any "infiltration of disloyal persons" in the U.S. government

- The 1950 Internal Security Act laid the groundwork for the insane trampling of civil liberties called McCarthyism

- The 1996 "Antiterrorism and Effective Death Penalty Act" deprives Americans of our constitutional protections of habeas corpus review in federal courts.

- The tyrannous "Patriot" Act instituted by Bush II creates, among other outrages, "roving wiretap" authority, unsubstantiated subpoena of anyone the FBI chooses and arrest of anyone who tells others of these illegal subpoenas, search and seizure of assets as long as it is claimed that the search is "related to terrorism or clandestine intelligence activities," etc, ad nauseam.

The Struggle of the Oppressed

Most of what we hear or read today perpetuates the dangerous delusion that we live in a democracy. Even iconoclasts who strip away the democratic myth to reveal the reality of plutocracy often end their discussions with generalized theories of reform which have no hint of reality to them. A more realistic point of view is to outline the elements of a commonwealth way of life and complete the American Revolution of freeing ourselves from the mental and political restraints of imperialistic capitalism: realizing a new culture.

First, we need to recognize that we don't live in a democracy, that the politicians who buy their way into office don't work for the good of people but for their own monetary gain. The richest one percent of Americans have gained over a trillion dollars in the past dozen years as a result of tax breaks.

With all its shortcomings, the United States still provides its citizens with a wide range of freedom, more than any other country in the world, primarily because of the Bill of Rights that the common people forced on the capitalist class. In our struggle to complete the American Revolution, the people have won some other important partial victories over plutocracy:

- The women's rights movement

- The civil rights struggle

- Vietnam war resistance

- The growing force of Internet-based news and analysis sources that are exposing the onslaughts of the Bush junta against our civil rights

- The 2006 mid-term election when the American people shouted their outrage at corruption and murder

A Training Program

We must begin training ourselves to understand that "democracy" is a concept that has been used throughout the world--including in America--as a scam to control the masses. Instead of a democracy--of whatever kind--we must begin working toward a commonwealth: a nation founded on law and united by compact of the people for the common good.

One of the reasons why ignorant and ill-intentioned thinkers have attacked Plato, is because he was forthright enough to reveal the reality of democracy--that it is in actuality the manipulation of the masses by an oppressor group who fools the common people into thinking they're ruling when they aren't.

> These will be some of the features of democracy. . . it will be, in all likelihood, an agreeable, lawless, parti-colored society, dealing with all alike on a footing of equality, whether they be really equal or not.

> —Plato, *The Commonwealth*

Plato had seen this form of swindle practiced on the citizens of Athens, and had seen the deadly results of such a fraud when a pseudo-democratic group sentenced his teacher and friend Socrates to death on trumped-up charges.

> Democracy is a pathetic belief in the collective wisdom of individual ignorance.

> —Henry Louis Mencken

Plato understood that a society must have either of two basic forms of government:

- Oligarchy: a government in which a small elite group rules for its own benefit

- Plutocracy: rule of those with wealth

- Tyranny: rule of a criminal cabal

- Commonwealth: a government in which political and economic principles and practices accrue to the benefit of all members of society

This form of government is ruled by some type of aristocracy, those with special knowledge and skill.

Plato believed that a commonwealth should be ruled by those persons who are seekers of wisdom--philosophers.

One of Plato's major works was entitled *Politeia*, the Greek word for Commonwealth. The title of this work has been mistranslated as *The Republic* when its actual title is *The Commonwealth*.

Plato saw clearly that the swindle called democracy is actually a form of tyranny--as has been born out in American history. The current demonic cabal is simply the most recent embodiment of this swindle. We can see this clearly both domestically and abroad:

- Within the United States the cabal stole the 2000, 2002, and 2004 elections; that the 2006 election resulted in the Democrats regaining both houses of Congress may prove to be a temporary situation; the Republicans are still intent on setting up permanent structures to make sure that fair elections are no longer possible

- the Bush II puppet junta pretends that the client-state dictatorships it set up in Afghanistan and Iraq are democracies

Bush and other junta members use the word "democracy" as a shibboleth to fool the ignorant American masses, pretending that they are spreading this magic form of government to as many nations as possible. "Democracy" has now become the mask for totalitarianism and imperialism.

As Howard Zinn has shown in *A People's History of the United States,*

> The American system is the most ingenious system of control in world history. With a country so rich in natural resources, talent, and labor power the system can afford to distribute just enough to just enough people to limit discontent to a troublesome minority. It is a country so powerful, so big, so pleasing to so many of its citizens that it can afford to give freedom of dissent to the small number who are not pleased. How wise to turn the fear and anger of the majority toward a class of criminals bred -by economic inequity -faster than they can be put away, deflecting attention from the huge thefts of national resources carried out within the law by men in executive offices.

The best argument against democracy is a five minute conversation with the average voter.

—Winston Churchill

We must train ourselves in the commonwealth way of life by:

1. Learning how to think critically

2. Gaining an awareness of our world, including an empowering historical perspective

3. Learning the skills of community organizing

4. Developing group decision-making skills

Learning to think critically involves examining our own self-delusions and incapacities and recognizing the essential ingredients of the commonwealth way of life. Certain of our delusions and incapacities make a commonwealth impossible at present.

- We've allowed ourselves to become consumed by egomania. Ego-obsession is the image we see everywhere, the individual feeling that he or she is the most important thing in the world. Movies, television, music, literature, all encourage us to feel that we are the center of the universe. We haven't learned to discriminate between ego obsession, self-respect, and servility. Yes, we want to attain a healthy respect for ourselves and avoid a demeaning feeling of servility, but most people have gone to the extreme of ego-mania--literally becoming obsessed with themselves. In a general social atmosphere of ego-obsession, a commonwealth life-style is impossible. People are not able to see beyond their own immediate, momentary interests to the good of a larger group interest which ultimately serves their individual well-being as well.

- We have allowed ourselves to become splintered into special interest groups and factions, based on ethnicity, age, gender, or other characteristics. A commonwealth is only possible when people see the improvement of their society as a common good and are willing to develop a genuine sense of solidarity with others. One of the major difficulties with our present culture is the inability and unwillingness of the wealthy rulers to work toward the good of all the people in our society. They act to serve only their own interests, gaining wealth and power. As we train for a commonwealth, we must realize a culture which will serve the interests of all its citizens, rich and poor, old and young, men and women, and people of all ethnic backgrounds and value orientations.

- We need to develop group decision-making skills as a foundation for the commonwealth way of life. This requires that we learn how to think critically, resolving issues through the use of evidence, not merely what we happen to feel or what some supposed authority has told us.

There are specific factors required for the commonwealth way of life.

1. First, we must realize that a commonwealth is not an external condition or system but a way of life. As such, it must be pursued, realized, and then continually maintained. By definition, it requires of its participants certain values, qualities of character, and capacities. Those values, qualities, and capacities must be central to one's whole life and being.

This means that it is not possible to practice a commonwealth life-style in one area of life--say on the job or in a civic organization--and yet remain acquiescent to or unmindful of the fascism of a political-economic system, or remain tyrannical in one's personal relationships.

This also means that a commonwealth, by its very nature, cannot be *given* to us by decree, or mandate, or vote, or constitution, or even political revolt. It is a capability for group decision-making which we must achieve for ourselves and which then requires continual effort and vigilance. A commonwealth is not an end to be realized once-and-for-all and handed from one generation to another. It is a process used by people in ordering their lives toward critical common goals such as constitutional liberties. Each generation's goals change, so a commonwealth life-style is a process which is never completed or achieved, any more than the process of learning is something we get the hang of and then stop doing.

2. A commonwealth can emerge only when certain persons decide to join with others in selecting and fulfilling common goals. To opt for a commonwealth must come out of the understanding that other seemingly simpler and more efficient processes of ordering a culture lead inevitably to the oppression of one group by another.

3. We gain this understanding by experiencing oppressive political, economic, and social organization in the family, the workplace, the community, and the nation. By experiencing the oppression and life-destruction which anti-commonwealth structures entail we gain an intense desire for the commonwealth way of life. We're presently experiencing

the oppression of wealth and power under the fascistic Bush II regime. Obscenely rich people are using political, economic, and military force to drive America into a society with two classes: the wealthy and the poor.

Americans have difficulty in understanding what a commonwealth means because we've lived, in the past decades, in a fairly affluent era ruled by a plutocracy masked as democracy. We're only now realizing that the United States isn't a democracy after all--it is a plutocracy controlled by a criminal cabal.

It's important to recognize the extent to which intelligent independence and self direction in any realm are an achievement. The ability to be an independent, self-directing personality is present in possibility in original nature; but this possibility is made an actuality only through the proper kind of education. The same is true of a group.

> Independent, self-directing group conduct is . . . an achievement. Merely to offer democracy to a group does not mean that the group is able to conduct itself democratically. Just as individual independence comes gradually, first in more restricted and then in wider areas of life, so independence in a group comes gradually, first in more restricted and then in ever and ever widening areas of conduct. Whether the group be a family, a gang, a class in school, or a nation, it cannot change suddenly with any success from complete autocratic control to entirely independent self-direction.

> —Harrison S. Elliott, *The Process of Group Thinking,* NY: Association Press, 1938, p. 12

Modern Times

Now that the conditions of widespread affluence and freedom of mobility are no longer profitable for the American plutocracy, some of the more unpleasant and inevitable features of their oppressive order are beginning to affect American citizens directly.

The harsh realities of unemployment, slave wages, tax-slavery, and government harassment will inevitably provide the kind of incentive we need to consider deeper values in life beyond mindless, superficial, addictive entertainment and sports--the "circuses" provided by the present rulers. Perhaps now we can begin to ask what a commonwealth is and how we can train for it.

We must first realize just what led to our present enslavement under a fascist plutocracy, what characteristics in us allowed for our self-delusion, our being controlled by lust for possessions and social acceptance, our willingness to let others rule us as long as we feel we are getting our share. If we can understand what personal qualities lead to enslavement we can then begin to understand their opposite: the positive qualities that make commonwealth self-rule possible.

The Commonwealth Way of Life

The commonwealth way of life is possible only with people who desire to work toward full human potential. A commonwealth cannot exist in a context where some always say: "I can't do that or I can't understand that, let someone else decide who can do more or who understands more."

A commonwealth is very difficult to initiate because at almost any moment in time a ruling group is faced with people who've been trained to be and feel incompetent. The ruling group's temptation at that point is to say: "Since the people clearly can't rule themselves, we'll rule them now and continue to rule them."

A commonwealth can only begin when a small group of persons -having suffered under an oppressive form of rule and having prepared themselves for self-rule -take over the direction of a group or culture. This preparation involves, among other things, the close examination of real, as opposed to assumed or imagined capacities, and the development of real competence. Even then there will be some persons in the community who can't yet participate effectively in decision-making. This is one of the major challenges of commonwealth self-rule. Will the leaders of commonwealth reform activate a process whereby others can learn to participate effectively in group decision-making or will they use the undeniable incompetence of others as an excuse for taking more absolute and final control?

It's hard for us to realize that we lack certain mental and behavioral skills required for a commonwealth way of life. We must train ourselves in the skills and understanding which a commonwealth requires.

A commonwealth can only come to those who are willing to work for the best and highest in human development for all. At almost any point in a nation's history it can be said: "Yes, there are problems here, but it could be worse. Instead of being a malcontent working for unnecessary change, be thankful for what you have." That has been said to every enslaved or oppressed group in human history. That's what the white owner said to his black slave, the British trying to mollify the oppressed colonists in America and India in the 1770s. The good is often enemy to the best. Today we hear: "What oppression? We never had it so good. Don't rock the boat." For many people, life under this present plutocracy, which they have been fully programmed to experience as a democracy, appears rewarding and complete.

But once having awakened to the conditions of oppression, people want to participate in a commonwealth structure of social order. As Harrison S. Elliott makes clear:

> It is he who does the thinking, who faces the problems, who makes the plans, who alone achieves both the growth and the happiness. Our present idea and practice of leadership reserve these supreme values to the leaders. Life has become, for a large number of people, pure drudgery. Men become "robots, " machines for executing other people's desires. The leaders grow, the individuals in the crowd decline.

Mr. Smith doesn't need to go to Washington; he and other American citizens need to complete the American Revolution and learn to refashion a government *of, by, and for* the people by training for a commonwealth. Mr. Smith and other citizens should look forward to the day when their skills are developed to the point that they can begin to make a difference in their community and their nation, taking back the government that's been stolen from them. As we learn to carry out the tasks and responsibilities of a commonwealth, as we're exploring in this book, we can begin to realize a new culture of shared values and rewards.

Chapter Twenty

Life As Awakening

By Norman D. Livergood

In this chapter we'll examine how the ordinary mental state of most humans is literally a form of dreaming while asleep. We'll discover precisely what this involves, how humans arrive at this state, and--most important--how we can escape from this delusory dream state and achieve a higher mode of consciousness.

By "ordinary consciousness," we mean the usual state of awareness, including the associated mental and emotional elements. If we ask the average person why he believes his ordinary consciousness is veridical, he'll say that it puts him in touch with reality in a way that "works" for him. "My usual way of thinking enables me to deal with objects, persons, and events in a manner that leads to successful outcomes. Since it 'works' for me why would I even consider the absurd idea that I'm living in an illusory world or a dream state?

I'm free from any such foolish notion."

None are more hopelessly enslaved than those who falsely believe they are free.

—Johann Wolfgang von Goethe

The difficulty is that the ordinary person isn't able--or willing--to acknowledge when his habitual consciousness (the dream state) leads him astray; when his view of the world causes him to mistake a dictatorial police state for a democracy, a mindless tyrant for a "fearless leader," and a pre-emptive, unjustified war for a struggle against terrorism and for the spreading of democracy.

The dream state of ordinary life is, of course, different from dreaming during regular sleep. This special state of dreaming sleep is an extraordinarily difficult condition to become aware of--or acknowledge. People in this dream world take it to be reality; they don't believe they're asleep--in fact they'll argue strenuously with anyone who says they're asleep and dreaming. This unusual dream world becomes a mass delusion when enough people accept the illusory domain as real. The demonic cabal presently creating this dream world defines reality for the sleepwalkers. So our task is to see through this illusory state.

Wake up! Snap out of it! Something's going on and you need to wake up! You've fallen into a trance or something, and you need to rouse yourself. You think you're awake but you're not -and as you've been sleeping, all kinds of hideous things have been happening.

I know that you think you're awake; your eyes are open, and you've been performing various motor functions and skills -after all, you are reading this. But you're still not really awake! You've been going through these actions as if you're in a trance, or under a spell or something, and you're not really awake; you're not really aware. It's very hard to explain the state you're in, but if you'd just snap out of it, you'd see what I'm talking about.

Let me put it another way. Things aren't really as you think they are. The thoughts you think aren't really your thoughts. You think them because somebody else wants you to think them. And the same applies to your actions. You do what ever it is you do because you've been programmed to do it. You don't realize it, but you've been programmed to think, act, and feel only within certain prescribed parameters. The bottom line, straight and simple, is: you are not really who you think you are -you think you are someone other than your own True Self.

You've been sold a complete bill of goods, right down to the very basics. What you believe, what you think is right or wrong, good or bad, what you should and shouldn't do, even who and what you think you are. But it's all a dream, an illusion, the result of the indoctrination and programming you've been subjected to. But underneath all this, the real YOU still exists.

You came into this life with a plan and a purpose. And you have an awesome power at your command. It lies silently inside, waiting. . . But you need to wake up and remember. Remember who you really are. Remember what you came here to do. And remember the awesome power. It is of great consequence that you do. I do realize that this must sound ty crazy to you. But let me assure you; it is the truth. I wish there was something I could say or do that could instantly snap you out of it, but it doesn't work that way.

Waking up is a process. Plato described it clearly in *The Republic*, (Book VII; The Cave) And even though that was over two thousand years ago, he wasn't the first. The Vedas, the oldest written records of mankind, are road maps left behind by awakened ones. They tell of the various techniques and methods they used to wake up from this somnambulistic, dream-like state that we human beings live in.

Imagine that! The very first entry in the journal of mankind is a call to awaken. It tells us that we human beings are not who we think we are; it calls upon us to awaken from this sleep-like state, and remember that we are so very much more than we think we are. And it describes the power. And ever since, artists, saints, and poets, throughout all the ages, have endeavored to call our attention to this higher and truer state of existence.

—Simon Hunt, *Spiritual-endeavors.org*

The Ordinary Dreaming State

Because our habitual state of dreaming sleep is so difficult to recognize and acknowledge, we'll need to examine this condition in detail and in as much depth as possible. The most insightful analysis of this state was carried out by Plato in a number of his dialogues. When we study Plato's dialogues mindfully we discover they possess an advanced technology enabling a prepared person to achieve a higher state of waking consciousness. We'll concentrate on Plato's *Theaetetus* and *Commonwealth*, because they refer directly to the ordinary state of dreaming sleep, reveal the nature of this condition, and provide the means of rising above such a state of delusion.

In the *Theaetetus*, Socrates asks: "How can you determine whether at this moment we are sleeping, and all our thoughts are a dream; or whether we are awake, and talking to one another in the waking state?"

Theaetetus: "Indeed, Socrates, I do not know how to prove the one any more than the other, for in both cases the facts precisely correspond; and there is no difficulty in supposing that during all this discussion we have been talking to one another in a dream; and when in a dream we seem to be narrating dreams, the resemblance of the two states is quite astonishing."

Socrates: You see, then, that a doubt about the reality of sense is easily raised, since there may even be a doubt whether we are awake or in a dream. And as our time is equally divided between sleeping and waking, in either sphere of existence the soul contends that the thoughts which are present to our minds at the time are true; and during one half of our lives we affirm the truth of the one, and, during the other half, of the other; and are equally confident of both.

The feeling of certainty we have about our experience--whether awake or asleep--is the same. It's naive for us to assume that our mere feeling of confidence in being fully conscious is enough to assure the veracity of our experience.

How We Are Put To Sleep

Many people wonder why Plato insisted in the *Commonwealth* that educational and artistic material used with young people should be strictly supervised. This wonderment arises from our naive assumption that our American public educational system is free from control by ideological dogma.

In fact, the opposite is true: American public educational institutions are entirely dominated by a system of misinformation and anti-intellectualism which has been imposed by the cabal which took control of education in the first decades of the twentieth century. The result has been just what they planned for: large masses of American citizens who are certifiably illiterate and lack any ability to think for themselves, thus allowing a criminal gang to take political and economic control of our nation.

Plato insisted that educational and artistic material should be supervised because young people learn from role models and become the kinds of people they read about and see in their everyday life.

> Since our students, the future leaders of the nation, imitate from their earliest childhood we should choose appropriate models for them to emulate, namely people who are courageous, self-controlled, virtuous, and free. We shouldn't encourage them to embody or imitate what is illiberal or shameful behavior because imitation gives rise to desire for that kind of reality. Imitation, continued from an early age, turns into habits and dispositions--of body, speech and mind.

> —*Commonwealth III (395 c-d)*

Instead of adopting Plato's teachings, Americans have allowed a depraved cabal to seize control of the four most powerful programming technologies in modern history: education, television, popular music, and movies. Through the insidious use of these instruments, American young people are programmed to value greed, egomania, money, power, fame, and cleverness in unscrupulousness, and are conditioned to crave and embody violence, ignorance, and anarchy.

> The average person in the US watches about four hours of television each day. Over the course of a year, we see roughly twenty five thousand commercials, many of them produced by the world's highest-paid cognitive psychologists. And these heavily produced advertisements are not merely for products, but for a lifestyle based on a consumer mind-set. What they're doing, day in and day out, twenty-five thousand times a year, is hypnotizing us into seeing ourselves as consumers who want to be entertained rather than as citizens who want to be informed and engaged. We need to take back the airwaves as a sphere of mature conversation and dialogue about our common future.

> —Duane Elgin, "On Simplicity and Humanity's Future," *IONS, Noetic Sciences Review*, December 2002

One of Plato's ideas we must take seriously is that we're not born with a fully formed psyche or soul, but through nurture and education develop into a specific kind of person. We begin with a capacity to develop and enhance our own psyche or soul through the kinds of experiences we encounter or orchestrate. We ingest cultural messages from our parents, teachers, and authority figures and these archetypes shape our psyches. Since our souls are constituted by the cultural messages we encounter, we must carefully supervise the kinds of concepts and exemplars we experience.

To comprehend the dream state of ordinary life we have to understand the distinct nature of the immature mind and how this mind is formed and controlled. In speaking of the undeveloped mind, Socrates says:

> The immature are incapable of judging what is the underlying meaning of an allegory (*hyponoia*) and what is not and the beliefs they absorb at that age are hard to erase and apt to become unalterable. For these reasons, then, we should take the utmost care to insure that the stories and myths that depict virtue are the best ones for them to hear.

> —*Commonwealth II (378d)*

Plato uses the Greek word *hyponoia*, which refers to the hidden meaning of a myth, the meaning and understanding coming from below. "Hypo" means "under," and "noia" is thought or mind. So *hyponoia* is literally "hidden, deeper, or underlying thought or meaning to which an allegory refers." This word has the same stem as that used to refer to hypnosis: a process in which a person is able to affect you in a strange way by somehow coming in under the radar of your own critical thinking, placing your ordinary consciousness in a state of suspension.

Plato is saying that an immature person cannot recognize that a myth or allegory is something that has a hidden, deeper, or underlying meaning *and effect*. The immature person is unable to recognize what that deeper meaning or effect is, what the story or myth or allegory is about, what it's doing to him. This peculiar lack of orientation and inability to distinguish meanings and detect effects is constitutive of the immature and infantile mind. In the cognizance of an undeveloped psyche, myths or allegories float free of their deeper symbology and inducement, they float free even of the recognition that they have underlying significance and control.

The mature, awakened mind possesses an exceptional capability of self-awareness, the "witness" aspect that allows it to stand apart and observe, ascertaining what is going on from a higher position of attentiveness. It is this extra-dimensional capability of awareness which Plato's dialogues enable us to develop, as they teach us to reflect on all aspects of our experience, not "falling asleep" in the immediacy of our sensations and thoughts.

Psychological and Intellectual Immaturity

To explain what immaturity means, Plato introduces us to a specific psychic type in the opening passage of Book I of the *Commonwealth*: the elderly person who's never achieved intellectual or psychological maturity. Cephalus, an older man, acknowledges that the stories and myths he experienced in his early years now haunt him, causing him to fear the retribution for sins which the myths have caused him to believe will occur after death. Cephalus, like millions of people in the modern world, never matured emotionally and mentally: fantasies frighten him because he cannot tell the difference between myth and reality. He never understood what those early brainwashing fables did to him and didn't work to overcome their negative effect.

Socrates explains that the impressions immature psyches take into their minds and emotions have a tendency to become fixed beliefs and habits, difficult to eradicate or change. A mature psyche has the capacity to distinguish truth from mere fantasy and appearance, propaganda from truth, to recognize stories as stories--and develop out of infantile illusions. Immaturity is the state of being asleep but presuming that you're awake; it is the inability to tell that you're NOT awake. Maturity is the capacity to distinguish true waking from vivid dream experiences. It's this discriminating capacity that goes to sleep when you go to sleep intellectually and emotionally. It's precisely because we can't tell that we're NOT awake that dream-experience—waking and sleep--has such power over us.

> The essential problem is that Americans have been lying to themselves for so many years now that they are completely incapable of telling the difference between the rather frightening truth and their mythological view of America. The roots of the problem go back to the 1930's, but the real problems began right after the Second World War, when the American government came under the control of the group of thugs who still run the country.

> There has been a carefully planned program of complete domination of all sources of information through total media control, the creation of the 'think tank' system to manufacture policy, the establishment of entrepreneurial right wing religion as a method of political control, the use of political contributions to buy politicians, and, if all else fails, simple violence. It is now a country where anyone who could do good is marginalized or assassinated, and changes in government are at least as likely to occur by coup d'etat than by the operation of democracy.

> There is no longer even the necessity to hide the fact that the country is run entirely for the benefit of certain large pools of capital. The essential lies that Americans tell themselves, which mainly have to do with class structure and, even at this late date, race, infect every major political issue in the country -crime and the incarceration industry, health care, the 'war on drugs', education, immigration including the racist response to 9-11, the environment, poverty and the extraordinary creation of what is really a new caste system consisting of a permanent underclass (something that has happened, unnoticed, only in the last few years), and even American foreign policy. Each year since around the time of Sinclair's broadcast [Gordon Sinclair's famous broadcast from radio station CFRB in Toronto in 1973] the situation has gotten worse, but lately the rate of deterioration appears to be increasing rapidly.

> Things have gotten so bad that the government is now fronted by a retarded (and I use that word in a technical sense) clown, who everyone treats as if he were a real President (the worst lie to yourself is when you have to pretend that the obvious idiot who leads you is entitled to do so). The lies are so

deeply ingrained into American thought that the vast majority of the population apparently is incapable of seeing that there is anything wrong, meaning that there is no possibility of change.

—http://www.xymphora.blogspot.com

In Book V (476c) of the *Commonwealth*, Plato explains that the incapacity of the immature mind to distinguish truth from fancy is essentially what it means to be in a dream state. While dreaming we take the dream-image of a person to be a real person. We take something similar to be the very thing to which it appears similar. His exposition explains how we can distinguish between the true waking state and the dream state.

What about someone who believes in beautiful things, but doesn't believe in Beauty itself and isn't able to follow anyone who could lead him to the knowledge of this Form? Don't you think his life is a dream rather than a wakened state? Isn't this dreaming: whether asleep or awake, to mistake resemblance for identity, to liken dissimilar things, to identify the expression of the Form as the Form itself, to think that a likeness is not a likeness but rather the thing itself that it is like? . . .

But take the case of the other, who recognizes the existence of Beauty and is able to distinguish the Form from the objects which participate in the Form, neither putting the objects in the place of the Form nor the Form in the place of the objects--is he a dreamer, or is he awake? He is wide awake.

And may we not say that the mind of the one who knows has knowledge, and that the mind of the other, who opines only, has opinion? Certainly.

So, to become mature we must learn how to:

- Distinguish resemblance from identity--for example, to distinguish between true democracy and the fake democracy that we now suffer under and which the cabal puppets lie pretend to be bringing to Iraq

- Avoid equating dissimilar things--for example, advancing in age is not equivalent to maturing

- Understand forms

- Abstain from identifying the manifestation of the Form as the Form itself: abstain from identifying our present Constitution (a plutocratic document) with the Ideal of a Commonwealth (a government of the people for the people)

- Realize that a likeness is a likeness and not the thing itself that it is like: realize that an illiterate, demented president is not a genuine American President

Maturity or awakeness is the capacity to stand apart from the immediacy of our experience and observe sensations and thoughts as they occur, reflecting on them, evaluating them, and thoughtfully choosing what our response will be. Plato assists us in attaining this kind of intellectual, emotional, and social maturity through his dialogues--but also through myths and fables as well.

Fables should be taught as fables, myths as myths, and miracles as poetic fancies. To teach superstitions as truths is a most terrible thing. The child-mind accepts and believes them, and only through great pain and perhaps tragedy can he be in afteryears relieved of them. In fact, men will fight for a superstition quite as quickly as for a living truth -often more so, since a superstition is so intangible you can not get at it to refute it, but truth is a point of view, and so is changeable.

—Hypatia (370-415 CE), a Perennialist teacher and head of the Neo-Platonist school in Alexandria; she was murdered on the orders of "Christian" Bishop Cyril (who was later canonized by the Church)

The Transformative Use of Myths

Plato is not suggesting that developing minds not be given myths, allegories, and fables from which to learn. He himself used myth to teach and transform his readers. As with all elements in the terrestrial world, the use that is made of myths and allegories is the key. *Hyponoia*--myths with deeper meanings deposited under the literal surface--have a noetic character: the reader or listener has to think his way across a semantic bridge, beyond which lies a realm of transcendent knowledge. Plato's myths and dialogues--which are stories--are highly advanced devices through which we are enabled to ascend to a higher consciousness.

Plato's use of dialectic and myth is so extraordinary that we have to work assiduously to grasp their deeper meaning and effect. The transformative elements of Plato's wizardry appear within the narrative of his dialogues, so it's easy to overlook them if we're not attuned to their characteristics and effects. We can learn a great deal by exploring Plato's strange myth which he develops in Book III of the *Commonwealth* (414c +). He refers to this myth as a "useful fiction" (not a lie) and says it is similar to old Phoenician tales about humankind's origin which people were encouraged to believe.

The "useful fiction" or myth is to be told to all the people, informing them that their early life was a dream, that the education and training which they received was initiation into an illusory dream world. In reality, they will be told, during all that time they were actually being formed and nurtured in the womb of the earth. When they were fully formed, the earth, their mother, caused them to ascend to a higher realm. So, the earth and their country being their mother and their teacher, they are responsible for defending her against attack, and her citizens are all to be regarded as a part of their earth family.

Plato's "useful fiction" also involves telling the people that God has framed them differently. Some have the power of command, and in the composition of these he has mingled gold, wherefore they are to receive the greatest honor. Others he has made of silver, to be auxiliaries. Others again who are to be husbandmen and craftsmen he has composed of brass and iron. And God proclaims as a first principle to all the people that their primary duty is to preserve the human species.

This myth fits into Plato's discussion of how the best kinds of humans can be produced through education and training--one of the major themes of the *Commonwealth*. Part of the educational process consists in observing students to see how their experiences affect them: who they know, what they read, and how they act. Do they, for example, swallow nonsense which is handed them and allow their beliefs to be formed by falsehoods?

We must first recognize that Socrates is presenting a myth about a myth: a story about how a story might be told to the people. Why would Socrates possibly tell such a fable to the populace? What effect would Socrates be trying to produce in the people to whom this myth was told? Why is he telling the story to his dialectical fellow-participants?

Part of the people's evaluation will be to see how they react to this story. Far from wanting the people to believe such a "useful fiction," Plato is encouraging a questioning attitude in them concerning how they were raised and what effect all the cultural "received truths" (principles, axioms, laws, customs, structures) had on them. He is showing that their culture's "useful fictions" have shaped all their beliefs, habits, values, tastes, desires, self-estimation, and countless other elements. "Who am I?" Plato wants them to ask; "How was I formed by my culture?" "What response have I made to the cultural myths which shaped me?"

Plato is encouraging them to question all their cultural values. "Why are there these class distinctions?" "For what purpose did my culture shape me in this particular way?" "How can I improve and transform myself, now that I have awakened to how I was structured by my culture?"

What is so deceptive about the state of mind of the members of a society is the "consensual validation" of their concepts. It is naively assumed that the fact that the majority of people share certain ideas or feelings proves the validity of these ideas and feelings. Nothing is further from the truth. Consensual validation as such has no bearing whatsoever on reason or mental health. Just as there is a "folie a deux" there is a "folie a millions." The fact that millions of people share the same vices does not make them virtuous, the fact that they share so many errors does not make the errors to be truths, and the fact that millions of people share the same forms of mental pathology does not make them sane.

—Erich Fromm, *Escape From Freedom*

Plato's myth is meant to awaken people to question what has happened to them, how they are currently being influenced, and what intelligent response they can make to their cultural engendering. It shows how easily public myths can, in some instances, completely structure the personality and social constraints of a culture. People are encouraged to become aware that they were earlier in an unrecognized state of sleep, were caused to ascend to a higher plane of awareness, but must now investigate and study their current state of consciousness to detect aspects of sleep or immaturity now present.

Maturity or awakedness is the constant, unending endeavor of discovering aspects of immaturity or sleep in yourself and rising above those to a higher awareness. One of the essential ways of telling if you're asleep is if you're regularly discovering traits and behaviors in yourself of which you were previously unaware, negative elements that controlled you without your being cognizant of them. For example, you may discover that you previously had fooled yourself into believing that you wanted to understand what is going on in the world, and you realize you hadn't really wanted to at all--as evidenced by your mindlessly accepting the cabal's propaganda.

Plato is using this unusual myth to explain the evolution of human experience. We're born as infants with very little self-awareness, living almost entirely in our immediate sensations and desires.

> The narcissistic orientation is one in which one experiences as real only that which exists within oneself, while the phenomena in the outside world have no reality in themselves, but are experienced only from the viewpoint of their being useful or dangerous to one. The opposite pole to narcissism is objectivity; it is the faculty to see people and things as they are, objectively, and to be able to separate this objective picture from a picture which is formed by one's desires and fears.
>
> —Erich Fromm, *The Art of Loving*

As we grow older, we enter what is called "adult life" and embrace the cultural myth that we've wakened to a new form of mature awareness. But part of what Plato's myth is telling us is that credulously swallowing this "adult life" myth involves merely "waking up" from one level of dream-life to enter another one. We're like someone in a dream who dreams that he wakes up. Thus although he considers himself awake, in reality he's still in a dream. As "adults," we're encouraged to believe that we're fully mature, that we now know what life is all about and have a total awareness of reality. The cultural myth of adulthood conditions us to believe that we've been initiated into the realm of civilized life and are heir to all the "received truths" which make us "enlightened" and "awakened."

Plato's "useful fiction" helps us realize that most cultural myths are for the purpose of "putting us to sleep," making us believe we're mature and awake when we're not, making us assume we understand reality fully when we don't. Plato's myth helps us make the comprehensive distinction between appearance and reality, myth and truth, cultural conditioning and true maturity. It makes us aware that most of life is mere appearance, a dream meant to keep us asleep and ignorant. Thus this "useful fiction" is psychologically and metaphysically revolutionary. It sows seeds of critical awareness and healthy skepticism at a "mythic level," making us wary of both the myths we've experienced and any future myths we might encounter. We seek to understand what it is to be truly awake and fully in touch with reality. And as we attain awakedness and genuine maturity, we enter an entirely new world.

> "The breakdown of the infantile adjustment in which providential powers ministered to every wish compels us either to flee from reality or to understand it. And by understanding it we create new objects of desire. For when we know a good deal about a thing, know how it originated, how it is likely to behave, what it is made of, and what is its place amidst other things, we are dealing with something quite different from the simple object naively apprehended.
>
> "The understanding creates a new environment. The more subtle and discriminating, the more informed and sympathetic the understanding is, the more complex and yet ordered do the things about us become . . . A world which is ordinarily unseen has become visible through the understanding."
>
> —Walter Lippmann, *A Preface to Morals*

Awakening From Relativism

Developing this higher level of awareness and discernment requires not only a positive expansion of our understanding and capabilities but ridding ourselves of negative elements. For example, we can only gain increased powers of discernment if we're unreservedly honest about ourselves and constantly seek to discover personality features that hold us back. We learn to recognize when we're rationalizing, equivocating, lying, projecting, or acting defensively.

Plato explains--*and effects*--escape from sleep in Socrates' discussion with Theaetetus and Theodorus in the dialogue *Theaetutus*. Cultural "sleep" in Plato's day as in ours is created by people becoming literally possessed by the Protagorean/Thrasymachan ideology:

- There is no objective truth; each individual is the determiner of truth and value for himself

- Whatever a society thinks useful, and establishes as the truth, really is the truth so long as the established order continues in power

- Justice is the interest of those in power: they decree what is legal or just

Plato's discussion of relativism is of immediate relevance because it has currently become the reigning ideology of American society. According to this creed, there is no way to determine the truth; truth is merely what a person happens to believe or what is imposed on society by the dominant powers; justice is the interest of those in power. Truth, under the rule of the current demonic cabal, is whatever they say is true. If they say there are weapons of mass destruction in Iraq and we must invade Iraq to make us safe from terrorists, then by golly, that's the truth. If that proves not to be borne out by inspection, so what. The truth is what they say is the truth—at the moment. Dubya's allowing the NSA to spy on Americans is legal--because he *says* it's legal.

It's interesting that Plato's refutation of relativism now has a modern application, because Protagorean relativism has seized the mind of many Americans:

- Since whatever a man thinks at the time is the truth for him, then no person can assess another person's judgment and see if it is right or wrong, so intelligent investigation of the truth becomes nonsense

- Every person is equal in wisdom to every other person: that's why we have so many uninformed idiots paraded in front of television cameras as though their complete ignorance is an indication of their grasp of the truth

- All arguments can be is forceful or entertaining, never true--(what pretends to be "argument" on TV is most often downright boring and the expression of uninformed beliefs)

Plato anticipated another contemporary falsehood: truth as determined by public opinion poll.

Socrates: "And how about Protagoras himself? If neither he nor the multitude thought, as indeed they do not think, that man is the measure of all things, must it not follow that the truth of which Protagoras wrote would be true to no one? But if you suppose that he himself thought this, and that the multitude does not agree with him, you must begin by allowing that in whatever proportion the many are more than one, in that proportion his truth is more untrue than true."

Theodorus: "That would follow if the truth is supposed to vary with individual opinion."

Socrates: "And the best of the joke is, that he acknowledges the truth of their opinion who believe his own opinion to be false; for he admits that the opinions of all men are true."

Theodorus: "Certainly."

Socrates makes it clear that truth is not determined by personal feeling, popular appeal or majority vote: it is an independent reality which must be discovered through objective investigation.

Socrates: "And does he not allow that his own opinion is false, if he admits that the opinion of those who think him false is true?"

Theodorus: "Of course."

The cultural sleep state many Americans allowed themselves to fall into involves the belief that truth is whatever their "leaders" tell them and right behavior is however their "leaders" act. It's okay for "rulers" to "out" a CIA agent if they don't happen to like what her husband says about their lying about weapons of mass destruction in Iraq. It's legal to allow elections to be fixed in Florida and Ohio and elsewhere because Bush and his supporters say it's legal.

An opinion on a point of conduct, not supported by reasons, can only count as one person's preference; and if the reasons, when given, are a mere appeal to a similar preference felt by other people, it is still only many people's liking instead of one. To an ordinary man, however, his own preference, thus supported, is not only a perfectly satisfactory reason, but the only one he generally has for any of his notions of morality, taste, or propriety, which are not expressly written in his religious creed.

—John Stuart Mill, *On Liberty*

The absolutely fatal danger of this kind of non-thinking inculcated by a culturally induced dream state is beyond measure. The very life and death of Americans is now being determined by such a cultural sleep state:

- Unthinking people are signing up for Bush's unlawful wars and dying by the thousands

- American workers in the millions are losing their jobs and falling into poverty and homelessness

- Constitutional freedoms are being destroyed wholesale before our eyes.

If you think all this talk about Americans being asleep is philosophical nonsense, the stark reality of this dream state is made dramatically evident when we see almost no Americans rising up to protect their lives and their country. In this current totalitarian mind-set, the cultural myth that truth is a personal whim allows unscrupulous leaders to dictate "truths" which will inevitably lead to our destruction.

How is it possible that the strongest of all instincts, that for survival, seems to have ceased to motivate us? One of the most obvious explanations is that the leaders undertake many actions that make it possible for them to pretend they are doing something effective to avoid a catastrophe: endless conferences, resolutions, disarmament talks, all give the impression that the problems are recognized and something is being done to resolve them. Yet nothing of real importance happens; but both the leaders and the led anesthetize their consciences and their wish for survival by giving the appearance of knowing the road and marching in the right direction.

While in our private life nobody except a mad person would remain passive in view of a threat to our total existence, those who are in charge of public affairs do practically nothing, and those who have entrusted their fate to them let them continue to do nothing."

—Erich Fromm, *To Have or To Be?*

Plato To the Rescue

What Plato's dialogues provide us--especially in such critical times as these we're living in--is a clear vision of what life is all about and a reassuring sense of the ultimate victory of transcendent, timeless truths. In the *Theaetetus*, Socrates finds two persons--Theodorus and Theaetetus--who have allowed themselves to be almost completely possessed by

Protagorean relativism. This is similar to the situation in which we now find ourselves, when we encounter millions of Americans who have allowed themselves to be culturally brainwashed into a mindless relativism: whatever leaders say is the truth is the truth.

But even in persons who have allowed themselves to be enslaved by destructive ideologies (think "compassionate conservatism") there are still deep, foundational soulelements through which to assist them to regain a truth-affirming self-empowerment.

- Humans recognize both wisdom and ignorance as characteristics of different people and seek the wise as their teachers.

- Humans are aware that there are great differences in the ability of specific persons to understand what is reality or truth.

- In relation to health and science, persons acknowledge that not all people possess knowledge of what is best--only some possess that knowledge; some people are superior to others in terms of knowledge.

- Humans recognize that a person who cannot give a reason for a thing, has no knowledge of that thing, that only when someone can provide a rational explanation does he possess genuine knowledge.

- Humans recognize that knowledge is correct judgment accompanied by knowledge of the difference between one object and other objects.

"We compel [the members of the jury] to hear both sides before casting their vote. We compel them to hear those two sides according to some rational rule of evidence and advocacy; and then, having taken these precautions, we take the further precaution of having the evidence summarized by an expert in the shape of the judge, who shows its relation to the law. Only then have we some hope that their decision may be broadly a sound one."

—Norman Angell, *The Public Mind*

From their own knowledge of mathematics, Theodorus and Theaetetus understand that there are experts in the area of ethics or morality as in all other fields. They're aware that truths--such as mathematical truths--are not determined by subjective whim and that a person can't merely make something true by saying it is. From their understanding of mathematics, they recognize that they are not knowledgeable in certain other areas, for example, in the field of determining what is true justice. They recognize that there are experts, such as Socrates, in the area of virtue, justice, and wisdom.

From their insight into geometry and other mathematical sciences, Theodorus and Theaetetus understand that one must have the humility of "knowing that one does not know" which makes a person ready to learn. They recognize that such psychological capacities constitute a kind of moral prerequisite in one's character, different from competence or expertise in a particular subject matter such as geometry. They agree with Socrates that morality is as stable and real a dimension of human knowledge as mathematics.

Socrates finds it possible, with such intelligent persons as Theodorus and Theaetetus, to clear up the smoke and mirrors of cultural relativism--the mind-state of being asleep instead of aware. From their knowledge of mathematics they know that there are principles that exist outside the terrestrial realm--Forms which are expressed only imperfectly through mundane entities such as the image of a triangle drawn on a sheet of paper.

They realize that when they see geometric images with their eyes, they are also--more importantly--seeing noetic Forms with their higher intellect. They know that geometric truths are not private understandings (whims or declarations) subject to public controversy, but universal conceptions valid for all. By extension, they are able to comprehend that there are similar universal and unchanging structures--such as justice--in the field of morality.

What Socrates is able to effect, through dialectic, is the ascent of Theodorus and Theaetetus from the subterranean cave of myth-thinking and relativism to an awareness of their Higher Self which recognizes excellence in humans and the transcendental existence of Forms which are manifested in mundane entities.

Socrates is in part a "physician of the soul." A soul made unhealthy (unjust, ignorant, presumptuous) by cultural myths does not see clearly--is asleep in a dream world. So the imposed unease of somnambulism--cultural sleep--must be cured because "seeing" transcendent realities requires turning one's whole soul toward the good, the Higher Forms. Only the healthy, psychically awake person is able to discern supersensible realities such as Beauty, Justice, Goodness, and Wisdom. Only an awakened person can see through the muck of everyday affairs to the divinely guided evolution of humankind.

> Real ability is to respect relative truth without *damaging* oneself by refusing to realize that it will be superseded. When you observe that today's controversies often reveal not relevance but the clash of the untaught with the wrongly taught, and when you can endure this knowledge without cynicism, as a lover of humankind, greater compensations will be open to you than a sense of your own importance or satisfaction in thinking about the unreliability of others."
>
> —Idries Shah, *A Perfumed Scorpion*

Plato is telling us that although we've awakened to a certain level of conscious experience, we must now develop the capacity to recognize life as a higher form of allegory. Waking up to conscious adult social life has involved merely entering a dream at another level where we're unable to distinguish between physical objects and the Forms which they manifest.

We must now move on to the next level where we acquire the ability to recognize terrestrial objects, events, and persons as higher allegories (*hyponoia*) pointing to deeper, hidden meanings. Earthly entities--such as beautiful people--are in fact manifestations of the Form Beauty.

Only if we make a concerted effort to examine our lives for elements which impede our development and keep us asleep, can we attain a higher state of awareness and awakedness to who we really are and the ability to understand life in higher terms:

- The physical world is itself a divulgence of the higher world of Forms.

- The Divine has the power to take all human actions and use them to assist us in our evolution.

- Who we are--at the highest level--are conduits of spiritual purposes which transcend any single person, group of persons, or any specific time period.

- The Divine manifests through everyone and everything.

- Each person receives exactly the experiences from which they can best learn what they need for their personal evolution--and at the same time for the evolution of all humankind.

- The Divine creates a world which provides precisely coordinated learning experiences transcendentally matched to our current needs and capabilities.

Nasrudin on phone: "Hello, psychiatric ward, my wife needs some help."

Nurse on phone: "What's the problem?"

Nasrudin: "Well, she thinks she's *not* a manifestation of the Divine, just a physical being."

Nurse: "Okay, we'll be right there to get you, uh, her."

Understanding Current Events From a Higher Perspective

What is the wise response to the collapse of our everyday world? We certainly don't want to bury our heads in the sands of indifference or ignorance, like so many who are now acting like mental ostriches. We can't escape into a fantasy realm, pretending that the ordinary world doesn't exist. At the same time we don't want to become so mentally brutalized by the daily horrors of the ordinary world that we allow their negative energy to create fear and hatred in us.

> We are such stuff as dreams are made on; and our little life is rounded with a sleep.
>
> —Shakespeare, *The Tempest*

We must recognize that the present political-economic-religious-social reality is merely a temporary scene in a vast drama being played out on Reality's eternal stage, that humankind's experience within history is being used to bring about its spiritual evolution. If the current mindless rulers delude themselves into believing that they control human life and human destiny, we're able to see through this chimera. We don't have to be taken in by their distortion of Reality. We can retain our own humanness, our ability to understand and our capacity to care for one another even in the face of the prevailing dog-eat-dog ideology.

> The illusion from which we are seeking to extricate ourselves is not that constituted by the realm of space and time, but that which comes from failing to know that realm from the standpoint of a higher vision. We are at length restored to consciousness by awakening in a real universe, the universe created by the One Mind as opposed to that perversion of it which has been created by our egocentric selves. We then see the visible world as the expression of the immanental life of God, the Divine in manifestation. In relating ourselves to it we live in that Presence subjectively in the depths of our mystical being. And in the properly integrated personality the two processes have become one.
>
> —Lawrence Hyde, *The Nameless Faith*, 1950

Beyond seeing through the cabal's propaganda haze that attempts to keep people ignorant and asleep, what are the higher purposes which Transcendental Power is realizing through this present world-anarchy? In what way is this seemingly totally negative power structure being used to further human evolution?

- The depraved *outrageousness--the enormity--the total disregard for human life*--shown by the cabal's actions are being used to awaken Americans to the fact that their very lives are at stake. Many people have allowed themselves to fall into so deep a somnambulism that only the most astounding events have a chance of awakening them. It was in this way that some Americans came partially awake during the 2006 mid-term election and expressed their outrage at the cabal's depravity.

- The more extreme the tyranny, the more direct the lessons to be learned. 9/11 has brought to the awareness of Americans that they will be murdered if they don't do something realistic in response--on their own, not by their leaders.

- An inhuman militaristic imperialism--with wars in Afghanistan, Iraq, and next in Iran--is teaching Americans that no one should die for the rulers' egomaniacal purposes, that perpetual war for ruler profits is no safeguard of American lives but--on the contrary--the senseless slaughter of Americans instead.

- The clearly negative character of George W. Bush is making clear to Americans that the presidency--and the entire structure of federal government--has been seized by a criminal gang. Dubya so totally lacks the intellectual and moral capabilities to lead effectively that it becomes abundantly clear that a cabal is in power--not the figurehead trotted out to show to the people.

- The utter criminality of the Bush junta and its cabal controllers is becoming so clear for all to see--with the revelations of the crimes of Libby (indicted) and Abramoff (convicted) and others--that Americans are awakening to the need to replace the rulers with decent, just leaders and institute new political and economic structures that will establish a government of the people for the people.

- The murder of Americans--in war and through economic repression--is providing the lesson that the American public--in large numbers--has become intellectually, morally, and vitally (life-or-death) *dysfunctional to the point of becoming suicidal*. The present outrages are making it clear that Americans are so out of touch with reality that they will allow others to lead them to their own destruction.

- The total seizure of all political and economic power by this demonic cabal is finally awakening Americans to the necessity of organizing themselves to create a more perfect union, that the course of human events has come to the point that it is now necessary for the American people "to dissolve the political bonds which have connected them with" their rulers and "to assume among the powers of the earth, the separate and equal station to which the Laws of Nature and of Nature's God entitle them."

There is an awakening to the necessity to realize a new culture, to enact once again what our Declaration of Independence calls for:

"We hold these truths to be self-evident, that all men are created equal, that they are endowed by their Creator with certain unalienable Rights, that among these are Life, Liberty and the pursuit of Happiness. That to secure these rights, Governments are instituted among Men, deriving their just powers from the consent of the governed. That whenever any Form of Government becomes destructive of these ends, it is the Right of the People to alter or to abolish it, and to institute new Government, laying its foundation on such principles and organizing its powers in such form, as to them shall seem most likely to effect their Safety and Happiness."

"The dreamer is not awake, he who is awake dreams not; for these things are the opposites of each other.

"He who thus understands, discerning the real from the unreal, ascertaining reality by his own awakened vision, knowing his own Self as partless awakening, freed from these things reaches peace in the Higher Self."

—Shankara, The Crest-Jewel of Wisdom

Chapter Twenty-One

Enlightening Groups

The Esoteric Process of Discovering
Truth Through Group Dialectic

By Norman D. Livergood

Throughout human history, arcane knowledge concerning *individual transformation and the discovery of truth through* esoteric *group processes* has been made available to select people through Perennialist teaching material and exercises.

In this chapter we focus on the paranormal capabilities of Perennialist operations to discover Truth through esoteric group processes, using the nomenclature of *enlightening groups*. Such Perennialist groups utilize the dialectical process as first developed by Socrates and Plato.

The symbiotic aspects of enlightening groups--group reasoning and group solidarity--have been applied by a few external social coteries over the centuries with outstanding success, but this civic wisdom has not been widely utilized. For the most part, humans have ignored this knowledge and allowed human predators--political, religious, military, and economic tyrants--to oppress them, causing untold misery. The group reasoning and group solidarity aspects of Perennial wisdom will be our focus in this chapter.

The current abuse of humans by political and economic tyrants has become so pervasive and ghastly that it's now essential for people to begin assimilating the Perennialist group symbiosis principles with which they can build a commonwealth to replace the current totalitarian dictatorship which I have titled the demonic cabal. This will not, of course, take place overnight, but it's essential for humans to begin now to understand these higher principles and learn to apply them in small experimental cells.

This arcane knowledge of group symbiosis is absolutely essential to humankind's survival and has been revealed by such Perennialist teachers as Hermes, Krishna, Pythagoras, Socrates, Plato, Jesus, Paul, Boethius, and Bernard of Clairvaux.

The Preserving Wisdom

In his dialogue *Protagoras*, Plato uses a teaching story to explain how humans, when they degenerated to the point of utter barbarism, were saved by a small, distinguished group of sages connected with the name of Hermes, who taught humankind the higher ordering principles of group solidarity and decision-making, delivering them from annihilation.

Protagoras Teaching Story

Humans very early in their history invented articulate speech and devised technical means for drawing sustenance from the earth. At first humans lived dispersed, not in clans or hamlets, but this lack of group unity led to their being destroyed by wild beasts and the elements. Humans had not learned how to cooperate for their own survival.

Finally, the human instinct for self-preservation brought them together into groups and villages, but lacking the higher ordering principles of government, they began to destroy each other. The Divine Principle feared that the entire human race would be exterminated, so Hermes was sent to humankind, bestowing the Forms of reverence and justice as the ordering principles of human groups, with the underpinning of the bonds of friendship and conciliation. The Divine instructed Hermes that he was to impart the sense of justice and reverence to all humans, for only in this way would they be able to survive.

The higher ordering principles of group solidarity and group reasoning, therefore, are elements of innate intelligence, allowing all humans to participate in group decision making. But even though these elements are innate, they can be overwhelmed by ignorance and personal vice, until they become non-functional--forgotten and atrophied.

Humans can degenerate to the bestial state of dog-eat-dog, disdaining reverence for unity, order, and justice. Therefore, when the majority of humankind loses the sense of civic and social virtue, to the point of civilization's being threatened, it becomes necessary for enlightening groups who know the Forms--to teach humans the arcane wisdom of group solidarity and group reasoning which will deliver them from extinction.

Plato's teaching story warns: Without the esoteric knowledge of group solidarity and group reasoning, humankind will perish.

The Esoteric Teaching of the Stratification of Groups

In the next chapter, we'll see how transformative groups are organized in a hierarchical structure, with the Perennialist teacher--the one who has achieved advanced awareness--directing the development of seekers and students. If a student attempts to usurp the role of the teacher, believing he can teach himself or others, the result is chaos.

At the same time, the teacher assists initiates (advanced students) to move ahead as quickly as possible to the point where they can take over much if not all of their own development--and assist in transformative work with others. We can identify this as the impetus toward egalitarianism.

Throughout the entire Perennialist operation, there is the necessary recognition of diverse functions and levels of capability. Without such differentiation, groups become dysfunctional and destructive. While some initiates are attaining the capability of directing their own and others' development, there is always the necessity of recognizing and implementing the distinction between teacher and novice in the ongoing transformative process.

The Perennial Tradition makes available to humans the arcane knowledge of how groups can work together for the benefit of all their members in the search for Truth. Though Perennialist enlightening groups are special aggregations of selected participants, the principles which these groups discover, practice, and disseminate are applicable to all human groupings. The Perennial Tradition sees the end and aim of evolution as the perfection of the One through the autonomous functioning of all its individual members. Perennialist groups revivify, adapt, and re-introduce esoteric principles of group operation that serve to promote the welfare of all members within any organization--including learning circles, cities, and society in general.

The Ultimate Application of Perennialist Principles to Society

Throughout our discussion of enlightening groups, we'll examine and explicate principles and procedures by which persons can learn to work effectively in face-to-face groups, always with the goal of exporting these unique ideas and methodologies to society as a whole as and when that becomes possible. Our re-discovery and re-adaptation of Perennialist principles begin with Plato in his *Commonwealth*.

> Our aim in founding the State was not the disproportionate happiness of any one class, but the greatest happiness of the whole; we thought that in a State which is ordered with a view to the good of the whole we should be most likely to find Justice.

One of Plato's seminal concepts was that of Justice.

Plato began his study of the social order with a definition and an analysis of the concept of justice. The state has no other and no higher aim than to be the administrator of justice. But in Plato's language the term justice does not mean the same as in common speech. It has a much deeper and more comprehensive meaning. Justice is not on the same level with other virtues of man. It is not, like courage or temperance, a special quality or property. It is a general principle of order, regularity, unity, and lawfulness. Within the individual life this lawfulness appears in the harmony of all the different powers of the human soul; within the state it appears in the 'geometrical proportion' between the different classes, according to which each part of the social body receives its due and cooperates in maintaining the general order. With this conception Plato became the founder and the first defender of the Idea of the Legal State.

—Ernst Cassirer, *The Myth of the State*

So the philosopher, in constant companionship with the divine order of the world, will reproduce that order in his soul and, so far as man may, become godlike. . . Suppose, then, he should find himself compelled to mould other characters besides his own and to shape the pattern of public and private life into conformity with his vision of the ideal, he will not lack the skill to produce such counterparts of temperance, justice, and all the virtues as can exist in the ordinary man.

—Plato, *Commonwealth IV*, 500

The guiding principle of a positively operating society is that each individual carries out the function for which his individual quality of consciousness enables him, one to one kind of work and one to another, every person functioning to the best of his ability. Thereby society becomes one unified, reciprocal whole.

A society should be lead by persons who have attained the specific skills of statesmanship--those persons Plato identified as philosopher-statesmen--who can order their own lives by an advanced knowledge of higher organizing principles (Forms). True statesmanship involves knowledge about societies as a whole and the maintenance of good domestic and foreign relations. This is a special capability, and a person cannot assume that he possesses these complex skills merely because he has wealth or power.

On the contrary, most often the rule of a society is taken over by the worst types of people, those with no ability to order their own lives or the functions of a society. One of the major catastrophes of our modern era is that citizens have lost the understanding that there are certain persons who, through training and character, possess the necessary capability to lead a society beneficially and effectively, while others only pretend to be able to do so.

Plato used a teaching story in the sixth chapter of the *Commonwealth* to illustrate the present plight of society. On a ship at sea, a group of mutinous sailors, with the help of a scheming villain, take control of the vessel. The villain is put in charge of the ship and acclaimed by the ignorant sailors to be a "great leader." Neither the villain nor the mutinous sailors possess the highly specialized skills of seamanship, assuming that the capabilities of a sea captain are negligible or non-existent. As can be imagined, the ship runs onto the shoals and is destroyed.

Until philosophers are kings, or the kings and princes of this world have the spirit and power of philosophy, and political greatness and wisdom meet in one, and those commoner natures who pursue either to the exclusion of the other are compelled to stand aside, societies will never have rest from their evils, nor the human race, as I believe, and then only will this our society have a possibility of life and behold the light of day.

—Plato, *Commonwealth* IV, 473d

Any buffoon can dominate and run roughshod over a group or a nation, given enough power and ruthlessness. But that's the very antithesis of what Perennialist esoteric principles teach in terms of developing groups and societies which succeed in serving the interests of all their members.

In today's world, the norm is groups--including nations--dominated by the worst types of persons: those who possess no moral principles at all and who do whatever they choose to gain control over people. Ordinarily, only when a nation comes to the crisis point of its despotic rulers bringing the nation and its people to the point of utter ruin, is a new type of leadership and a new set of ordering principles sought.

At present, the myth which controls most Americans is that they live in a democracy. What they usually mean by that is that the people get to vote for their representatives, who will in turn make most if not all political and economic decisions for them. In the 2000, 2002, and 2004 elections the entire voting system in the United States was taken over by criminal factions within the Republican party. Florida election rigging in 2000 resulted in the Katherine Harris-Jeb

Bush-Supreme Court coup d'etat. Karl Rove's Nazis rigged both the 2002 and 2004 elections, with massive vote fraud in key states such as Florida and Ohio.

Fortunately, in the mid-term 2006 election, the Democrats were able to make sure that most of the voting results were honestly recorded. However, if America is ever to become a true commonwealth, it will be necessary to rid ourselves of the voting machines--returning to paper ballots--and bring the criminal Republican factions that rig elections to justice.

At times, societies devolve to the point where the people are so debilitated by miseducation, misinformation, and moral degeneracy that they're incapable of recognizing a demonic ruler for what he is. Unfortunately, that's largely the situation we're now living in.

> Paradoxically, a society of simple tools that allows men to achieve purposes with energy fully under their own control is now difficult to imagine. Our imaginations have been industrially deformed to conceive only what can be molded into an engineered system of social habits that fit the logic of large-scale production. We have almost lost the ability to frame in fancy a world in which sound and shared reasoning sets limits to everybody's power to interfere with anybody's equal power to shape the world.

> —Ivan Illich, *Tools for Conviviality*

Even in such desperate times as these, persons associated with the Perennial Tradition persist in working to overcome ignorance, tyranny, and destruction, while providing lost knowledge to those persons who are still capable of appreciating it and using it to attain personal and social transformation in special enlightening groups.

The Search for a More Perfect Union

Because sub-human predators have seized political and economic power worldwide, humans are now literally an endangered species--as in Plato's *Protagoras* allegory. They've lost the life-or-death capability of living in consensus communities where the goal is the welfare of all. Unless this lost wisdom is revivified in peoples' minds and actions, the entire species could degenerate to the sub-human state of barbarity.

All people are seeking a better way to live together than in the monarchies, fake democracies, plutocracies, and dictatorships that we now are forced to endure. All of us have suffered under despotic and incompetent leadership in one group or another--including at present our nation under the criminal cabal. So we know first hand what personal grief such tyrannous presidents, bosses and managers can cause group members. Though a truly representative democracy would be a vast improvement over the various forms of tyranny people now suffer under, what we're exploring in this chapter is the training in and application of principles leading to a very special kind of group--what we're calling an enlightening group--totally unlike 99% of the organizations we now find in society.

The procedures we're exploring and developing here point to a new kind of organizing principle--group reasoning--which forms the basis for consensus decision-making and action. Such groups are completely different from organizations that elect representatives and allow those persons to think and act for them.

In this chapter, we're not attempting to show how current flawed and despotic political systems can be propped up or revised. We're not concerned with such systems as representative democracy. In his *Commonwealth*, Plato showed how democracy can be taken over by criminal elements and used to manipulate the people in any way a tyrant chooses--just as American democracy has been taken over by such despots as John Adams in 1796 and the current cabal beginning in the early decades of the twentieth century. What we're discussing are principles of consensus decision-making, an entirely different system from the theory of representative democracy.

Counterfeits of Group Reasoning

Before we explore the principles and procedures of group reasoning, we first need to see what this process is *not*. By examining some of the structures and processes that are counterfeits of or divergent from group reasoning, we'll get a better idea of what it *is*.

1. Group reasoning is not a form of democracy.

In supposed representative democracies such as the United States, the thrust is not to secure participation but to win assent. The so-called "representatives of the people" do not attempt to secure genuine consideration of various issues by the people, but approval of candidates or proposals which will be reflected in opinion polls and voting. Consequently, the process is propaganda and salesmanship, not reasoning. The people are led to make their choices with as little rational discussion as possible. No favorable consideration is given to reasonable alternatives. Thus, in this present society individuals are trained from an early age to look to their representatives for the direction of their thought and action and to dissociate reasoning from social life.

Group reasoning involves all members deciding and acting on their own, not through a representative. They learn how to make intelligent group decisions by actually participating in the process.

2. Group reasoning is not debate or argument.

> In debate, one desires to know what another person thinks in order that he may devise arguments to convince him he is wrong. In discussion, one wishes to know what the other person thinks in order that he may get more light on his own problem or may cooperate with the other persons in solving their common problem.

> —Harrison S. Elliott, *The Process of Group Thinking*, 1938

3. Group reasoning is not a form of mindless association of people in an indoctrination process:

Association in groups can be used for the purpose of brainwashing and conditioning. There are powerful elements within group dynamics that allow indoctrination of participants into whatever ideology the manipulators choose. Numerous studies of group behavior demonstrate that the emotional and intellectual aspects of group interchange can be used to program the minds of humans. One of the most revealing descriptions of the debilitating aspects of indoctrination groups is provided by the first-hand account of a German man who was forced to participate in a Nazi training group in the late 1930s.

> Comradeship can become the means for the most terrible dehumanization--and . . . it has become just that in the hands of the Nazis. They have drowned the Germans, who thirst after it, in this alcohol to the point of delirium tremens.

> They have made all Germans everywhere into comrades, and accustomed them to this narcotic from their earliest age: in the Hitler youth, the SA, the Reichswehr, in thousands of camps and clubs--and in doing this they have driven out something irreplaceable that cannot be compensated for by any amount of happiness.

> Comradeship is part of war. Like alcohol, it is one of the great comforters and helpers for people who have to live under unbearable, inhuman conditions. It makes the intolerable tolerable. It helps us cope with filth, calamity, and death. It anesthetizes us. It comforts us from the loss of all the amenities of civilization. Indeed, that loss is one of its preconditions. It receives its justification from bitter necessities and terrible sacrifices. If it is separated from these, if it exercised only for pleasure and intoxication, for its own sake, it becomes a vice. It makes no difference that it brings a certain happiness. It corrupts and depraves men like no alcohol or opium. It makes them unfit for normal, responsible, civilian life. Indeed it is, at bottom, an instrument of decivilization. The general promiscuous comradeship to which the Nazis have seduced the Germans has debased this nation as nothing else could.

> —Sebastian Haffner, *Defying Hitler*, 2000

4. Group reasoning differs fundamentally from consensus decision-making, majority-vote decision-making, and polling.

The Symbiotic Group

All esoteric knowledge seems commonplace to ordinary minds, and this is nowhere more true than with the arcane knowledge of group symbiosis. To the person who assumes he knows how groups operate, this Perennialist wisdom appears lackluster and simplistic. But let the ordinary person attempt to apply these higher operating procedures in an actual group setting, and he'll quickly discover how complex and enigmatic they really are. If he's intelligent--and honest--enough to comprehend and acknowledge what occurs, he'll recognize that his untutored efforts are incapable of applying these hidden precepts successfully.

One of the first operating principles of an *enlightening group* is that the persons involved must be interested in *learning* how to cooperate in a group setting to accomplish goals chosen by all its members. The members must all be active participants, not mere observers. In enlightening groups the persons who set the goals are responsible for realizing them. It's only reasonable that those who share the responsibility of carrying out group goals should have the opportunity to share in planning what's to be done.

The other element included in that first principle is that the members must all be *eager to learn* the essential skills required for effective group participation, leading to the success of each member and of the organization as a whole. They must recognize that persons do not develop such specialized skills in the ordinary course of human experience--that they require technical training in the principles and procedures involved.

Granted, many current groups *claim* that all members are equal and that the group is working toward goals which will fulfill the needs of all participants. But as most of us experience, these claims are entirely spurious: there are hidden agendas, subtle--and sometimes not so subtle--manipulation of group processes, and almost always the president or boss has determined beforehand what the group is to finally agree on--his or her preselected outcome.

Once it's recognized by all participants in an enlightening group that this is to be a situation in which the goals are "owned" by all and work toward the fulfillment of all, not just a directing or ruling faction, then they recognize that this is something so new that it will require a very different type of training in a unique process of group reasoning.

The flawed principles of American representative democracy--subverted by a plutocracy-created U.S. Constitution--were doomed from the start because American citizens were never trained in democratic principles and were never meant to govern themselves. A fully effective society can only be formed out of competent individuals--those who know how to think and act for themselves and how to reason in a group to make group decisions.

Some early American leaders--such as Patrick Henry, George Mason, Luther Martin, John Francis Mercer, and Elbridge Gerry--were trained in consensus decision-making in face-to-face state assemblies where they hammered out ideas and proposals in a fashion similar to what we're exploring here. These specific leaders were trained in group reasoning and the result was the Declaration of Independence, the Bill of Rights, and such consensus-driven documents as the Pennsylvania state constitution of 1776. Also, all the persons mentioned above had learned from effective group training to think for themselves, so they all rejected the fatally flawed American Constitution when it was concocted by a few unscrupulous autocrats.

Group Reasoning

Group reasoning is the process by which an organization decides and plans as a whole--not just in theory or pretense but in actuality. Group reasoning involves, in the discussions and decisions of the group members, the same kind of process which an individual follows when he's reasoning effectively.

> The person whose judgment we trust is the one who does not act on impulse or authority or tradition. He is the one who takes into consideration present and past experience; who enriches his judgment with emotion, and who tempers his emotion with judgment. He is the one who honestly examines the evidence and weights various courses of action. His decision represents his conviction as to what is most worthwhile.
>
> —Harrison S. Elliott, *The Process of Group Thinking*, 1938

The aim of group decision-making is to secure the active participation of all members to the limit of their capacity in the conduct of all the group's activities.

The first thing groups have to realize is that effective organizational leadership is a specialized skill that must be learned; it's not an innate talent that persons possess by nature. Neither individual nor group reasoning is an endowment; they're the result of training and experience. To develop the capability of forming reliable and effective group decisions, we have to study relevant material and participate in specialized exercises.

> Independent, self-directing group conduct is . . . an achievement. Merely to offer democracy to a group does not mean that the group is able to conduct itself democratically. Just as individual independence comes gradually, first in more restricted and then in wider areas of life, so independence in a group comes gradually, first in more restricted and then in ever and ever widening areas of conduct. Whether the group be a family, a gang, a class in school, or a nation, it cannot change suddenly with any success from complete autocratic control to entirely independent self-direction.
>
> —Harrison S. Elliott, *The Process of Group Thinking*, 1938

The Principles and Processes of Group Reasoning

All participants must learn the principles and processes of group reasoning and apply them in specific activities for a group to be successful. However, what's regarded as "successful" in other kinds of groups is not what Perennialist teachings point to. An enlightening group operates for the purpose of *discovering the truth*. That may seem simplistic, but it's actually complex and very demanding. Most contemporary groups not only do not have truth as their goal, but assume that there's no such thing as truth. Truth is currently viewed as Thrasymachus and other sophists in Plato's dialogues erroneously defined it: whatever a person or a group *feels* or *thinks* is true. People not only believe there is no "objective" truth, independent of opinion or force, but that no group, large or small, could ever possibly *agree* on what is true.

So it should be clear that we're exploring a very different kind of reality: a group which works together to discover what is the truth for all members as a whole, agreeing on group values, goals, and modes of action. Such a group, when you experience one in operation, seems almost miraculous. Here are persons with very disparate backgrounds and experience all making sure that the issues important to the group are clearly defined and understood, that the important factors in the situations are brought out and recognized, that the possibilities as to what to do are stated and the real reasons for each felt, that the points of agreement are recognized and the differences understood and explored, that the discussion moves toward an integration of fact and opinion to a conclusion with which all agree. And then they make certain that attention is given to ways and means for putting the group decision into effect.

From that description it may begin to be clear how exceptional group reasoning really is and what unusual understanding and skill it requires. This is a process which brings all persons involved into a group discussion and group decision-making situation, with the more able, the more mature cooperatively interacting with the less able and the less mature, in a process in which all have the full opportunity to contribute in proportion to their ability. In such advanced group discussions, participants come with open minds, expecting to receive new light on problems in working with others in search for viable group solutions.

The ideas and proposals of each member of the group stimulate and modify the thinking of the others. When individual group members pool the knowledge and experience they have, more resources and more varied points of view are made available than when a single individual is thinking alone. Group members learn and develop as the group reasoning process continues, members sharing their thoughts and feelings with all the others, so their contributions increase in productivity and effectiveness.

Group Formation and Group Leadership

An enlightening group is formed by a Perennialist teacher. The novices (beginning students) and initiates (advanced students) must learn the erudite principles and procedures of group reasoning. The teacher's responsibility is to organize the group, orchestrate the ongoing group operations, bring the group to successful realizations of goals and understanding, and make sure that members are experiencing personal transformation while at the same time gaining increased skill in group reasoning processes.

The Perennialist teacher supervises the procedures of the group rather than dictating group conclusions and decisions. This is the catalytic element she interjects, encouraging the development of genuine freedom within the group as it learns to think and decide for itself. She sees that the novices and initiates develop skills in the various leadership processes, encouraging them to practice their skills in the ongoing operation. For example, an effective group of any type requires evaluation and monitoring: judging the effectiveness of specific participants and pointing out to them their counterproductive behaviors in reference to group process. The teacher encourages all participants to join in the evaluation and monitoring tasks, so she is not the only one carrying out these responsibilities, and the group quickly learns to evaluate and monitor itself.

Group reasoning is a highly complex fusion of many processes: cooperating, discussing, forming consensus, making changes in ideas and attitudes, arriving at decisions and goals, agreeing on ways and means to carry out goals and decisions, and forming solidarity of a positive kind.

Group Discussion

In group reasoning and decision-making, participants must freely share their ideas, thoughts, and feelings because it's necessary that each member of the group be aware of what the others are thinking and feeling. Consequently, group reasoning requires not only that the individuals consider the issues and questions, but that they share with each other the progress of their thinking.

The group leader makes sure that all ideas from the participants come into the circle of discussion on an equal basis, not as cases to be defended but as possible parts of the whole truth. The attitude of an enlightening group toward an expressed idea or feeling is the same as that of a genuine scientist toward what appears as a piece of suggestive evidence. The scientist doesn't immediately reject it and think of ways to disprove it. He considers it objectively, giving it full weight and examining its possibilities.

The enlightening group welcomes and encourages each suggestion, while at the same time drawing out its implications and subjecting those to evaluation. But all this is done in the manner in which scientific evidence is subjected to criticism: through impersonal, objective evaluation. An enlightening group has the earnest desire to see that it doesn't miss any contribution to the solution of the group issues or questions, no matter how unpromising they may seem when they first appear.

Group discussion involves the statement of all relevant issues and problems, within a specific context, in relation to the concerns of the group members.

In whatever form the problem faces the group, it is important first to recognize that it is not sufficient just to state the problem. Time must be taken for a description of the situation as it appears to various members of the group. It is not enough to open the discussion by a mere statement of the question. . . Even when the question is drawn sharply and is very specific, to go at once to discussion without time for understanding the issue in the setting it has for this particular group makes for needless argument and misunderstanding.

A question for discussion always represents a problem in a setting. There are differences in the actual setting and in the importance given to the various factors by one group as compared to another. This is why that which is seemingly the same question is never the same for two groups in different situations or indeed for the same group at different times. . . A problem must always be considered as it manifests itself to the particular group facing it.

There is another reason for taking time to describe the situation fully. If a group is to discuss a question in a rewarding manner, each person must not only be aware of the problem as it appears and feels to him but must also understand and feel it as it looks to the others in the group. The chairman does not know what the issue means to the members of the group, nor does any member of the group know what it means to the others, until there has been enough time for discussion so that there is this mutual understanding of the important factors in the situation and the problems involved. More than this, a description of the important factors means that various persons emphasize different factors until the situation and its problems come to take on meaning which they otherwise would not have. Unless time is taken really to develop the problem, important elements in the situation will be overlooked . . . Further, no problem has fully the glow of life and reality until the group has taken time to describe the situation and come to feel the problem anew.

These important factors in the situation become the tests to be applied to any solution to determine the degree to which it will seem to the group an answer to their problem. The search for the solution becomes the effort to meet the demands brought by these factors.

—Harrison S. Elliott, *The Process of Group Thinking,* 1938

Throughout the group discussion phase of the operation, the leader encourages participants to describe the issue or problem in the third person and without personal advocacy. Ideas are expressed objectively--"This appears to be a possible problem or solution"--instead of in personal language such as: "I believe" or "I propose." What the group is doing at this point is seeking to discover the best description of its problems, issues, and possible solutions, so participants can most effectively contribute through discriminating thoughts and suggestions. Using impersonal language in expressing their ideas, participants thus speak more objectively and at the same time more honestly, since their observations or suggestions are not seen as something they have to defend or advocate. An open-ended discussion involves participants avoiding early--or fixed--commitment to a point of view. Group reasoning involves modification of opinions and feelings as the process evolves.

Participants propose descriptions and solutions while also indicating *why* they consider the factors mentioned to be important and viable. This allows for various points of view to emerge and for the issues and problems to be defined in a variety of ways. This process avoids turning the discussion into an argument or debate, placing the proceedings on the plane of giving evidence for possible descriptions or solutions.

At some point during the discussion the leader will provide a summary, so the group can view its accomplishments in an objective manner. The summary will include an outline of the ideas, issues, problems and proposals that have emerged. The important factors are highlighted so that now the group can focus on possible solutions to the problems identified and ways to evaluate those solutions. The summary points out areas of agreement and disagreement and recognizes unifying factors which have arisen during the discussion.

The Search for Solutions to Group Problems

Following the summary of the proceedings, the group can begin to search for solutions to its identified problems.

The chairman must be sure to state the question of search for solution in relation to the summary of the first stage of the discussion so that it will be evident that it is not a general search for an answer to a general problem but a specific search for what to do in the situation under consideration. The point here is to be sure that every option or proposal which seems important to members of the group is recognized and considered, even though it may not seem important to the leader.

It is important also to be sure that any proposals of which a group is ignorant but which might appeal, are brought before it in some way. The proposed courses of actions must include not only those which are live options because of the experience of the group, but others which have grown out of the richer experience of other groups in the past or present. In short, the group seeks to meet its particular situation in the light of the best experience to date in meeting similar situations. Any person making a proposal makes it because on the basis of experience it seems to him likely to work out effectively in this situation.

— Harrison S. Elliott, *The Process of Group Thinking,*1938

Enlightening groups discover solutions which are for the members new-born, creative resolutions that arise out of the richness and versatility of the proposals brought before them. Originality and creativity in an enlightening group grow out of abundance rather than out of paucity of experience and thought.

As this phase proceeds, the group eliminates those possible solutions which are not real options, combines proposals which seem viable, and narrows the options to the most likely possibilities. As the discussion continues, the reasons given for a particular proposal are not mere intellectual arguments but concrete considerations charged with the emotion of real life. Discussion of the proposals involves a prediction of the likely consequences and comparison of these possible outcomes. In other words, the group is forming hypotheses.

The reasons for proposals are based on evidence based on experience or on predictions which have some foundation in reality. Proposals are tested by asking: Why does it appear that this possible solution would work out this way? What evidence is there in experience that this proposal would bring the results suggested?

The group can now begin to finalize its efforts and come to a conclusion.

All that has happened thus far in the discussion makes toward reaching a conclusion which will be considered best by all concerned and which will conserve the values and points of emphasis considered important. The conclusion includes always two parts: a decision as to a specific course of action which forms a definite answer to the problem; and the reasons that this has been chosen. It is 'what' we shall do, plus a 'why' we do it. The 'why,' the 'because,' represents the facts, the viewpoints, the goals or purposes on which the group is now united.

Integration represents the result of the magnifying of differences, of seeking to bring out into the open every contribution, of attempt to build into the conclusion the very best of all.

In reaching a conclusion, the group should search for some new alternative rather than merely make a choice from the possibilities which they saw when they began the discussion.

—Harrison S. Elliott, *The Process of Group Thinking*, 1938

"Now the body is not one member but many. If the foot should say, "Because I am not a hand I don't belong to the body," does that alter the fact that the foot is a part of the body? Of if the ear should say, "Because I am not an eye I don't belong to the body," does that mean that the ear really is no part of the body?

After all, if the body were all one eye, for example, where would be the sense of hearing? Or if it were all one ear, where would be the sense of smell? But God has arranged all the parts in the one body according to his design. For if everything were concentrated in one part, how could there be a body at all? The fact is there are many parts, but only one body. So that the eye cannot say to the hand, "I don't need you!" nor, again, can the head say to the feet, "I don't need you!" On the contrary, those parts of the body which have no obvious function are the more essential to health: and to those parts of the body which seem to us to be less deserving of notice we have to allow the highest honour of function. The parts which do not look beautiful have a deeper beauty in the work they do, while the parts which look beautiful may not be at all essential to life! But God has harmonised the whole body by giving importance of function to the parts which lack apparent importance, that the body should work together as a whole with all the members in sympathetic relationship with one another. So it happens that if one member suffers all the other members suffer with it, and if one member is honoured all the members share a common joy.

—1 Corinthians 12:14-26

The foregoing outline of the operations carried out by an enlightening group describes most--but not all--the processes of group reasoning. Ineffable alchemical, creative, and spiritual effects occur at the same time as the more easily explicable events.

The Alchemy of Group Symbiosis

When an enlightening group reaches a consensus decision, an alchemical process has occurred. The "solution" contains all the original elements in the group, but they've been magically modified in the process--combined but not lost. Something entirely unique and unforeseen has appeared. All the original elements in the group have been included in the procedures and outcome. Certain dross has been eliminated. All valuable elements have been included in a solution which is actually something entirely new. The unified outcome is different from any single contribution and yet includes the best from all the ideas, proposals and solutions presented. The conclusion is not necessarily an either/or dichotomous selection, it may be a combination or something entirely new.

The Creative Element in Enlightening Groups

It's impossible to understand the creative power of an enlightening group unless one has participated in the process.

> We need to see groups at work . . . to appreciate how the give and take of a pure discussion, which is not a debate, throws new light on old ideas, shifts emphases, corrects aberrations, and even softens emotional antagonisms. The die-hard debater ready to beat the world into submission finds that he is not facing opponents at all. The group is eager to get all that he has of value to contribute. A simple idea presented by a humble member is taken up with care and handled gently lest a promising infant be destroyed by too rough handling at the start. Such ideas caught up by the group grow to unexpected proportions, and make for cooperation in a search for truth. Groups made up of very ordinary people have proved essentially creative to a degree that could hardly have been hoped for beforehand.

—Harrison S. Elliott, *The Process of Group Thinking,* 1938

The Spiritual Domain

An enlightening group, through the direction of a Perennial teacher, operates in the spiritual dimension.

> A group reaches the spiritual plane when it is conducting its discussion in a recognition of and a search to conserve the very highest and best the group knows.

> When a group is seeking most earnestly to find what is best or truest to their highest conception; and when they are doing this in a situation of real concern in a spirit of fellowship, there is indeed a high level of spiritual experience.

> The group becomes dynamically spiritual when the members are willing not only to search for a course of action which will be true to the highest values they have recognized and the deepest meanings that have come to life for them, but when they are willing to reexamine these values and search for still higher and better purposes.

> Something happens which is in the highest sense dynamic when a group in fellowship and in confidence lays hold of the previously unreleased resources within itself. At such a time there comes insight as to what to do, and strength and ability to carry out the purposes, which represent more than the mathematical total of the resources of the members of the group when taken separately. Such release of spiritual power is a manifestation of the divine resources all around us which are at the command of all those who in a group process meet the conditions of spiritual creativity.

—Harrison S. Elliott, *The Process of Group Thinking,* 1938

Enlightening groups are harbingers of an earthly commonwealth toward which we aspire and at the same time reveal a heavenly fellowship which already has being in a celestial realm.

> Even though the commonwealth described does not exist in the terrestrial domain, there is a model of it in the sovereignty of the higher realm for anyone who wants to look at it and make himself its citizen on the strength of what he sees. It makes no difference whether it is or ever will be somewhere in the terrestrial realm, for he takes part in the practical affairs of that commonwealth in the higher realm and no other.
>
> —Plato, *Commonwealth X*, 592b

Because the destructive forces of tyranny and oppression seek to destroy all overt positive activities, enlightening groups led by Perennialist teachers operate somewhat "invisibly" at present. As the time arrives when new creative energies can help to build a commonwealth in which all human potential can be realized, the wisdom of these enlightening groups is now being made available to humankind. Part of the preparatory training for participation in enlightening groups is now being provided online.

Chapter Twenty-Two

Transformative Groups

By Norman D. Livergood

As the world plunges headlong into the maelstrom of totalitarianism and the collapse of civilization, Perennialist teachers organize Transformative Groups, making arcane wisdom available to humankind essential for the species' survival.

The Perennialist transformative group is one of two ordering structures most effective for adapting higher knowledge to the present time, the other being the enlightening group format. The arcane knowledge of personal transformation and group symbiosis is absolutely essential to humankind's survival and has been revealed by such Perennialist teachers as Hermes, Krishna, Pythagoras, Socrates, Plato, Jesus, Paul, and Boethius.

The Esoteric Teaching of Transformative Groups

Perennialist savants all teach the esoteric wisdom of *individual transformation, group solidarity, and group reasoning.* You may have wondered why advanced spiritual teachers all create close-knit coalitions of seekers and initiates--Egyptian hierophant temples, Pythagoras' community, Plato's Academy, the esoteric Christian communities, the Neo-Platonic academies in Alexandria, the Cathedral schools, St Bernard's Cistercian Order, the Cambridge Platonist group, and so on. There are multifarious reasons for this as we shall see, but three of the major purposes for forming a very select circle are:

- To provide a new organ of transformation utilizing a unique adaptation of the Perennial wisdom, to which students may seek admittance after undergoing prerequisite preparation

- So the teacher can create a hierarchy of levels within the group through which to carry on her transformative operations

- To teach, through experience, the veiled mysteries of how groups of people can think and interact together at a higher level of consciousness

Transformative groups--ageless spiritual aristocracies which disseminate wisdom to humankind in each historic era--conduct themselves according to Perennialist precepts. Thus, they contain in their very existence and modes of operation the mystery of how transformation is carried out through group activities and how human groups can function at the highest level.

Super-normal elements manifest themselves in all advanced Perennialist groups:

- The mystical state of group higher consciousness which occurs in Platonic dialectical interchange

- The paranormal capabilities experienced in enlightening groups

- The development of extra-normal cognition in physical exercises

These same paranormal phenomena become apparent whenever Perennialist knowledge of group symbiosis is put into practice.

This creative result [of higher group thinking] will take place in proportion as the group has reached in its discussion the spirit of worship, whether or not it is a religious group and uses this term. What happens is that a truly spiritual atmosphere pervades the group process. The essential difference between a group discussion which is truly religious and one which is irreligious is at this point: that, in a discussion which is religious, the group is earnestly seeking to find in any situation that which represents for that group the highest and best that they know or can discover.

—Harrison S. Elliott, *The Process of Group Thinking*, 1938

Like all esoteric knowledge, the principles of Perennialist transformation, group solidarity, and group reasoning seem prosaic and lackluster to the ordinary mind. This is one of the many reasons why esoteric teaching is reserved for those who have demonstrated the ability to understand and appreciate higher knowledge.

The Perennialist Principles of Distinct Human Groupings

The knowledge of how to organize students and followers into separate general (exoteric) and select (esoteric) groups is part of the hidden Perennialist wisdom concerning how humans must be arranged in order for them to realize their full potential. Plato saw "true philosophers" as a supra-human group distinct from the general public who had no interest in higher knowledge.

The genuine practitioners of philosophy will be but a small remnant . . . Those who belong to this small class have tasted how sweet and blessed a possession philosophy is. . . The many refuse to believe that philosophy is worthwhile, for they have never seen genuine philosophy realized; they have seen only a conventional imitation of philosophy, consisting of words artificially brought together, not like these of ours having a natural unity.

—Plato, *The Commonwealth*, Book 6

The Perennialist savant Jesus of Nazareth taught about an Empyreal Fellowship which he said is not visible because its essence is "within us." The Greek words referring to this Empyreal Fellowship in the New Testament have been mistranslated "Kingdom of heaven" or "Kingdom of God:"

- *basileia*: fellowship, brotherhood, governance, sovereignty, royal power, dominion, a rule or reign, kingdom, an exercise of authority
- *ouranos*: the realm of Higher Being--the Empyrean, heaven

As we examine Jesus' life and teachings, it is unmistakable that he was a sage within the Perennial Tradition proclaiming the sovereignty of the Empyreal Realm and organizing his followers in *transformative groups,* a general circle of followers and a more select cell of apostles. Jesus clearly made the distinction in his teachings between those that were for the general public and the esoteric, those reserved for a select group of initiates.

Then when they were by themselves, his close followers and the twelve asked about the teaching stories he used, and he told them: "The secret of The Empyreal Fellowship has been given to you. But to those who from lack of effort or interest are not deserving of receiving esoteric knowledge, everything remains in allegories, because even when they are allowed to see, they do not make the effort to discern the hidden wisdom; and when they're allowed to hear, they don't go beneath the surface to understand the deeper truth. They are not given more profound information, so that their rejection of knowledge will not make them any more blameworthy than is just."

So Jesus taught the masses his message through the use of teaching stories, through which their minds could comprehend at whatever level they were. He did not speak to the people in general at all without using allegories, although in private he divulged the esoteric meaning of his teachings to his disciples.

—*Mark 4*

The Necessity of Transformative Groups

Before exploring the hidden wisdom concerning individual transformation, it's necessary for us to comprehend why such transformative groups are absolutely essential relative to present circumstances.

- As the world is falling apart, it is only such advanced brotherhoods that have the higher knowledge as to how to transform human character while at the same time preserving the essentials of human civilization.

- Transformative groups provide the most effective organizational and strategic means for struggling against personal and social ignorance and tyranny.

- These coalitions of advanced thinkers provide effective laboratories for experimentation and training in consensus decision-making which will produce innovative concepts and procedures to use in resuscitating human culture.

- These initiate echelons provide a sustaining environment of open, positive interpersonal interchange in which individuals can develop to their fullest.

- Transformative fellowships provide security in numbers and commitment.

- Transformative groups provide the substructure of a new society for future generations.

These groupings of initiates provide a supportive experimental environment in which new ideas, art forms, and approaches can be tried, tested, and nurtured.

The Requisite Capabilities of Transformative Groups

Initiate echelons or transformative groups are composed of persons who have developed to the point of possessing super-normal powers:

1. Social and spiritual awareness

2. The capability of working in the spiritual world to bring about effects in the material world

3. The ability to commune with kindred souls

4. An awareness of and a participation in the struggle between the old world and the new world

The four areas above are explored in detail in the co-author's (Livergood) new book: *Portals to Higher Consciousness*. In this chapter, we'll concentrate on transformative operations related to an advanced group.

The difficulty with discussing transformative groups is that these esoteric fellowships are completely unknown to and beyond the comprehension of the average person, yet most people assume they know what they are when we speak of them. They presume that the phrase "transformative groups" refers to ordinary collections of people. As is often the case with uninformed people, the mere fact that they're familiar with the words describing a reality leads them to assume that they comprehend what that reality is. Since they feel they know the meaning of the words "transformative" and "groups," they assume they fully comprehend what "transformative groups" must mean. It's similar to an unenlightened person presuming they understand precisely what is meant by "Platonic dialectic" because they believe they understand what is meant by the terms "Platonic" and "dialectic."

The Varieties of "Spiritual" Groups

It's necessary, therefore, to distinguish between various types of groups which claim to be "spiritual" or religious. It's difficult for many people to realize that most of the groups that claim to assist individuals develop higher awareness are in fact counterfeits. Participants in such groups may *feel* they're "making great personal improvement," or "becoming closer to God," or "getting in touch with their inner self," or some such self-delusion. But the ultimate test is whether or not the person experiences *genuine transformation* or not.

Transformation is the touchstone of spiritual development. Transformation refers to:

- Metamorphosis of a person from one level of consciousness to a higher one

- Regeneration: the reunion of personal consciousness with the Universal Mind involving "spiritual death" and rebirth

  - Actual transmutation of the psychic and physical elements within our present frail and imperfect nature into a divinized condition

  - Achieving contact with a Higher Consciousness so that one experiences intuition, inspiration, and bliss

What is achieved is not some nice, minor revision in one's mental framework or one's behavior, it is a physical and mental rebirth into the full consciousness of one's divine nature and powers as a "Son or Daughter of God."

Transformation involves the constant, unending endeavor of discovering aspects of immaturity or sleep in yourself and rising above those to a higher awareness. One of the essential ways of telling if you're experiencing transformation is if you're regularly discovering traits and behaviors in yourself of which you were previously unaware, negative elements that controlled you without your being cognizant of them.

In reference to our touchstone of transformation we can distinguish between various types of groups which claim to be "spiritual:

- Cults: groups created by deluded, egomaniacal persons who create dependency in their followers, manipulating them for their own selfish interests, making the group into a personality cult

- Religious coteries dominated by self-appointed "spiritual masters," priests, ministers, rabbis, mullahs, or "counselors" who produce phony feelings in their victims of "spiritual upsurge," "release from mental turmoil," "merging with other people," and other bogus sentiments and impressions--to the extreme of brainwashing the followers to destroy their religious or political enemies

- Conduit groups which transmit transformative knowledge but are affected by the knowledge to a limited degree, sometimes almost not at all

- Deteriorated or derelict groups: those which once possessed a measure of transformative knowledge or force but have lost the original impetus or endowment

- Genuine transformative groups whose teachers have been able to attain personal transmutation and have achieved the capability of assisting their students to attain personal transformation as well

Conduit groups exhibit interesting characteristics, serving as channels through which transformative knowledge is transmitted, while experiencing little or no personal growth. These groups serve a limitedly useful purpose in making higher knowledge available to others, whether or not they benefit from their action. Very often such groups are created by a self-deluded "master" who has experienced little personal transformation and is incapable of assisting his followers to achieve spiritual regeneration.

The Perennial Tradition possesses a transcendent power whose operations are amazing to observe. Even when false teachers try, unsuccessfully, to distort or misuse its concepts and methods, the tradition is able to use this failed effort as part of its teaching to show students how *not* to behave and how its detractors inadvertently assist its own operations. An interesting example of the Perennial Tradition's indirect operation is how the death of a teacher becomes a part of the total process of transformation.

"But if a Sufi Teacher dies, or there is a gap in the teaching, what then? The interesting thing is that that very gap is a part of the training. You may explain certain things to a child: shall we say tell him not to do certain things. Then you will pretend to go out of the house and observe him. According to how well he has learned, so will he react. . .

After the disappearance from the field of a Sufi teacher, the followers will divide themselves into groups, in accordance with their strengths and weaknesses. Some will assume control of others. They may be good or bad, and this will be shown by their reactions to the second teacher when he arrives. If they realise that he is their teacher, then they have merely been developing themselves and can mature. But if they have become atrophied, they will be too blind to recognise the *baraka* (spiritual force) of the very man for whose appearance they have been prepared. They may attach themselves, in default, to some other group. Again, well and good: providing that they return to the mainstream of teaching when it is offered to them again. . . . They will realise, if they are sufficiently developed, that the person who appears to be the 'second' teacher is in reality the first in importance. If, however, they have developed a too-strong attachment for the husk, they will try to guard the husk, and they will be lost to the activity.

—Zealander Abdur-Rahman Siddiqi, "Finding, Losing and Finding the Way,"
The Sufi Mystery (Edited by N. P. Archer)

A genuine teacher does not begin teaching or forming a transformative group out of personal desire or egotism. Her own transformation process, directed by her teacher (which we recognize may be her everyday life-experience or previous transformative material) unfolds in such a way that her *work* leads to her receiving inspiration to take up teaching and forming a group. Specious "teachers" concoct teaching systems to magnify their sense of self-importance. With a genuine teacher, the need for involvement with a teaching group emerges through the natural—and supernatural--course of events.

Transformation as the Touchstone

By using transformation as our touchstone, we're able to discern the precise nature of groups which claim to be "spiritual." This assumes that persons applying the touchstone actually understand the essence of transformation and have themselves experienced spiritual death and regeneration to a higher level of awareness and power. If we discover no genuine transmutation and spiritual growth in the leaders and members of a group, we can be sure we're dealing with a cult, ordinary religious group, conduit group, or derelict organization--the blind leading the blind.

Transformation is an ongoing, never-ending process. If we don't see continual change and improvement in the leaders and members, then the group has devolved to an inert, impotent organization--no matter how alive and thriving it may seem on the outside. The counterfeit organization may achieve widespread fame, publishing books, presenting lectures, its leaders appearing on TV talk shows; but its inner barrenness and deceit will be clearly evident to the spiritually discerning.

There is no worse moral transgression than to imagine that an inner and true virtue does not exist to be perceived, by falsely identifying and attributing merit to an external appearance as that inner and true virtue.

From our discussion, it should be clear that the prospective student has his work cut out for him in sorting through the many counterfeit groups and teachers to find the authentic. He should view this as a challenge in developing a genuine capability of discerning the Real.

Specific changes in attitude and perspective are necessary before a seeker can hope to be admitted to study with a genuinely transformative teacher. Among other things, the seeker must realize that "things are not what they seem" and that how he sees himself is largely an ego-serving illusion, among other things. Perennialist teachers make it clear that preparatory screening and study is required before a would-be student can benefit from or be admitted to advanced teaching. An applicant to a program of study must have certain qualifications, just as a person applying for admission to a medical school must have undergone prerequisite training in biology, chemistry, anatomy, and other essential fields of study.

The ancient Gnosis we may define as that knowledge of the nature of Man and of his place in the Universe which transcends the mere appearance of things as presented to the senses and the intellect, and which contacts Reality in a region of pure Truth. The beginning of this knowledge, therefore, is the realization that things are not what they seem; and no one who is a crude realist . . . can make any approach to this super-knowledge.

—William Kingsland, *The Gnosis or Ancient Wisdom in the Christian Scriptures*

A transformative group thus provides two kinds of material for students:

- Teachings of a preparatory nature to assist the prospective student to make essential changes and improvements in his character, attitudes, and behavior

- Transformative material which is used in instructing students after they are admitted to an advanced program of study

"Perennialist knowledge is like a powerful medicine, which cures strong bodies and kills weak organisms. At one and the same time, this puissant wisdom elevates the mentation which can understand, overcoming its shortcomings, while also killing the weak understanding of some people."

—Ibn Hazm, al-Tahiri, a Perennialist teacher of Cordova

We can be certain that a group that omits screening and doesn't require preparation of a prospective student, has the characteristics of one of the false "spiritual groups" we discussed above. Since such a group does not have the capability of engaging in genuine transformative operations, it's reduced to conditioning the mind of its victims to accept its dogmas without thought. The benighted converts will be programmed to blind loyalty to the leader.

It might seem that such fake groups would be easily recognizable, but if we examine the actual workings of most organizations--professions, educational institutions, businesses, among many others--we'll discover that they have essentially the same characteristics as the false "spiritual groups" in terms of how they recruit, train, manage, and evaluate their members.

A genuine transformative teacher must provide some kind of experiential material at every stage of a study program. Even preparatory material must include procedures which allow the prospective student to experience what transformation actually involves. A teacher who merely talks about transformation, providing nothing but written material of a didactic nature, is one who clearly has not attained personal transformation himself and doesn't know how to assist students achieve spiritual insight. The Perennialist teaching operation is not the mere delivery of a body of knowledge, its essence is providing whatever is needed to assist students in their spiritual development, which must include experiential operations: study material and active exercises.

Counterfeit teachers give the excuse that experiential exercises can only be made available in a face-to-face situation in a specially chosen group. There are some experiential procedures, it is true, which can only be carried out in a context of personal interchange. But a genuinely transformative teacher provides experiential material throughout his teaching, including his preparatory operations--especially since both asynchronous and real-time interchange is now possible via the Internet.

Students must have enough intelligence and insight to know that a genuine teacher is not going to be a popular figure. He will not be found on prime-time television. Wealth and fame will not be of interest to him. However, because wealth and fame are the primary contemporary cultural criteria of success, a genuine teacher may *make it appear* that he is interested in these to deflect unsuitable students from pursuing him as a teacher.

In fact, a genuine teacher may use any appropriate means to discourage unsuitable students, so that students are required to develop finely-tuned discernment to "find" an authentic teacher. The student is learning to use his inner sense of discernment to discover a teacher whose reality is authentic.

It is not a teacher's responsibility to proclaim himself a great spiritual authority--quite the opposite. A genuine teacher will seem to most people to be a failure--because he is not preaching to thousands in Yankee Stadium like Billy

Graham. He will seem excessively unassuming and retiring, because the popular model for a guru is self-advertisement and self-promotion of every possible kind.

There was once a young woman who sought out a Perennialist teacher and said to her: "I wish to achieve enlightenment--how can I achieve my wish?"

The Perennialist teacher heaved a great sigh and replied:

"There was once a young woman, just like you. She wished to achieve enlightenment and this wish had great power. Suddenly, she found herself sitting, as I am, with a young woman, like you, seated before her, asking, 'How can I achieve enlightenment?'"

Spiritual Resonance

One of the primary transformative factors in the Perennial Tradition is called "resonance." "We may describe an oscillator as any object that moves in a regular, periodic manner. We may call a vibrating string an oscillator, or a weight hanging from a spring, or a pendulum--anything that performs a repetitive, periodic movement, that is, vibrates. We may generalize and say that oscillators produce a sound or a note, whether audible or not, as long as they alter their environment in a periodic manner. That environment may be tissue, as in the heart-aorta oscillating system, water, air, electrical fields, gravitational fields, or anything else.

"Suppose we tune two violins, then put one of them on the table and play a note on the other. If we watch carefully we shall see that the same string that we are playing on one violin is also humming on the violin that we placed on the table. Clearly, there is a 'sympathetic resonance' between the two."

—Itzhak Bentov, *Stalking the Wild Pendulum*

The Perennialist teacher sends out a certain "signal" or "frequency" through his special knowledge of how to operate at a higher level of consciousness. He will produce finely tuned written material, images, and psychic missives that possess a specific frequency, which will resonate with those students who are "attuned" to his messages. Resonance operates unrestrictedly to bring a teacher and a student together who are of the same spiritual frequency. Which means that if you have within you the resonance of deceit or greed, it is to that kind of teacher, with those same inner qualities, that you will be drawn. Like calls to like, truth to truth.

Bees have a natural instinct for sensing a flower through scent. They do not lose this sensing capability, so they do not have to be told about it or learn how to use it. There are very few humans today who are perceptive enough to sense the resonance of a Perennialist teacher. This is a capability which has become dormant through ignorance and neglect. Not many humans are aware of this power and have to receive a teaching about it to make them aware of it's dormant existence.

Different types of seekers are drawn to corresponding types of groups. Those prospective students who want excitement and emotional stimulation will be attracted to a derivative group of the kind that appeals to their weaknesses.

Qualities Required in a Seeker

We are examining how a Perennialist teacher operates to make it possible for a properly attuned student to "find" him. Before a seeker can approach a genuine teacher he must develop the inner desire for personal transformation. In other words, he must develop a kind of *divine discontent*. He must have a genuine--not half-hearted--desire to improve himself—a sense that he is less than he could be, is less in control of himself than he should be, that much of what he thinks he knows really isn't true, and an awareness of just how much he doesn't know.

This implies that the prospective student must be a genuine seeker--a person who is searching for a teacher who will help him achieve transformation. It is not for the teacher to in any way seek the prospective student--through trying to appear erudite or wise or "brilliant." Only if the student possesses the awareness that he must humbly *request* help from the teacher will he be able to approach him. Any other attitude--say the feeling that the teacher should feel honored to have such an outstanding student--makes it impossible for him to approach the teacher in a functional manner.

The teacher knows that the seeker has a *need* to ask humbly to receive correctly and successfully. He is aware that prospective students approach the teaching with improper attitudes. For example, some persons assume that the mere delineation of prerequisites for a program of study is a veiled attempt on the part of a teacher to solicit students.

The student must be discerning enough to realize that he does not know how to approach the teacher, what he needs, how he can learn to learn, or what the process will be in his transformation.

Nobody can hope to arrive at illumination if he thinks that he knows what it is, and believes that he can achieve it through a well-defined path which he can conceive at the moment of starting.

—Idries Shah, *The Sufis*

From the beginning of the process of seeking a genuine teacher, through entry into an advanced study group, to personal effort toward spiritual awareness, both the teacher and the students must constantly work to achieve personal transformation. At times, one's special "teacher" is ordinary life-experience itself. This comes about through realizing and acting on certain spiritual truths:

- The Divine has the power to take all human actions and use them to assist us in our evolution.

- The Divine manifests through everyone and everything.

- All persons receive exactly the experiences from which they can best learn what they need for their personal evolution--and at the same time for the evolution of all humankind.

- The Divine creates a world which provides precisely coordinated learning experiences transcendentally matched to our current needs and capabilities.

Everything stands for God and you see only God in all the world. . . If this is lacking, if you are not looking for God and expecting him everywhere, and in everything, you lack the [inner] birth.

—Meister Eckhart

The following extra-dimensional operation illustrates the principles delineated in this chapter. It involves both a transformative teaching story (which the reader may perhaps actually experience) and a situational learning episode at the same time.

The Treasure Is There to Be Served, Not to Be Stolen

Three applicants for admission into an advanced study program are attending the Thursday evening group meeting of a Perennialist teacher. They are all three unaware of what they need, but eager to ask questions and solicit special attention from the teacher. As the meeting opens, the teacher says to the students.

"Of the four new persons experiencing this transformative operation, one will receive nothing, one will discern some of its meaning, another will comprehend more of its effects, and the fourth, if she actually experientially enters into the episode, will gain the ability to derive her own understanding of the operation, beyond mere knowledge of its details."

The teacher then turns to the three applicants. "Promise me one thing, and I will provide you what you need for personal transformation."

The three applicants readily agree.

"You shall," continues the teacher, "promise never to ask me to do anything *for* you, then I'll provide you everything you need."

One of the applicants immediately exclaims, "I knew it, you're nothing but a fraud, just like my friends said you were!" He leaves immediately.

The second applicant says: "From your statement I understand, for the first time, that I am incapable of knowing what I need."

The third applicant replies: "Thank you. From what you have said I understand that you cannot do anything *for* me, only provide me prescribed experiences which will help me to achieve transformation along with my own efforts."

"Yes," the teacher agrees, "but the prescription is non-refillable."

After an extended moment of silence, one of the students, after being recognized by the teacher, asks: "Who is the fourth person of whom you spoke, and how will she have gained understanding beyond knowledge?"

"The fourth person," the teacher replies, "is you, the reader of this transformative operation. You will have gained understanding if you entered into the experience with the proper attitude and desire."

Chapter Twenty-Three

The Saving Remnant

By Norman D. Livergood

In each era, small groups of advanced thinkers have helped humankind to evolve, revealing what persons are capable of, while battling the forces of degradation, ignorance, and indifference. But the ongoing struggle against negative elements is ultimately insufficient--as one form of mental, social, and spiritual tyranny replaces another in historic succession. *Humans must at last attain the understanding and capability that will enable them to create a higher social order—a new culture.*

The only viable way for this to occur is for an advanced group to constitute itself as a "saving remnant" that will leaven the larger society with its higher knowledge and power, creating a new culture—a commonwealth.

In chapter nineteen we examined how the realization of a commonwealth must come about. In this chapter we're concentrating on the role of a saving remnant in assisting in this process of creating a benevolent social order—a new culture.

In a time when a demonic international cabal tyrannizes the ordinary world, we wonder how humankind will ever gain the understanding and the power to throw off this reign of terror and establish a commonwealth for the good of all its members.

From time immemorial, humans have been dominated by small despotic groups characterized by ruthlessness and depravity, with a benevolent leader here and there thrown in for good measure. A somewhat progressive industrial capitalism that came into dominance in the eighteenth century has devolved into a baleful vulture capitalism and a positive but flawed American democracy has now degenerated into a barbaric totalitarianism.

As people have been mentally conditioned in autocratic social control and interaction, "the struggle of all against all," the knowledge and capability relative to effective group solidarity and decision-making has essentially been lost.

The Concept and Realization of the Saving Remnant

The concept of the "saving remnant" is constituted by allegory, metaphor, and analogy, deriving its meaning from a number of sources. In this chapter's use of the concept, "saving" does not refer to orthodox religious "salvation" whereby a believer has faith in and devotion to a "savior" who "delivers" him from an angry deity who wishes to punish him for his sins.

In our use of the term, "saving" refers to protecting, maintaining, preserving, or rediscovering something of value. The concept of remnant in this chapter refers to a small surviving, transformative, and enlightening group, in somewhat the same terms used by Gerald Sykes in his book *The Saving Remnant.*

> A Remnant means, both originally and in the sense in which it is used here, a group of people who have survived or can survive a great catastrophe, while an elite means a group of socially superior persons. The origin of one word is religious, of the other social. In its flowering a society may produce an elite. It is only in a time of extreme trial that it is called upon to produce a Remnant. . . .

A saving remnant, then, is a small group which discovers, applies, and disseminates transmutational principles within its own domain, proving the truth and efficacy of its precepts by its own practices, then leavening the larger culture within which it exists, creating a commonwealth.

The Necessity of a Saving Remnant

As the world descends into anarchy, it is only such an advanced brotherhood that has the higher knowledge of how to transform human character while at the same time preserving the essentials of human civilization. An enlightening, transformative group provides the most effective organizational and strategic means for struggling against personal and social ignorance and tyranny.

This coalition of advanced thinkers provides an effective laboratory for experimentation and training in consensus decision-making which will produce innovative concepts, procedures, and leaders to assist in building an advanced human culture. This initiate echelon provides a sustaining environment of open, positive interpersonal interchange in which individuals can develop to their fullest.

A transformative fellowship provides security in numbers and commitment and provides the pattern for a new society for future generations. This grouping of initiates provides a supportive experimental environment in which new ideas, art forms, and approaches can be tried, tested, proved, nurtured, and disseminated.

A transformative group--an ageless spiritual aristocracy which disseminates wisdom to humankind in each historic era--conducts itself according to Perennialist precepts. Thus, it contains in its very existence and modes of operation the mystery of how transformation is carried out through group activities and how human groups can function at the highest level.

The Felt Need for Preservation

The progress of civilization has largely been the work of creative and conscientious men and women, forgotten by history and derided by power brokers and scholastics. The criminal cabal has been able to destroy the minds of a great number of Americans, to the point that they are blind to the debauched, lethal condition of the nation and the world. They're aware of almost nothing of what's happening in the world, what's happening to the psyches of the world's peoples, and therefore see no need for preservation.

Since the brain-dead masses throughout the world see no need for deliverance from the totalitarian cabal, they make exceptional people--those who could rescue them from the death-throes of their suicidal ignorance--superfluous and unrecognized.

What further evidence do we need of the degrading ends of our acquisitive existence, when it has reduced our defenses and self-justifications to a level which, by any normal standard of judgment, has lost all the essential marks of civilization? What shall we say of ourselves, and of our philosophy and 'way of life,' when, looking for the spokesmen of the best in the traditions of Western culture, we find that we have made them into *superfluous men*? How many of those who are acknowledged to be individuals of cultivation and sensibility are able to make their voices heard? How many try to make themselves heard? You hear a Bertrand Russell in England, a Lewis Mumford in the United States. A Schweitzer speaks from Africa. There are one or two more, perhaps, who would qualify as of this group, but the Saving Remnant among contemporaries is indeed a desperately tiny few. . .

Here, you might say, in Gerald Sykes' phrase, is 'the politics of shipwreck,' which is the only kind of politics worth practicing, these days. [Sykes'] conception of the Remnant reminds us somewhat of the endeavor of Pythagoras in founding his school at Krotona. The Greek philosopher sought to train individuals in a way of life that would enable them to go out into society and lift it to a higher level by the leverage of their personal example.

—Walker Winslow, "The Irrelevance of the Cold War," *MANAS Journal,*
November 28, 1962

The saving remnant assists the larger culture to recognize its critical need for knowledge and awareness by which it can be delivered from the murderous intentions of the current cabal which is running rampant over the face of the earth.

The mass society must first recover from its moral insensibility, and this can happen only as more and more of its members stop submitting to mass ompulsions. The Remnant, in short, must grow.

—Winslow, Op. Cit.

"In an essay on this subject, Albert Jay Nock identified the few who understand this problem as members of what he, following the Book of Isaiah, called the Saving Remnant, in which he placed Plato and Marcus Aurelius along with the Hebrew prophet. To structure his analysis, Nock rendered Isaiah into modern English. (The time of Isaiah was after the rule of King Uzziah of Israel, who reigned for fifty-two years [808-756 B.C.], a period of notable prosperity.) Nock relates:

In the year of Uzziah's death, the Lord commissioned the prophet to go out and warn the people of the wrath to come. "Tell them what a worthless lot they are," He said. "Tell them what is wrong, and why, and what is going to happen unless they have a change of heart and straighten up. Don't mince matters. Make it clear that they are positively down to their last chance. Give it to them good and strong, and keep on giving it to them. I suppose perhaps I ought to tell you." He added, "that it won't do any good. The official class and their intelligentsia will turn up their noses at you, and the masses will not even listen. They will all keep on in their own ways until they carry everything down to destruction, and you will probably be lucky if you get out with your life."

Isaiah had been very willing to take on the job; in fact, he had asked for it; but this prospect put a new face on the situation. It raised the obvious question why, if all that were so, if the enterprise were to be a failure from the start, was there any sense in starting it? "Ah," the Lord said, "you do not get the point. There is a Remnant there that you know nothing about. They are obscure, unorganized, inarticulate, each one rubbing along as best he can. They need to be encouraged and braced up, because when everything has gone completely to the dogs, they are the ones who will come back and build up a new society, and meanwhile your preaching will reassure them and keep them hanging on. Your job is to take care of the Remnant, so be off now and set about it.'

—"The Weight of Orthodoxy," *MANAS*, March 21, 1984

Humans must overcome their tendency to ignore and marginalize persons with wisdom, gaining essential respect for those adepts capable of preserving civilization and developing a higher social order. The desire for a commonwealth must come out of the understanding that other seemingly simpler and more efficient principles of social order lead inevitably to the oppression of society by a tyrannous faction. We gain this understanding by experiencing oppressive forms of despotism in the family, the workplace, and the community. By experiencing the oppression and life-destruction which these forms entail we gain an intense desire for the commonwealth way of life.

Unlike Isaiah's concept of the saving remnant as the "obscure, unorganized, inarticulate" residue that happens to survive catastrophe, our concept of a transformative, enlightening group in this chapter refers to a deliberately created, carefully developed grouping with advanced knowledge and capability.

A Deliberately Created Saving Remnant

Every civilization has contained within it the principle that certain advanced persons have constituted the means by which a society has been preserved and advanced: Sargon of Babylonia, Hermes (Thoth) of Egypt, Moses of the Hebrew nations, Pericles of Greece, and the Roman Emperor Marcus Arelius--to name only a few. At some point in the nation's history the people have been "taken captive" by some hostile, malevolent force, necessitating the extraordinary efforts of a Patriarchal Leader to preserve a remnant by which to rebuild the society. Much of this epochal history is mere myth, with little if any foundation in reality and is always based on the happenstance of a Preserver appearing on the scene.

But in truth, as we've explored in previous chapters, throughout history humankind *has* been preserved and its mind and spirit advanced through the arcane wisdom of Perennialist teachers. They have initiated the great impulses that move humanity forward, leaving their mark, as in the examples of Perennialist-inspired leaders like Frederick II and teachers such as Diotima, Hypatia, Boethius, Rumi, and Bernard of Clairvaux. "Great persons" have been a force for good throughout human history, as Thomas Carlyle, H. L. Mencken and others have made clear.

But never has an individual leader or a group been able--yet--to develop a *lasting* civil order based on the principle of serving the interests of all its citizens. In the history of the United States, Thomas Jefferson and Franklin D. Roosevelt saved the country from collapsing into totalitarianism (Federalist party tyranny) and economic disaster (the Great Depression of 1929). But America was soon again overpowered by domestic and European moneyed interests in the nineteenth century, represented by the Belmonts and the Rothschilds, and the result was the American Civil War and the severe depression of 1893. Since the presidency of Franklin D. Roosevelt, the international cabal, typified by the Rockefellers, the British royals, and Harriman interests--including their Bush puppets--have controlled the American economic and political systems to the detriment of the people, while amassing great wealth and power for themselves. Even worse, the demonic cabal now has seized power through the coup d'etats of JFK's assassination and the 2000 and 2004 rigged elections, and threatens to retain unending power through violence and corruption.

We are historically at a time, therefore, when we can no longer merely hope and wait for a "Great Leader" to come along, someone who might pull us out of our present catastrophic condition. If humankind is to be preserved from utter destruction by this demonic cabal, we must deliberately create a saving remnant that will rescue us from our plight, an advanced group which will demonstrate higher knowledge, disseminating this wisdom through which to build a new culture in which the good of all its members is the operating principle.

Getting the Concepts and the Facts Straight

One of the reasons why ignorant, ill-intentioned, and cabal-financed frauds such as Karl Popper and Leo Strauss have attacked Plato is because he was forthright enough to reveal the reality of democracy--that it is in actuality the manipulation of the masses by an elite group that fools the common people into thinking they're ruling when they aren't.

Plato had seen this form of swindle practiced on the citizens of Athens, and had witnessed the deadly results of such a fraud when a pseudo-democratic group sentenced his teacher and friend Socrates to death on trumped-up charges.

Plato provides the best solution regarding the tensions between various factions in a society and how best to order a nation to benefit all citizens. A nation, Plato recognized, can no more be governed by "the people" than a ship at sea can be controlled by the crew or passengers. Leadership--of a ship or a nation-state--requires special expertise that can only be gained by knowledge and experience. A society, Plato recognized, is always ruled by an elite, of whatever kind.

If we examine history with a discerning eye, we discover that power and initiative have always been exercised by a cohesive minority (elite) who are marked off from the mass of the population by some particular skill, quality, or insight.

Human beings do not organize themselves spontaneously; things only happen when a small group decides to act in moving the larger collection forward. Whether it be a book club or a nation, someone has to decide what the group will do, who will be members and who won't, when and where it will meet, and all the other minutiae that most members of a collective never suspect have to be done. Most human beings have neither the time, the interest, nor the opportunity to act unless led by a small elite.

> In all societies-from societies that are very meagerly developed and have barely attained the dawnings of civilization, down to the most advanced and powerful societies-two classes of people appear--a class that rules and a class that is ruled. The first class, always the less numerous, performs all political functions, monopolizes power and enjoys the advantages that power brings, whereas the second class, the more numerous, is directed and controlled by the first, in a manner that is more or less legal, now more or less arbitrary and violent.
>
> —Gaetano Mosca, *The Ruling Class*

The term "elite" is a neutral term, referring to any small leadership group, whether its goals are positive or negative relative to the larger collective it controls.

> Human society is not homogeneous, it is made up of elements which differ more or less, not only according to the very obvious characteristics such as sex, age, physical strength, health, etc., but also according to less observable, but no less important, characteristics such as intellectual qualities, morals,

diligence, courage, etc. . . . Just as one distinguishes the rich and poor in society even though income increases gradually from the lowest to the highest, one can distinguish the elite in a society, the part which is aristocratic, in the etymological sense, and a common part . . . The notion of this elite is dependent on the qualities which one seeks in it. There can be an aristocracy of saints, an aristocracy of brigands, an aristocracy of scholars, an aristocracy of thieves, etc.

—Pareto, *Manual of Political Economy*

A commonwealth must be lead by a philosophical aristocracy, Plato maintained. Those best able to direct the course of a society are those who are trained in the search for wisdom (philosophy) and live their lives as protectors of the people. But instead of recognizing this insight as the guide for a nation-state, throughout history small groups of ignorant, self-deluded, power-mad pretenders have seized political-economic-social control, ignoring those who truly know how to order a society.

Plato recognized that a nation would have to be composed of extraordinarily intelligent people to put philosopher-leaders in charge of their public institutions. Nonetheless, Plato contended that only if persons seeking true wisdom (philosophers) were the guardians of society would all people prosper, because philosophers seek the good of all the people in a society instead of a wealthy few.

Every step in human progress--social and spiritual--has been brought about by a handful of innovators who have discovered new and more productive ways of carrying out necessary tasks. The new methods and concepts both revise and replace the older, traditional techniques and ideas. Innovators, from Socrates to Jesus to Einstein, have been perceived by traditionalists as anti-social revolutionaries.

So history, namely change, has been mainly due to a small number of "seers,"--really gropers and monkeyers--whose native curiosity outran that of their fellows and led them to escape here and there from the sanctified blindness of their time.

—James Harvey Robinson, *The Mind in the Making: the Relation of Intelligence to Social Reform,* 1921

Previous Efforts Toward Commonwealth

A considerable number of utopian groups have attempted to create a more exemplary society: New Harmony, Amana, Brook Farm, Oneida, to name but a few. Similar efforts toward a benevolent social order have been made by more advanced persons and groups such as Pythagoras' community at Krotona, Plato's Academy, Jesus' preaching of the sovereignty of a Higher Realm, Hypatia's Neo-Platonic school at Alexandria, and the colonial leaders' creation of the United States. It may seem that these previous, unsuccessful attempts by a variety of groups to create a lasting commonwealth prove that such a goal is unrealistic. The reality is quite otherwise.

The efforts by the utopian societies were doomed to failure from the beginning because of their rigid adherence to preconceived dogmas and their authoritarian social structures. Whether it be the doctrinaire socialism of Robert Owens, George Ripley's dogma of the abolition of domestic servitude, or the unyielding doctrines of perfectionism and "male continence" on the part of John Humphrey Noyes, dogmatic creeds and prejudices led to the inevitable failure of these ventures.

The creation of the United States Constitution through a coup d'etat of a tyrannous group lead by Alexander Hamilton and John Adams, bent on creating a document which would favor the rich and powerful, doomed American "democracy" to failure from the beginning.

Earlier efforts by Perennialist teachers or those inspired by Perennialist teachings were primarily for the purpose of preserving humankind and assisting in its intellectual and spiritual advancement and evolution. In some instances, principles and practices of a commonwealth were articulated by these advanced groups, such as Plato's *Commonwealth*, but the purpose of those efforts was not to create an actual new society but to assist in developing humankind's intellectual and philosophical capabilities so that a commonwealth could be created when that became a possibility and a necessity.

The philosopher remains quiet, minds his own affair, and, as it were, standing aside under shelter of a wall in a storm and blast of dust and sleet and seeing others filled full of lawlessness, is content if in any way he may keep himself free from iniquity and unholy deeds through this life and take his departure with fair hope, serene and well content when the end comes." "Well," he said, "that is no very slight thing to have achieved before taking his departure." "He would not have accomplished any very great thing either," I replied, "if it were not his fortune to live in a state adapted to his nature. In such a state only will he himself rather attain his full stature and together with his own preserve the common weal.

—Plato, *The Commonwealth, Book 6*

The Invisible Saving Remnant

As our present "dark age" grows ever more barbaric, it may be necessary for the saving remnant to organize itself as an "invisible" group in which to preserve and disseminate the Perennial wisdom. Alexis Carrel, a twentieth-century Nobel Prize winner, thought that such a "survival society" might have to adopt the structure of earlier organizations such as the Knights Templar.

A group, although very small, is capable of eluding the harmful influence of the society of its epoch by imposing upon its members rules of conduct modeled on military or monastic discipline. Such a method is far from being new. Humanity has already lived through periods when communities of men and women separated from others and adopted strict regulations, in order to attain their ideals. Such groups were responsible for the development of our civilisation during the Middle Ages.

There were the monastic orders, the orders of chivalry, and the corporations of artisans. Among the religious organisations, some took refuge in monasteries, while others remained in the world. But all submitted to strict physiological and mental discipline. The knights complied with rules varying according to the aims of the different orders. In certain circumstances, they were obliged to sacrifice their lives. As for the artisans, their relations between themselves and with the public were determined by exacting legislation. Each corporation had its customs, its ceremonies, and its religious celebrations. In short, the members of these communities renounced the ordinary forms of existence. Are we not capable of repeating, in a different form, the accomplishments of the monks, the knights, and the artisans of the Middle Ages?

—*Man, the Unknown*, 1935

You do not know and will never know who the Remnant are, or where they are, or how many of them there are, or what they are doing or will do. Two things you do know, and no more: first, that they exist; second, that they will find you.

—Albert Jay Nock, *Free Speech and Plain Language*, 1937

The Supernal Features of the Saving Remnant

Though ordinary humans are rapidly losing the ability to understand reality, a small contemporary group is accessing supernormal knowledge through portals into Higher Consciousness. These are the true representatives of Plato's vision of philosopher-leaders and our current conception of a saving remnant. They are making knowledge available about what is actually going on in the world--beyond what the cabal media lies say is going on.

And, of critical importance, they are preserving higher knowledge in books and Web sites which will be available when conditions have degenerated to the point where a rudely awakened mass of people will suddenly say: "How can we get out of this intolerable situation? What knowledge do we need to rebuild a sane and progressive world?"

These supra-humans have undergone a spiritual transformation through initiation into a Higher Consciousness and are harbingers of the evolutionary Supra-Human. The foundations of this transformational knowledge lie within the Perennial Tradition. These savants are now creating a saving remnant--a new culture--which is overcoming the current Dark Ages and laying a foundation for a future commonwealth—a new culture.

After humankind had degenerated during the Dark Ages, Perennialist teachers made available to the West the teachings which spurred Renaissance literature and art, science, and the Enlightenment. The Enlightenment provided the impulse which brought about the American revolution and its transformative documents, the Declaration of Independence, the Preamble to the Constitution, and the Bill of Rights.

These and the additional embodiments of the Perennial tradition--the Hermetic, Platonic, and Esoteric Christian, among others--have inspired humankind ever since and today give proof to people worldwide that a New World is being realized in an invisible way and is overcoming the demonic cabal.

> This Remnant may remind our children and grandchildren of a truth known to our ancestors: individual 'freedom' expresses itself as harmonious, integrated social behavior. If you refer to an etymological dictionary, you will discover – as I did many years ago – that the words 'peace, ''freedom,'' love,' and 'friend' have interconnected origins. Our allegedly "primitive" predecessors understood what our college indoctrinated minds have long since forgotten, namely, that a peaceful society is one in which free men and women live as friends with genuine love for one another.

> —Butler Shaffer, "The Sociopathic Cult," *LewRockwell.com*, January 24, 2005

The Saving Remnant's Secret Weapon: Dialectic

The reason why previous efforts toward commonwealth failed is that the groups making this attempt did not possess an understanding of higher social ordering principles or capability in a methodology by which to create and maintain a saving remnant. A transforming and enlightening group--a saving remnant--possesses knowledge of and experience with transcendent procedural capabilities known as dialectic: Plato's mystical science which he termed *maieutic psychagogy*:

- Maieutic: *maieûtikos*, midwife, one who assists in the delivery of a new being

- Psychagogy: *psuchagôgê*, from Greek, *psûché*, soul, and *agogê*, transport to or lead out of; the science of helping to bring out (give birth to) new elements (ideas, beings) from a person's soul or to infuse (transmit into) a person's soul, elements from a higher level of being

Most persons--including almost all academic philosophers--have failed to understand the transcendent nature of dialectic. They assume they know--from a superficial reading of Plato's dialogues--what this phenomenon means: merely the debating and arguing that go on in ordinary academic discussion. So they find it difficult to fathom why Plato made such a huge fuss over this element within his philosophical teachings, indicating that only dialectic made it possible for the philosopher to apprehend higher knowledge. It's a challenge for us to understand what a supernal phenomenon dialectic really is.

Genuine participants in dialectic practice an extraordinary kind of *shared mystical experience* in which they serve for each other as psychagogic midwives, overseeing the process of the divulgence of, the bringing into being of new elements: ontological episodes, ideas, feelings, inspirations, and images. Experienced participants in dialectic enter an altered state of consciousness.

As we see in Plato's dialogues, Socrates at times had to work to bring other participants into a heightened state, since they were largely unfamiliar with the experience. But his presence and his actions were able to bring them into this higher state--so much so that the participants sometimes spoke of being entranced, charmed, or bewitched.

> Menon: You seem to me to be a veritable wizard, casting your spells over me, and I am truly getting bewitched and enchanted, and YOU HAVE STOPPED MY WORLD. And if I may venture to make a jest about you, you seem to me both in your appearance and in your power over others to be very like the flat torpedo fish [electric eel], who torpifies those who come near him and touch him, as you

have now STOPPED MY WORLD. . . . And I think that you are very wise in not venturing away from home, for if you performed your necromancy in other places as you do in Athens, you would be cast into prison as a sorcerer.

—*Meno*

As is clear from the *Phaedo* and other dialogues, Plato believed that we can only discover truth when we are in our higher consciousness.

"Then when does the soul attain truth?-for in attempting to consider anything in company with the ordinary bodily consciousness she is obviously deceived.

"Yes, that is true.

"Must it not, then, be by reasoning in our soul, if at all, that any of the things that possess true being become known to it?

"And surely the soul then reasons best when none of these things disturb it--neither hearing, nor sight, nor pain, nor pleasure of any kind; but it retires as much as possible within itself, taking leave of the body; and, so far as it can, not communicating or being in contact with it, it aims at the discovery of that which has true being."

Such statements as this--occurring throughout Plato's dialogues--should make it clear to us that the search for truth cannot take place in the ordinary bodily consciousness. Yet academics and scholastics, throughout history, have ignored Plato's declaration and thoughtlessly assumed that what Plato was describing in the dialogues was merely two or more people, in their ordinary state of consciousness, conversing about philosophical concepts.

If we're to take Plato at his word, a dialogue involves the participants attempting to gain a genuine understanding of "that which has true being"--eternal Forms. Since Plato makes it clear that eternal Forms *cannot* be discovered or understood in the ordinary mind-state, a dialogue can occur only when the participants are in a heightened mode of consciousness.

Plato makes this very clear in the *Phaedo*. He is explaining to them that they have had experience with Forms and since they could not have had this experience in their ordinary state of consciousness, it must have been in a higher state.

"Is there or is there not an absolute justice?

"Assuredly there is.

"And an absolute beauty and absolute good?

"Of course.

"But did you ever behold any of them with your eyes?

"Certainly not.

"Or did you ever reach them with any other bodily sense? (and I speak not of these alone, but of absolute greatness, and health, and strength, and of the essence or true nature of everything). Has the reality of them ever been perceived by you through the bodily organs? or rather, is not the nearest approach to the knowledge of their several natures made by him who so orders his intellectual vision as to have the most exact conception of the essence of that which he considers?

"Certainly.

"And he attains to the knowledge of them in their highest purity who goes to each of them with the soul alone, not allowing when in the act of contemplation the intrusion or introduction of sight or any other sense in the company of reason, but with the very light of the soul in her clearness penetrates into the very light of truth in each; is not this the sort of man who, if ever man did, is likely to attain the knowledge of true being?"

Dialectic is the only philosophical method which seeks for wisdom by (anagogically) transporting our foundational underpinnings so that our Higher Self ascends to the Origin.

—Plato, *The Commonwealth*

The Mystical Dialectic

We can identify other essential features of the Socratic shared mystical experience which Plato called dialectic maieutic psychagogy:

1. In the experience itself, participants were aware that they were in a state of heightened consciousness: inspiration or divine rapture.

> "And now, dear Phaedrus, I shall pause for an instant to ask whether you do not think me, as I appear to myself, inspired? Phaedrus: Yes, Socrates, you seem to have a very unusual flow of words."

> Socrates: Listen to me, then, in silence; for surely the place is holy; so that you must not wonder, if, as I proceed, I appear to be in a divine fervor, for already I am getting into inspired poetry." [We must be aware that Socrates is speaking somewhat ironically. But he is also speaking of the reality of a heightened state of consciousness which participants experienced in dialectic.]

2. Maieutic psychagogy involves Socrates (or other advanced teacher) helping other participants to give birth to realities from within them. Plato believed that the human soul possesses latent knowledge which could be brought out and elucidated by a special kind of interchange which he called dialectic--a bringing to birth from the depths of a person's higher being. The maieutic art of Plato's Socrates involved his drawing his interlocutors into stating and reflecting upon the implications of their uncritically held opinions and their joint examination of these opinions to see if they were stillborn or viable.

> Indeed, the secret of your system has just this instant dawned upon me. I comprehend the principle you use in communicating your questions. You lead me through the field of my own knowledge, and then by pointing out analogies to what I know, help me understand that I really know some realities which hitherto, as I believed, I had no knowledge of.

> —Xenophon, *Oeconomicus*

3. In the shared mystical experience of dialectic, Socrates and Plato acted as a spiritual midwife, assisting the other persons to bring their own ideas into being, as we see in *Theatetus*:

> You are not bearing in mind, my friend, that I have no knowledge; I cannot claim any such ideas as my own, no, I am barren as far as they are concerned. But I am acting as your midwife, and that is why I am chanting and serving up morsels of my own wisdom for you to taste. This will continue until I have played my part in bringing your very own notion out into the world. Once that stage is over, I will examine the idea to see whether it turns out to be viable or stillborn.

> And so with dialectic; when a person starts on the discovery of the absolute by the light of reason only, and without any assistance of sense, and perseveres until by pure intelligence he arrives at the perception of the absolute good, he at last finds himself at the end of the intellectual world, as in the case of sight at the end of the visible."

> —Plato, *The Commonwealth*

4. In the shared mystical experience of maieutic psychagogy, Socrates, Plato, or an equally advanced dialectician plants idea-seeds in other participants' souls and then watches as they come to fruition.

Socrates: Is there not another kind of word or speech far better than this, and having far greater power --a son of the same family, but lawfully begotten? Phaedrus: Whom do you mean, and what is his origin?

Socrates: I mean an intelligent word graven in the soul of the learner, which can defend itself, and knows when to speak and when to be silent.

Phaedrus: You mean the living word of knowledge which has a soul, and of which the written word is properly no more than an image?

Socrates: But nobler far is the serious pursuit of the dialectician, who, finding a congenial soul, by the help of science sows and plants therein words which are able to help themselves and him who planted them, and are not unfruitful, but have in them a seed which others brought up in different soils render immortal, making the possessors of it happy to the utmost extent of human happiness.

—Plato, *Phaedrus*

5. Plato's explanation of the nature of maieutic psychagogy in his *Seventh Letter* makes it clear that dialectic is a mystical experience.

After much effort, as names, definitions, sights, and other data of sense, are brought into contact and friction one with another, in the course of scrutiny and kindly testing by men who proceed by question and answer without ill will, with a sudden flash there shines forth understanding about every problem, and an intelligence whose efforts reach the furthest limits of human powers . . . After much converse about the matter itself and a life lived together, suddenly a light, as it were, is kindled in one soul by a flame that leaps to it from another, and thereafter sustains itself.

The mystical aspect of dialectic is evidenced by the sudden flash that shines forth, the light that is kindled in one soul which leaps to another and then sustains itself. As a Master--such as Socrates or Plato--creates the dialectical atmosphere and brings his inner wisdom to bear on the shared mystical experience, a literal enlightenment takes place. Such an experience cannot be contrived by merely trying to set up a "debate" or a "philosophical conversation." There must be a real magician--a genuine philosopher--present to bring about the flash of intuitive illumination eventuating in attunement with true reality, the "activation of the subtleties."

To read a Platonic Dialogue is to participate in a dramatic experience, and what readers cull from these experiences and refer to as *The Philosophy of Plato* can never be stated in the indicative mood, as if it were so much objective information on matters of fact. Plato's 'secret' is not factual at all. No application of scholarly technique enables the reader to extract from *The Dialogues* a concentrate which can be distilled into a specific essence. Plato's "philosophy" has no prescriptive formula. There is nothing, nothing whatever, which you might conceivably discover, write down, and pass around in a printed book which could be set upon library shelves and put into the hands of young students. It is like poetry or music. You have to experience it directly, in and for yourself.

—Rupert C. Lodge, *The Philosophy of Plato*, 1956

6. Given the nature of the spiritual birth process in dialectic, only a prepared student can effectively participate. Plato makes this clear in his *Seventh Letter*:

The process however of dealing with all of these, as the mind moves up and down to each in turn, does after much effort give birth in a well-constituted mind to knowledge of that which is well constituted. But if a man is ill-constituted by nature (as the state of the soul is naturally in the majority both in its capacity for learning and in what is called moral character)-or it may have become so by deterioration not even Lynceus could endow such men with the power of sight.

7. The mystical experience of maieutic psychagogy involves the participants in a process which teaches how to develop and take part in the process; it involves learning by doing. Socrates and Plato taught how the mystical dialectic can be entered into, how it can be carried out (allowing higher knowledge to flow through oneself), and how to continue this process in one's life. Something occurred within the dialectic experience which remained with those who were prepared to take up the philosophical-mystical life.

Let us review the whole development of this dialogue [*Phaedo*], in which Socrates brings his hearers to behold the eternal in human personality. The hearers accept his thoughts, and they look into themselves to see if they can find in their inner experiences something which assents to his ideas. They make the objections which strike them. What has happened to the hearers when the dialogue is finished? They have found something within them which they did not possess before. They have not merely accepted an abstract truth, but they have gone through a development. Something has come to life in them which was not living in them before. Is not this to be compared with an initiation? And does not this throw light on the reason for Plato's setting forth his philosophy in the form of conversation? These dialogues are nothing else than the literary form of the events which took place in the sanctuaries of the Mysteries. We are convinced of this from what Plato himself says in many passages. Plato wished to be, as a philosophical teacher, what the initiator into the Mysteries was, as far as this was compatible with the philosophical manner of communication. It is evident how Plato feels himself in harmony with the Mysteries! He only thinks he is on the right path when it is taking him where the Mystic is to be led.

—Rudolph Steiner, *Christianity as Mystical Fact*

8. We can experience Plato's dialogues as noetic dramatizations of dialectical interactions which hold in suspension the question of the validity or invalidity of the counter-claims, while allowing us to feel the full force of the arguments. The dialogues allow us to see that philosophy, for Plato and Socrates, was not a body of true or false doctrines, of sound or unsound arguments. Philosophy, Plato makes clear, is not the power, rhetorical or logical, to win arguments or to make the weaker case appear the stronger, which it was for the Sophists such as Zeno and Protagoras. We can experience dialogue as a means of learning to philosophize dialectically and as meditation exercises on essential philosophic themes.

9. Practicing genuine dialectic requires that there be at least one person at an advanced level within the Perennial Tradition, and prepared participants willing and able to actively engage in the experience to the fullest extent. Such dialogues require that each participant speak openly and honestly, holding nothing back out of fear of contradiction or personal criticism. A person cannot participate in a true dialogue if he tries to plan his tactics ("I'll hold back on this argument until the end of the debate . . ."), hedge his bets ("I dare not say that, because they would criticize me for such a weak argument. . ."), or seek to defeat an opponent ("His argument on this point is weak; I'll hit him with this overwhelming fact . . .").

10. The participants within a true dialogue reside in a higher intellectual dimension. The power of genuine dialectic occurs because all persons are fully and honestly invested in what they're saying. Their divergent contributions vigorously interact--sometimes colliding--then coalesce in a harmonious understanding--even if it's a comprehension that they don't fully understand a particular concept or reality. Each participant must, like Zorba dancing, "undo his belt" and surrender to a higher energy, allowing the free flow of the give-and-take of the dialogue to lead whither it will. The most fruitful dialogues of this nature are those in which more than one participant is an advanced teacher.

Dialectic Within the Saving Remnant

We've seen some of the numinous qualities of dialectic. Now we must examine how this paranormal phenomenon operates within a saving remnant. Dialectic is so misunderstood a concept and so arcane in its essential nature that only persons who have experienced this heightened state of consciousness can hope to understand it or participate in it. Some of the transcendent aspects of dialectic are so enigmatic and inexplicable, that it requires extraordinary discernment to understand or practice this methodology. For example, dialectic allows participants to communicate by supernormal means which are not completely explained by such terms as telepathy or insight.

It's an astounding experience to become aware of the "opening up" of artistic elements (literature, music, art, conversation, humor) simply because you're within a dialectic environment with an advanced person or persons. Even in a dialectic milieu composed of two participants, a book or a piece of music or a painting can suddenly reveal completely new, previously unexperienced--and unanticipated--aspects. Interaction and communication within a dialectical group embody an uncommon, supernormal openness, considerateness, and honesty which can be experienced in no other atmosphere. Once a person has experienced this kind of interaction, the "small talk" and inanity of ordinary conversation seems unrewarding and repugnant.

> Those who understand Higher Wisdom do not speak in an ordinary manner. Those who speak in an ordinary manner do not grasp Higher Knowledge. Close the mouth; shut the door.
>
> —Lao-tzu, Oriental Teacher

A saving remnant is a group which survives during a time of Pandemonium: anarchy and tyranny. Dialectic, as a super-normal methodology for discovering truth and arriving at symbiotic group consensus, is absolutely essential if the group is to gain understanding of what is happening and determine how to respond effectively. That is, dialectic not only provides knowledge but also discernment as to what strategies will be effectual in realizing the group's goals.

The dialectical process in a transformative, enlightening group has part of its purpose in training persons in the dialectical procedures, feelings, attitudes, and mind-set, so they may become leaders both within the saving remnant itself and also in the larger society. Dialectical training produces these effects:

- Participants are better able to "see" and "listen to" others--in the group and outside. Ego distractions no longer blind and deafen us, and we suddenly discern deeper meanings within persons, events and objects, making us capable of responding to them in entirely new, more potent ways.

- Participants in dialectic are more capable of disclosing feelings and ideas, both those which they are aware of when the interchange begins and those newly realized elements which appear as the dialectical process proceeds.

- Dialectical interchange makes it possible to come to agreement on facts and strategies in a more comprehensive manner. As the group focuses on questions, problems, and issues, the diversity of thought and understanding within the participants produces symbiotic resolutions and realizations which no other atmosphere can produce.

- Participants gain an increasingly effective capability of "seeing" the main thread in a procedure, event, or problem which allows them to lead others in a line of thought or a direction of action that eventuates in enhanced understanding and effective activity.

- Leadership capabilities within the dialectical setting include discernment of subtle elements such as ambience, pacing, meaning, and resonance. This allows participants to gain the capability of weaving a common fabric of thought and action, a cross-patterning of all the participants' contributions into a lovely and efficacious tapestry.

- One of the major discoveries which a saving remnant makes through its use of dialectic is the most effectual way to leaven the larger society with its own inspirations and approaches, leading ultimately to a commonwealth.

Take your practiced powers and stretch them out until they span the chasm between two contradictions. . . For God wants to know Himself in you.

—Rainer Maria Rilke, "As once the winged energy of delight"

Afterword

The Triumph of a New World Culture

By Norman D. Livergood

Culture, in its most comprehensive meaning, includes knowledge, belief, art, morals, law, custom, and other capabilities and habits acquired by humans as members of a society.

In essence, culture is the sum of all technology and values that make up human life. The definition of culture changes relative to how we interpret human life and human values. If we define human life as mere physical existence and if we base our value system on nothing more than ego-satisfaction, our culture is materialistic regardless of how technologically advanced we might be.

In this book we've explored the foundation of human culture in higher metaphysical knowledge as preserved in the Perennial Tradition and seen how the modern world's loss of contact with this elemental source is the chief reason for our world culture's extraordinary and perilous disintegration.

Throughout the book, we've distinguished between human culture in general (civilization) and specific cultures (such as the American culture). This definition of world culture as synonymous with civilization differs from that of many thinkers.

> Our present civilization quite obviously lacks any unifying principle. The degree of unity which the vague term 'modern civilization' implies is in many ways a 'unity of disunity', the peoples involved being given a superficial coherence by the spread of technology and by common acceptance of certain ways of thought whose very nature is to create further disintegration.
>
> —Alan W. Watts, *The Supreme Identity*

The Perennial Tradition's concept of culture includes both the material and spiritual dimensions. Material culture is not an end in itself but provides opportunities for inner, spiritual development. Cultural development is defined not as possessions and dominance, but inner growth expressed through personal morality and societal well-being.

American culture is being deliberately destroyed by a barbaric cabal that has taken control of the United States. The cabal is busily obliterating America's institutions and values.

If your house were being deliberately burned down by arsonists or your car stolen by a gang of thieves, you'd be outraged and do whatever it took to stop this assault. But an even more precious possession of ours is being deliberately destroyed right before our eyes--our American culture. And most U.S. citizens aren't lifting a finger to stop it!

It may seem rather extremist to say that our American culture is being deliberately destroyed, but I challenge you to look honestly at the facts and then describe them in any other way. We all wish this destruction weren't going on, but we can't make it disappear just by burying our head in the sands of ignorance and denial.

The destruction of American culture by this barbaric horde started in the early part of the twentieth century and has continued at a faster pace ever since. Realizing a new culture requires an electorate that understands what is actually happening in the world, beyond what the ruler-owned media tell us is happening. If American citizens receive an effective education, we learn to inform ourselves and can see through the propaganda, the dictatorial actions, and the outcomes of the non-constitutional acts of our rulers.

Beginning in the early part of the twentieth century, American ruling groups began to create a pseudo-educational system which produces students no longer capable of understanding such key concepts and factors as "freedom," "government of the people," "critical thinking," etc.

The demonic cabal wanted a working class that was merely trained to do a particular job, not think about social or political issues. They created an educational system focused on training instead of learning. So today we have an American citizenry that can't even see that Bush II has lied to them repeatedly and has committed unspeakable acts of moral depravity.

In history the way of annihilation is invariably prepared by inward degeneration . . . Only then can a shock from outside put an end to the whole.

—Jakob Burckhardt, *Force and Freedom*

The demonic cabal, using its current Bush II puppet government, is systematically and deliberately destroying our American culture. But such attempts to destroy cultures and civilizations have occurred before, and the ultimate victory is always won by the progressive and positive forces. Sooner or later, humankind reawakens to its spiritual heritage-- preserved by Perennialist sages during the twilight periods of cultural decline.

The Triumph of Civilization

It may seem that barbarism is currently winning in its attempts to destroy civilization, so we must utilize a wider perspective in understanding how the principles of civilized behavior are ultimately triumphant. It's absolutely essential that we re-examine the principles of civilization as bequeathed by Plato and other teachers within the Perennial Tradition to discern the veiled pattern in world history. Over many centuries mankind has seen varied types of imperialism attempt to seize world dominance, only to result in their own self-destruction.

Civilization is the maintenance of social order through persuasion, not force. The ideals of civilization are the heritage of both the East and the West. In spite of--and in some ways because of--the varied attempts by tyrannous rulers over the centuries to enslave humankind, our species is evolving toward the development of an enlightened consciousness:

- Engaging in humane civility

- Practicing moral self-discipline

- Appreciating beauty

- Developing an autonomous self which is able to think and act on its own initiative

- Seeing through the current social myths and diversions

- Understanding the necessity of life-long self-education

- Recognizing the necessity of social action, including discerning what the social situation requires and creating a program to realize social reform

- Developing genuine feelings of compassion and regard for one's fellow human being

"The creation of the world is the victory of persuasion over force." Plato

We Must Understand History's Lessons

To understand how humankind is evolving toward the development of an enlightened consciousness, we must examine the essence of the historical struggle for understanding and freedom, simplifying historical processes so they become easily comprehensible.

Overall, the direction of human evolution has been an upward helical path with each new cycle achieving a higher advance :

- Savagery: a pre-cultural level marked by total absence of restraint

- Untamed and bestial dominance

- A recovery of Perennial wisdom and the development of a new culture

The recovery of the Platonic embodiment of the Perennial Tradition in the twelfth century allowed a new movement to develop in the eighteenth century called the Enlightenment.

The Enlightenment was in essence a re-discovery of the knowledge and values preserved by Perennialist seers. We can appreciate the work of the eighteenth century Enlightenment thinkers--especially American philosophers Benjamin Franklin, Thomas Jefferson, Patrick Henry, James Madison, and James Monroe. Their study of the Enlightenment Tradition made it possible for them to create an entirely new nation and establish its foundations on the fundamental civil liberties set forth in the Declaration of Independence, the Preamble to the Constitution and the Bill of Rights.

Enlightenment liberalism set the individual free politically, intellectually, and economically. The political universe was demystified, as the magical power of thrones, scepters, and crowns was replaced by rational acts of consent. The individual (understood, of course, in the Enlightenment as male and propertyowning) did not receive government and authority from a God who had given his secular sword to princes and magistrates to rule by his divine right. Nor did the individual keep any longer to his subordinate place in a divinely inspired hierarchy, in which kings and noblemen had been placed above him as 'your highness' who were society's natural governors. Government was voluntarily established by free individuals through a willful act of contract. Individuals rationally consented to limit their own freedom and to obey civil authority in order to have public protection of their natural rights. Government's purpose was to serve self-interest, to enable individuals to enjoy peacefully their rights to life, liberty, and property, not to serve the glory of God or dynasties, and certainly not to dictate moral or religious truth.

—Isaac Kramnick (Editor), *The Portable Enlightenment Reader,* 1995

The Perennial Wisdom

The Higher Realm has created the physical universe and has overseen the evolution of humankind. Even the worst destruction of civilizations cannot obliterate the wisdom which humankind has realized (understood and brought to manifestation) from the Higher Realm of eternal values and forms.

There are always preservers and custodians of the hidden Perennial Wisdom. As humankind advances in terrestrial and spiritual understanding, advanced savants make available teachings for personal transformation. Only those humans who prepare themselves through self-awareness and self-discipline are initiated into these Mysteries.

It is possible for any man or woman to enter into that ancient fellowship of those who seek to become the servants of the great preservers of the secret records of antiquity. Krishna taught Arjuna in the fourth chapter of the Bhagavad Gita that after the greatest – now forgotten – civilizations of long ago came and went, "the mighty spiritual art" was lost.

Though it was lost, collectively speaking, it was never lost to all because these hierophants assiduously preserved it. It has been called the Wisdom-Religion. It is the divine wisdom maintained by those few who embody it, who are its self-conscious custodians, tribeless and raceless, genuinely free men proud to belong to the family of man. They differ from the exhaustless potentiality of the Divine Mind only as divine thought differs from divine ideation. It is the difference between a library and men who in using the library and in reflecting and ideating upon its books, magically bring them to life. . . The faculty of self-conscious awareness in the human being never seems to be exhausted, even by the whole catalogue of abuse of that power.

—D. K. Mavalankar, "Order and Chaos," Theosophy Trust Website

When the Perennial Tradition is forced to go underground during times of extreme tyranny and devastation, it preserves the priceless heritage of wisdom and understanding.

In eras of cultural destruction, such as we are now experiencing, humankind's fate often seems hopeless. The low level of culture to which America has now devolved is revealed by the proliferation of mindless human savages who not only cannot understand an author such as Shakespeare, but have lost even the desire to understand transformative art or literature. Such a statement is not meant to defame humankind, but to provide a straightforward, honest appraisal of our present decadent state.

It is important to realize that even when the fires of culture burn low--almost to ashes--the Perennial Wisdom is still being preserved by wise sages. These savants continue to teach selected initiates--often in ways invisible to the savage culture. As these initiates achieve the prerequisite understanding and skill required, the hidden wisdom is made available to them.

Both Spengler and Toynbee refer to similar effects in the revival of Classical (Greek and Roman) knowledge in the West. Referring to a "Western Dark Age," Arnold Toynbee, in *The Study of History*, comments that renaissance of the Classical literature did not become accessible "until the Westerner was competent to read its contents."

World citizens are presently facing the ravages of deliberate cultural destruction by politicians and their corporate controllers. We are entering a period when much of the Perennialist wisdom will have to go underground, to protect it from destruction by savages and barbarians--now called "compassionate conservatives."

Those among humankind who can understand the enduring importance of the higher knowledge and values must preserve this priceless heritage. These few will have to carry out cloaked operations to safeguard and disseminate the hidden wisdom. This book constitutes a call to action in this regard, and will resonate with those who have developed advanced powers of discernment.

About the Authors

Dr. Norman D. Livergood is an author, publisher, and teacher living in Vista, California. After receiving his bachelors degree from Phillips University, he completed a Master of Divinity, Master of Arts, and a Doctorate in philosophy at Yale University. His interest in psychology led him to pursue a masters equivalent in that field. In 1989 he completed a second doctorate in artificial intelligence at The Union Institute. He has taught at a variety of universities across the United States, from Yale University to the University of California, San Diego. In 1993 through 1995, he served as Professor and Chair, Artificial Intelligence, at the United States Army War College. Dr. Livergood has carried out extensive research and published in the fields of philosophy, philosophy of religion, artificial intelligence, political-economic philosophy, and distance learning. He is webmaster of the Internet site: *http://www.hermes-press.com*.

Michelle Mairesse is a freelance writer who has published a book on botanical medicine and articles on art, literature, politics, linguistics, and the environment. She completed her undergraduate degree in English Literature at Los Angeles State University and then did graduate work in English Literature at the University of California Los Angeles. Michelle is Executive Editor of Hermes Press.

Index

ITAA 39

J

Japan 8, 17, 18, 25, 28, 29, 31
Jesus xix, 141, 153, 154, 167, 189
JFK 1, 3, 103, 105, 166
Jihad vii, 8, 54, 55

K

Kabbalah 1
Kennedy 3, 6, 8, 90, 103, 104, 105
Kidan 41
Konstantinos 41
Korea 11, 17, 28, 41, 60, 69
Korean 32
Kosovo 1, 94
Kuhn-Loeb 2
Kurd 10
Kurdish 9, 78

L

Lebanon 6, 8, 9, 10, 11, 12
Leningrad 24
Li-Woan Yang 41
Lockheed-Martin 39
London 8, 30, 36, 191
Loney 33

M

Madsen 54, 190
Mahfouz 3, 54, 56, 57, 59, 60
Mahoning County 46
Maliki 6
Manuel 54
Medellin 54
Mid-East 189
Middle-East 8, 12, 98
Middle East 6, 8, 9, 25, 27, 31, 33, 59, 60, 64, 91, 190, 191, 193
Mideast 53, 60, 61
Mitofsky International 48
Mortham 36
Moscow 26
mujahideen 53
Mumford 109, 110, 111, 164
Muslim xiii, 53, 54, 56, 88, 98, 189

N

New Delhi 26
New Yorker 30, 31, 37

T

Taliban 9, 53, 54, 55, 56
Tanzania 55
Tawney 20
Taymiya 54
Tigua 40

U

Ukraine 46, 48
UN 27, 31
Unilect 39
United Nations 6, 46, 64, 77
UN Security Council 31
Urosevich, Bob 42
US-Israeli 6
USS Cole 55

V

Vietnam 1, 3, 11, 17, 24, 43, 60, 62, 63, 103, 106, 107, 122
Voltaire 6
Volusia County 37
Voting 37, 39, 40, 42, 43, 49, 50
Voting Experiment 39

W

Wahabism 3
Wahhabi 53, 54
West Point 7
Wire Fraud 41
Wolfowitz 32, 61, 63

Y

Yadavaran 31
YEI 41
Yemen 55, 86, 88
Yemeni 55
Yukos 26

IF YOU LIKED THIS BOOK, YOU WON'T WANT TO MISS OTHER TITLES BY DANDELION BOOKS

Available Now And Always Through
www.dandelionbooks.net And Affiliated Websites!!
TOLL-FREE ORDERS—1-800-861-7899 (U.S. & CANADA)

Non-Fiction – Uncensored & Unfettered

It's All about Control: The God, Jesus and ET Coverup Conspiracies, by Tony Stubbs… Three major conspiracies are controlling the people of planet Earth: This book provides the truth-serum and tools for breaking free from a cruel, cleverly contrived mind-control game that for centuries has been keeping the human race in bondage to the Religion, War and Finance industries. (1-893302-95-4)

Adam & Evil: The God Who hates Sex, Women and Human Bodies, by The Heyeokah Guru… EXPOSED: 'Jesus Christ' is a mythological figure, not a person The Virgin Mary is the Earth, not a young woman who never had sex; Heaven and Hell are right here! We create them ourselves. The truth at last about one of the greatest conspiracies in the world! (ISBN 1-893302-94-6)

The Host & The Parasite: How Israel's Fifth Column Consumed America, by Greg Felton… "The United States became midwife to a war crime when it endorsed the creation of Israel in 1948 and blackmailed European nations into supporting it," writes Felton. "From this time forward, the Zionist parasite began leaching off the U.S." A definitive study of "Israel's conquest of America and its use of the U.S. economy, government and military to terrorize the Muslim world." (ISBN 1-893302-97-0)

Overthrow of the American Republic – The Writings of Sherman H. Skolnick, by Sherman H. Skolnick… Known as "America's leading judge-buster," the late Sherman H. Skolnick was one of America's most courageous and outrageous journalists. This collection of his internet writings also includes 24 articles that were never published on his website. This 600-page book which contains over 80 Skolnick articles, is a complement to Skolnick's *Ahead of the Parade*, published by Dandelion Books in 2003. (ISBN 1-893302-22-9), $33.95 + S & H ; 2 –book Skolnick package

*Ahead Of The Parade: A Who's Who Of Treason and High Crimes – Exclusive Details Of Fraud And Corruption Of The Monopoly Press, The Banks, The Bench And The Bar, And The Secret Political Police,*by Sherman H. Skolnick… One of America's foremost investigative reporters, speaks out on some of America's current crises. Included in this blockbuster book are the following articles: Big City Newspapers & the Mob, The Sucker Traps, Dirty Tricks of Finance and Brokerage, The Secret History of Airplane Sabotage, Wal-Mart and the Red Chinese Secret Police, The Chandra Levy Affair, The Japanese Mafia in the United States, The Secrets of Timothy McVeigh, and much more. (ISBN 1-893302-32-6)

Taboo: A Memoir – Confessions of Forbidden Love, by Tom Hathaway… A brave and honest exploration of the primal lust of our psyches, *Taboo* points the way to a new sexual frontier. Women who want to know what men really want must read this erotic rhapsody. A 21st Century *Lady Chatterly's Lover* by a prolific new author whose name will soon become a household word. (ISBN 1-893302-87-3)

Tracking Deception: Bush Mid-East Policy, by William A. Cook… "Bill Cook writes with vivid urgency as he excavates the Augean muck of the Bush years, subjecting the president and his gang to an excruciatingly tight close-up, where every flaw, every imperfection, every touch-up is exposed to all who dare to look."—Alex Cockburn, *Counterpunch* Editor-in-Chief [from the Introduction] (ISBN 1-893302-83-0)

Exopolitics: Political Implications Of The Extraterrestrial Presence, by Michael E. Salla, Ph.D…. According to Dr. Michael Salla and many other experts in the field of ET research, for almost 70 years the US government has engaged in an extensive "official effort" of disinformation, intimidation and tampering with evidence in order to maintain a non-disclosure policy about extraterrestrial presence. (ISBN 1-893302-56-3)

America Speaks Out: Collected Essays From Dissident Writers John H. Brand, Meria Heller, John Kaminski, Norman D. Livergood, Wayne Madsen, Kurt Nimmo, Albert D. Pastore, Michael

E. Salla, Sherman H. Skolnick & John Stanton... A collection of essays extracted from works recently published by Dandelion Books. (ISBN 1-893302-63-6)

America 2004: A Power But Not Super, by John Stanton [Foreword by Bev Conover, Editor - onlinejournal.com, Introduction by Karen Kwiatkowski, Lieutenant Colonel, USAF(Ret.)]... Stanton explains how Bush has adroitly fused state, religious (faith-based government) and business interests into one indistinguishable tyrannical mass... his explanation of how this has been accomplished is eye-opening. (ISBN 1-893302-26-1)

Stranger than Fiction: An Independent Investigation Of The True Culprits Behind 9-11, by Albert D. Pastore, Ph.D... Twelve months of careful study, painstaking research, detailed analysis, source verification and logical deduction went into the writing of this book. In addition to the stories are approximately 300 detailed footnotes. Pastore: "Only by sifting through huge amounts of news data on a daily basis was I able to catch many of these rare 'diamonds in the rough' and organize them into a coherent pattern and logical argument." (ISBN 1-893302-47-4)

Unshackled: A Survivor's Story of Mind Control, by Kathleen Sullivan... A non-fictional account of Kathleen Sullivan's experiences as part of a criminal network that includes Intelligence personnel, military personnel, doctors and mental health professionals contracted by the military and the CIA, criminal cult leaders and members, pedophiles, pornographers, drug dealers and Nazis. "I believe my story needs to be told so that more people will understand how 'Manchurian Candidate' style mind-control techniques can create alter-states in the minds of unwitting victims, causing them to perform deeds that are normally repugnant." (ISBN 1-893302-35-0)

Another Day in The Empire: Life in Neoconservative America, by Kurt Nimmo... A collection of articles by one of Counterpunch's most popular columnists. Included in this collection are: The Son of COINTELPRO; Clueless at the State Department; Bush Senior: Hating Saddam, Selling Him Weapons; Corporate Media: Selling Dubya's Oil War; Iraq and the Vision of the Velociraptors: The Bleeding Edge of Islam; Condoleezza Rice at the Waldorf Astoria; Predators, Snipers and the Posse Comitatus Act, and many others. (ISBN 1-893302-75-X)

Palestine & The Middle East: Passion, Power & Politics, by Jaffer Ali... The Palestinian struggle is actually a human one that transcends Palestine... There is no longer a place for Zionism in the 20th century... Democracy in the Middle East is not safe for US interests as long as there is an atmosphere of hostility... Suicide bombings are acts of desperation and mean that a people have been pushed to the brink... failure to understand why they happen will make certain they will continue. Jaffer Ali is a Palestinian-American business man who has been writing on politics and business for over 25 years. (ISBN 1-893302-45-8)

Ben-Gurion's Scandals: How The Haganah And The Mossad Eliminated Jews, by Naeim Giladi... The painful truth about the Zionist rape of Palestine and deliberate planting of anti-Semitism in Iraqi Jewish communities during David Ben-Gurion's political career in order to persuade the Iraqi Jews to immigrate to Israel. (ISBN1-893302-40-7)

America, Awake! We Must Take Back Our Country, by Norman D. Livergood... This book is intended as a wake-up call for Americans, as Paul Revere awakened the Lexington patriots to the British attack on April 18, 1775, and as Thomas Paine's *Common Sense* roused apathetic American colonists to recognize and struggle against British oppression. Our current situation is similar to that which American patriots faced in the 1770s: a country ruled by 'foreign' and 'domestic' plutocratic powers and a divided citizenry uncertain of their vital interests. (ISBN 1-893302-27-X)

America's Nightmare: The Presidency of George Bush II, by John Stanton & Wayne Madsen...Media & Language, War & Weapons, Internal Affairs and a variety of other issues pointing out the US "crisis without precedent" that was wrought by the US Presidential election of 2000 followed by 9/11. "Stanton & Madsen will challenge many of the things you've been told by CNN and Fox news. This book is dangerous." (ISBN 1-893302-29-6)

America's Autopsy Report, by John Kaminski...The false fabric of history is unraveling beneath an avalanche of pathological lies to justify endless war and Orwellian new laws that revoke the rights of Americans. While TV and newspapers glorify the dangerous ideas of perverted billionaires, the Internet has pulsated with outrage and provided a new and real forum for freedom among concerned people all over the world who are opposed to the mass murder and criminal exploitation of the defenseless victims of multinational corporate totalitarianism. John Kaminski's passionate essays give voice to those hopes and fears of humane people that are ignored by the big business shysters who rule the major media. (ISBN 1-893302-42-3)

Seeds Of Fire: China And The Story Behind The Attack On America, by Gordon Thomas… The inside story about China that no one can afford to ignore. Using his unsurpassed contacts in Israel, Washington, London and Europe, Gordon Thomas, internationally acclaimed best-selling author and investigative reporter for over a quarter-century, reveals information about China's intentions to use the current crisis to launch itself as a super-power and become America's new major enemy…"This has been kept out of the news agenda because it does not suit certain business interests to have that truth emerge…Every patriotic American should buy and read this book… it is simply revelatory." (Ray Flynn, Former U.S. Ambassador to the Vatican) (ISBN 1-893302-54-7)

Shaking The Foundations: Coming Of Age In The Postmodern Era, by John H. Brand, D.Min., J.D.… Scientific discoveries in the Twentieth Century require the restructuring of our understanding the nature of Nature and of human beings. In simple language the author explains how significant implications of quantum mechanics, astronomy, biology and brain physiology form the foundation for new perspectives to comprehend the meaning of our lives. (ISBN 1-893302-25-3)

Rebuilding The Foundations: Forging A New And Just America, by John H. Brand, D.Min., J.D.…Should we expect a learned scholar to warn us about our dangerous reptilian brains that are the real cause of today's evils? Although Brand is not without hope for rescuing America, he warns us to act fast–and now. Evil men intent on imposing their political, economic, and religious self-serving goals on America are not far from achieving their goal of mastery." (ISBN 1-893302-33-4)

The Last Days Of Israel, by Barry Chamish… With the Middle East crisis ongoing, *The Last Days of Israel* takes on even greater significance as an important book of our age. Barry Chamish, investigative reporter who has the true story about Yitzak Rabin's assassination, tells it like it is. (ISBN 1-893302-16-4)

The Last Atlantis Book You'll Ever Have To Read! by Gene D. Matlock… More than 25,000 books, plus countless other articles have been written about a fabled confederation of city-states known as Atlantis. If it really did exist, where was it located? Does anyone have valid evidence of its existence – artifacts and other remnants? According to historian, archaeologist, educator and linguist Gene D. Matlock, both questions can easily be answered. (ISBN 1-893302-20-2)
Cancer Doctor: The Biography Josef Issels, M.D., Who Brought Hope To The World With His Revolutionary Cancer Treatment, by Gordon Thomas…Dr. Josef Issels treated more than 12,000 cancer patients who had been written off as "incurable" by other doctors. He claimed no miracle cures, but the success record of his revolutionary "whole person treatment" was extraordinary… the story of his struggle against the medical establishment which put Dr. Issels in prison, charged with fraud and manslaughter. (ISBN 1-893302-18-0)

Non-Fiction – Conscious Solutions

A Rediscovery of Free Will: An Un-Doing, by Frederick J. Smith, M.D.… Have you had your 10 "Hits of Joy" today? Have you had your 5 "Moments of Peace"? Is your intuition running, and available to you? Are your 'hunches' reliable? Can you get yourself into the 'zone'? Are you able to, each day, open your heart and let the love out, at least once, without fear or caution? These and more, are the Practical Payoffs of investing your time, energy, and focus in "a rediscovery of free will." (ISBN 1-893302-98-9)

Living with Soul: An Old Soul's Guide to Life, the Universe and Everything, Vol. I, by Tony Stubbs… Who are we? Where did we come from? Why are we here? Master teacher and sage Tony Stubbs urges us to "go to the Source… look in the mirror." In the first of a two-volume compendium of comprehensive spiritual teachings, Stubbs expertly documents his lessons and observations with excellent anecdotes, charts and other graphics. (ISBN 1-893302-85-7)

Living with Soul: An Old Soul's Guide to Life, the Universe and Everything, Vol. II, by Tony Stubbs... Learn how to work with energy and make it work for you by discovering your own energy patterns or bio-rhythms. Explore reincarnation, death, grief, near-death experiences, life on the "other side" and many other multi-dimensional experiences. Also learn more about the coming U.S. disclosures concerning extraterrestrials, UFOs and many over-ups that may have "Earthshattering" repercussions for those who until now have been unwilling to accept that "we are not alone." (ISBN 1-893302-86-5)

Unveil the Past: Heal the Future through Hypnotherapy, by Doris Small Proiette, DCH, Ph.D.... Amazing stories from Dr. Proiette's clinical records about the healing power of past life regression that reaffirms the power of the mind and the ability for every human being to release themselves from unwanted feelings and belief systems. Dr. Proiette's books supports statistics that show Hypnotherapy as the leading technology for helping people heal their issues of disease and dysfunction. (ISBN 1-893302-96-2)

Portals to Higher Consciousness: Exploring the Spiritual Domain, by Norman D. Livergood... What is the process that serious students use to actually realize—bring to manifestation—their Higher Consciousness, "through which they are able to contact Reality in a region of pure Truth." If you're interested in investigating higher consciousness, put on your hiking clothes and join this spiritual expedition (1-893302-92X)

Creation and Metempsychosis (The Evolution of the Soul): An Introduction to the "Psychological Key of Man," edited and compiled by Q. Dean Sloan... A compilation of theosophical metaphysics that provides the technical metaphysical rationale for Creation itself, as well as Creation of the human soul ("crown chakra") and is based on the psychology of the 7 rays. "The 'petals' in the crown chakra unfold slowly over a long series of lives, and we achieve perfection only when they have completely unfolded." (ISBN 1-893302-90-3)

The Perennial Tradition: Overview Of The Secret Heritage, The Single Stream Of Initiatory Teaching Flowing Through All The Great Schools Of Mysticism, by Norman D. Livergood... Like America, Awake, this book is another wake-up call. "It was written to assist readers to awaken to the Higher Spiritual World." In addition to providing a history of the Western tradition of the Perennial Tradition, Livergood also describes the process that serious students use to actually realize--bring to manifestation--their Higher Consciousness. "Unless we become aware of this higher state, we face the prospect of a basically useless physical existence and a future life--following physical death--of unpleasant, perhaps anguished reformation of our essence." (ISBN 1-893302-48-2)

Progressive Awareness: Critical Thinking, Self-Awareness & Critical Consciousness, by Norman D. Livergood... how to avoid being manipulated by our emotions and ideas and how to start thinking for ourselves; increase your skills for understanding, critical thinking, self-awareness, critical consciousness, and enlightened discernment. (ISBN 1-893302-80-6)

My Name is Esther Clara, by Laurel Johnson... Esther Clara's lifetime spanned two world wars and the inventions of electricity, telephones, automobiles, airplanes, radio, TV, computers and many other conveniences that have become basic necessities of modern American life. An authentic first-hand account of 20th Century rural America audio and videotaped before her death and adeptly reconstituted by master storyteller and book reviewer, Laurel Johnson. (ISBN 1-893302-89-X)

Romance Stew: The Way to a Woman's Heart, by Becky Ruff . . . If you've ever tried to cook up a man or woman in your life, you're going to love Becky Ruff's colorful description of her multiple Cauldron Crashes. Today's excess of Internet "match" websites provides sizzling opportunities for relationships of every flavor. Like any women with a healthy appetite, Ruff decides to taste them all. She regales the reader with her unpredictable Kitchen Capers that keep manifesting the same fatal endings yet leave her feeling far from being a *femme fatale*. (ISBN 1-9789611-0-2, 978-0-9789611-0-7)

Why Don't You Love Me? I'm the Best Choice: Repairing Heartache, Finding the Right Mate & Not Making the Same Mistakes the Next Time, by Debi Davis... Everyone has a perfect mate waiting for them and it may not be the person you are trying to hold onto now. Learn how to manifest that perfect partner... for you by clearly identifying the qualities you're looking for and making sure you show the world a true and honest portrait of who you are. (ISBN 1-893302-91-1)

The Compassionate Surgeon, by Joop Schokker, M.D. . . . Do you or someone you love need an operation? Scared? Don't know where to turn for advice? Let Dr. Joop Schokker guide you through the process and answer such questions as: What should you expect before, during and after surgery? What should you ask of, and expect from, your surgeon? What can go wrong and how will your surgeon fix it? When is surgery unnecessary? What are your chances of full recovery? (ISBN 0-963294-76-8)

*Executive Parenting: Risks & Solutions for the Working Parent-What you may not know . . . but will wish you did!,*by Debi Davis & Ellen Sherman, Ph.D....Health expert Debi Davis and Marriage and Family Counselor Dr. Ellen Sherman have combined their knowledge and experience to deliver a comprehensive manual for child-rearing in the 21st century. (ISBN 1-893302-93-8)

The Courage To Be Who I Am, by Mary-Margareht Rose... This book is rich with teachings and anecdotes delivered with humor and humanness, by a woman who followed her heart and learned to listen to her inner voice; in the process, transforming every obstacle into an opportunity to test her courage to manifest her true identity. (1SBN 1-893302-13-X)

The Making Of A Master: Tracking Your Self-Worth, by Jeanette O'Donnal... A simple tracking method for self-improvement that takes the mystery out of defining your goals, making a road map and tracking your progress. A book rich with nuggets of wisdom couched in anecdotes and instructive dialogues. (ISBN 1-893302-36-9)

Fiction with Flare

Waaaay Out There! Diggertown, Oklahoma, by Tuklo Nashoba...Adventures of constable Clint Mankiller and his deputy, Chad GhostWolf; Jim Bob and Bubba Johnson, Grandfather GhostWolf, Cassie Snodgrass, Doc Jones, Judge Jenkins and the rest of the Diggertown, Oklahoma bunch in the first of a series of Big Foot-Sasquatch tall tales peppered with lots of good belly laughs and just as much fun. (ISBN 1-893302-44-X)

Waaaay Out There! Arbuckle Treasure Hunt, by Tuklo Nashoba... The second in the WAAAAY OUT THERE series that takes Clint Mankiller and his deputy, Chad GhostWolf, Bubba and the rest of the Diggertown gang high up in to the Arbuckle Mountains on a hunt for buried Spanish gold. Maps, hidden chests and dangerous Werewolves are all part of the adventure that even manages to turn up the old man who originally buried the gold! Buckle up for some more great laughs and lots of campfire fun. (ISBN 1-893302-65-2)

Drifters: The Final Testament, Volume One, by Michael Silverhawk... Within the DRIFTERS trilogy is a powerful secret, a key that unlocks our human potential! Can one man "make a difference" not only in his own life but for everyone else on the planet? Is it possible for a single human to transform chaos into order, darkness into light? (ISBN 1-893302-57-1)

Ticket to Paradise, by Yvonne Ridley...Judith Tempest, a British reporter, is searching for the Truth. But when it starts to spill out in her brilliant front page reportage of Middle East suicide bombing in retaliation for Israeli tanks mowing down innocent Palestinian women and children, both 'Tempest' and 'Truth' start to spell 'Trouble'-- with a capital 'T', joke her friends and colleagues. A non-stop mystery thriller that tears along at a reckless pace of passion, betrayal, adventure and espionage. (ISBN 1-893302-77-6)

Synchronicity Gates: An Anthology Of Stories And Poetry About People Transformed In Extraordinary Reality Beyond Experience, by Stephen Vernarelli... An inventive compilation of short stories that take the reader beyond mere science, fiction, or fantasy. Vernarelli introduces the reader to a new perception of reality; he imagines the best and makes it real. (ISBN 1-893302-38-5)

The Alley of Wishes, by Laurel Johnson… Despite the ravages of WWI on Paris and on the young American farm boy, Beck Sanow, and despite the abusive relationship that the chanteuse Cerise endures, the two share a bond that is unbreakable by time, war, loss of memory, loss of life and loss of youth. Beck and Cerise are both good people beset by constant tragedy. Yet it is tragedy that brings them together, and it is unconditional love that keeps them together. (ISBN 1-893302-46-6)

Freedom: Letting Go Of Anxiety And Fear Of The Unknown, by Jim Britt… Jeremy Carter, a fireman from Missouri who is in New York City for the day, decides to take a tour of the Trade Center, only to watch in shock, the attack on its twin towers from a block away. Afterward as he gazes at the pit of rubble and talks with many of the survivors, Jeremy starts to explore the inner depths of his soul, to ask questions he'd never asked before. This dialogue helps him learn who he is and what it takes to overcome the fear, anger, grief and anxiety this kind of tragedy brings. (ISBN 1-893302-74-1)

The Prince Must Die, by Gower Leconfield… breaks all taboos for mystery thrillers. After the "powers that be" suppressed the manuscripts of three major British writers, Dandelion Books breaks through with a thriller involving a plot to assassinate Prince Charles. *The Prince Must Die* brings to life a Britain of today that is on the edge with race riots, neo-Nazis, hard right backlash and neo-punk nihilists. Riveting entertainment… you won't be able to put it down. (ISBN 1-893302-72-5)

Come as You Are, by Sarah Daniels… "Tongue-in-cheek" entertainment at its wackiest—and most subtle. If anyone ever doubted that sex makes the world go around, author Sarah Daniels will put your mind, and body to test. Non-stop humor, humanness and wisdom are bundled together to deliver one of life's most important unheeded lessons: each of us has a unique destiny to discover, and until we find and embark on that destiny, life may be one bowl of cherry pits after another. Adult language and scenes. (ISBN 1-893302-15-6)

Unfinished Business, by Elizabeth Lucas Taylor… Lindsay Mayer knows something is amiss when her husband, Griffin, a college professor, starts spending too much time at his office and out-of-town. Shortly after the ugly truth surfaces, Griffin disappears altogether. Lindsay is shattered. Life without Griffin is life without life… One of the sexiest books you'll ever read! (ISBN 1-893302-68-7)

The Woman With Qualities, by Sarah Daniels… South Florida isn't exactly the Promised Land that forty-nine-year-old newly widowed Keri Anders had in mind when she transplanted herself here from the northeast… A tough action-packed novel that is far more than a love story. (ISBN 1-893302-11-3)

Adventure Capital, by John Rushing…South Florida adventure, crime and violence in a fiction story based on a true life experience. A book you will not want to put down until you reach the last page. (ISBN 1-893302-08-3)

A Mother's Journey: To Release Sorrow And Reap Joy, by Sharon Kay… A poignant account of Norah Ann Mason's life journey as a wife, mother and single parent. This book will have a powerful impact on anyone, female or male, who has experienced parental abuse, family separations, financial struggles and a desperate need to find the magic in life that others talk about that just doesn't seem to be there for them. (ISBN 1-893302-52-0)

Return To Masada, by Robert G. Makin… In a gripping account of the famous Battle of Masada, Robert G. Makin skillfully recaptures the blood and gore as well as the spiritual essence of this historic struggle for freedom and independence. (ISBN 1-893302-10-5)

Time Out Of Mind, by Solara Vayanian… Atlantis had become a snake pit of intrigue teeming with factious groups vying for power and control. An unforgettable drama that tells of the breakdown of the priesthood, the hidden scientific experiments in genetic engineering which produced "things" -- part human and part animal -- and other atrocities; the infiltration by the dark lords of Orion; and the implantation of the human body with a device to fuel the Orion wars. (ISBN 1-893302-21-0)

ALL DANDELION BOOKS ARE AVAILABLE THROUGH *WWW.DANDELIONBOOKS.NET*… ALWAYS. NEW: TOLL-FREE ORDERS 1-800-861-7899 (U.S. & CANADA)

LaVergne, TN USA
11 December 2009
166704LV00002B/24/A